MEXICO
and
Central America

To my mother

MEXICO
and
Central America

A Handbook for the Independent Traveller

FRANK BELLAMY

TWO CONTINENTS: NEW YORK
WILTON HOUSE GENTRY: LONDON

First published 1977
© Frank Bellamy 1977
All rights reserved.

Published in Great Britain by
Wilton House Gentry Limited,
Wilton House, Hobart Place, London SW1.
ISBN 0 905064 14 3

Published in the United States of America by
The Two Continents Publishing Group,
30 East 42 Street, New York, New York 10017.

Library of Congress Cataloging in Publication Data
Bellamy, Frank
   Mexico and Central America
   Includes index.
   1. Mexico – Description and travel – 1951 – Guide-books.   2. Central
America – Description and travel – 1951 – Guide-books.   3. Southern
States – Description and travel – 1951 – Guide-books.   I. Title.
F1209.B44   917.2'04'82   76-55108
ISBN 0-8467-0272-X
ISBN 0-8467-0336-X pbk.

Filmset by Computacomp (UK) Limited, Fort William.
Printed and bound in Great Britain by
William Clowes & Sons, Limited,
London, Beccles and Colchester.

Acknowledgements

I wish to acknowledge, with thanks, the invaluable assistance of Joe Clare, who has provided me with copious notes without which the Central American section would not have been possible, and the Mexico section less comprehensive. I have quoted directly from his notes on the following pages: 63–70, 76–7, 79–82, 90–91, 93, 94–5, 105–6, 108–14, 118–19, 123–4, 128, 135–6, 140–1, 142–3, 143–4.

Contents

Illustrations

Maps

Maps drawn by Frank Bellamy

Notes on Currencies

All local prices quoted in this book have been adjusted to take into account the general rate of inflation in the countries concerned, up to December 1976. The recent devaluation of the Mexican peso will obviously benefit US and European travellers: however, readers should note that according to unofficial sources Mexico's rate of inflation in 1976 was considerably higher than the officially quoted figure of 15 per cent, and that a high rate of inflation may continue for some time.

We give below rates of exchange for all the currencies quoted in this book, as at mid February 1977. Remember that rates change frequently and check with your bank before departing.

	One US dollar	One pound sterling
Barbados (dollar)	2.00	3.39
Belize (dollar)	2.00	3.39
Colombia (peso)	36.45	61.94
Costa Rica (colon)	8.57	14.59
El Salvador (colon)	2.50	4.25
Guatemala (quetzal)	1.00	1.70
Honduras (lempira)	2.00	3.39
Mexico (peso)	22.55	38.42
Nicaragua (cordoba)	7.03	11.94
Panama (balboa)	1.00	1.70
US (dollar)	1.00	1.74
Venezuela (bolivar)	4.29	7.29

Introduction

The prime purpose of this book is to guide the independent budget-conscious traveller through one of the most beautiful and stimulating parts of the world.

A number of different itineraries are possible, using the route information given in this book. The traveller's final choice will depend on personal preference, and the length of time at his disposal.

I have taken El Paso as the starting point for the Mexican itinerary, as the route down through the Copper Canyon and along the Pacific Coast is far superior to the inland route. Some travellers may prefer to forgo these pleasures and fly direct to Mexico City, thus missing out north Mexico altogether.

The Central American itinerary is followed by a brief chapter giving details of a more adventurous way home, via South America and the Caribbean.

As an appendix, I have included full details on travelling through the southern USA from Miami to El Paso. Cheap trans-Atlantic flights from Miami make this the most sensible route for travellers from Europe, and I hope it may also appeal to citizens of the USA and Canada who have not visited the deep south before.

My own journey, on which this book is largely based, finished in Merida, from where I returned to Miami. Details of my own experience and research have been supplemented by Joe Clare's on the spot reports on Central America and parts of Mexico, which I have reproduced verbatim.

I had a great trip. I hope you do.

Part 1
Preparing for the Trip

Financial planning

Excluding long-distance connections, this trip can cost you anything upwards of US$380 for a three-week journey in Mexico only, to US$730 for a six-week journey through Mexico and Central America. The itineraries below are based on the routes described in this book. If you follow our suggestions re transport, accommodation, meals, you should find that your total expenditure (excluding shopping sprees, etc.) falls within the price range quoted.

The biggest savings can be made by careful planning of your long-distance flights. United States and Canadian citizens should check with a good travel agent or airline what incentive flights are available. Europeans have a bewildering variety of trans-Atlantic fares available to them, some unofficial. Details are given in Appendix 1: North American Connections (pages 155–7), Trans-Atlantic Flights for non-US Travellers (pages 157–60), and Homeward Bound (pages 161–2). You should note that many of the cheapest flights require an advance booking of two months.

You should take with you traveller's cheques in US dollars, in denominations of $10 and $20. Also take at least $10 in cash. The total value of your traveller's cheques will depend on your itinerary, duration of trip and how much you have purchased of your surface travel in advance. Reading this book all the way through in advance of your trip will help considerably with your financial planning.

Suggested itineraries

Three weeks (21 days): El Paso/Mexico City/Merida: $380/$450

Day 1 El Paso/Chihuahua
  2 Chihuahua
  3 (Chihuahua/Los Mochis/
  4 (Acaponeta/Playas de Novilleros
  5 Playas de Novilleros
  ·6 Playas de Novilleros
  7 (Playas de Novilleros/
  8 (Tepic/Mexico City
  9 Mexico City
  10 Mexico City (Teotihuacan)
  11 Mexico City
  12 Mexico City
  13 Mexico City/Oaxaca/Mitla

17

Mexico and Central America

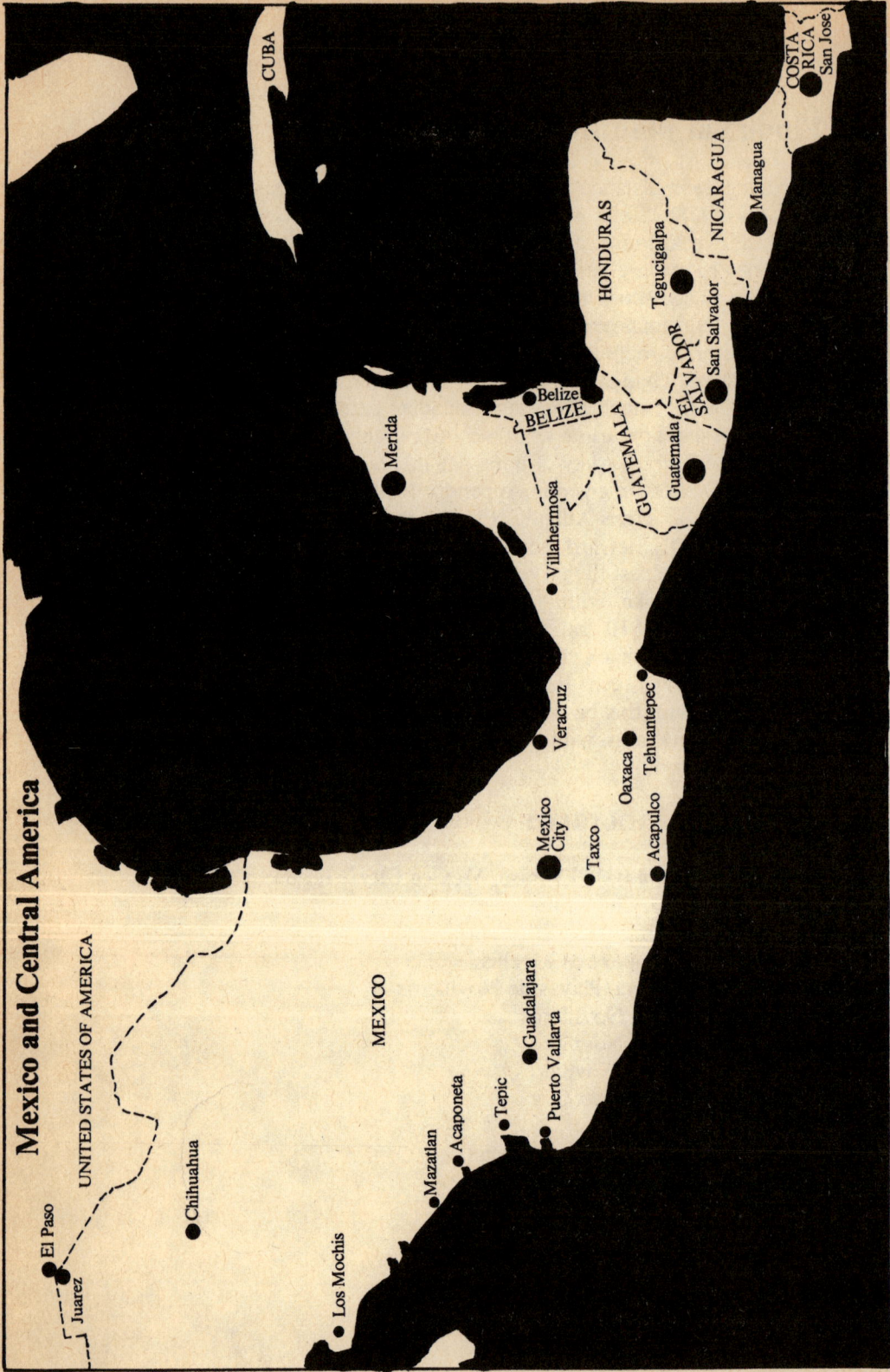

UNITED STATES OF AMERICA

El Paso
Juarez

Chihuahua

Los Mochis

MEXICO

Mazatlan
Acaponeta
Tepic
Guadalajara
Puerto Vallarta

Mexico
City
Taxco

Acapulco

Oaxaca
Tehuantepec

Veracruz

Villahermosa

Merida

CUBA

Belize
BELIZE

GUATEMALA

Guatemala

EL SALVADOR
San Salvador

HONDURAS

Tegucigalpa

NICARAGUA

Managua

COSTA
RICA
San Jose

14 Mitla/Oaxaca
15 (Oaxaca/
16 (Merida
17 Merida
18 Merida (Chichen Itza)
19 Merida (Uxmal)
20 Merida
21 Depart Merida

Three weeks (21 days): alternative itinerary from Day 12 above:
Day 12 Mexico City/Oaxaca
13 Oaxaca/Mitla/Oaxaca
14 Oaxaca (Monte Alban)
15 (Oaxaca/Coatzacoalcos/
16 (Cuidad del Carmen
17 Cuidad del Carmen/Merida
18 Merida (Chichen Itza)
19 Merida (Uxmal)
20 Merida
21 Depart Merida

Four weeks (28 days): El Paso/Guadalajara/Mexico City/Merida: $450/$480
Day 1 El Paso/Chihuahua
2 Chihuahua
3 Chihuahua/Los Mochis/Mazatlan
4 Mazatlan (Playas de Novilleros)
5 Mazatlan/San Blas
6 San Blas
7 San Blas/Matanchen/San Blas
8 San Blas/Puerto Vallarta
9 Puerto Vallarta/Guadalajara
10 Guadalajara/Ajijic
11 Ajijic
12 Ajijic/Chapala
13 Chapala
14 Chapala/San Miguel de Allende
15 San Miguel de Allende/Mexico City
16 Mexico City
17 Mexico City (Teotihuacan)
18 Mexico City

19

19   Mexico City
20   Mexico City/Oaxaca/Mitla
21   Mitla/Oaxaca
22   (Oaxaca/
23   (Merida
24   Merida
25   Merida (Chichen Itza)
26   Merida (Uxmal)
27   Merida
28   Depart Merida

Note: days 19 to 28 correspond to days 12 to 21 of the three-week itinerary.

Five weeks (35 days): El Paso/Guadalajara/Mexico City/Acapulco/ Merida: $500/$550

Day   1   El Paso/Chihuahua
     2   Chihuahua
     3   Chihuahua/Los Mochis/Mazatlan
     4   Mazatlan (Playas de Novilleros)
     5   Mazatlan/San Blas
     6   San Blas
     7   San Blas/Matanchen/San Blas
     8   San Blas/Puerto Vallarta
     9   Puerto Vallarta/Guadalajara
    10   Guadalajara/Ajijic
    11   Ajijic
    12   Ajijic/Chapala
    13   Chapala
    14   Chapala/San Miguel de Allende
    15   San Miguel de Allende/Mexico City
    16   Mexico City
    17   Mexico City (Teotihuacan)
    18   Mexico City
    19   Mexico City
    20   Mexico City/Taxco
    21   Taxco
    22   Taxco/Acapulco
    23   Acapulco
    24   Acapulco
    25   Acapulco/Oaxaca/Mitla
    26   Mitla/Oaxaca

27 Oaxaca (Monte Alban)
28 (Oaxaca/Coatzacoalcos/
29 (Cuidad del Carmen
30 Cuidad del Carmen/Merida
31 Merida
32 Merida (Chichen Itza)
33 Merida (Uxmal)
34 Merida
35 Depart Merida

Three weeks (21 days): Merida/Panama: $350/$380

Day 1 Arrive Belize*
     2 Belize/Guatemala
     3 Guatemala
     4 Guatemala
     5 Guatemala/El Salvador
     6 El Salvador
     7 El Salvador/San Miguel
     8 San Miguel/Tegucigalpa (Honduras)
     9 Honduras
    10 Honduras
    11 Honduras
    12 Tegucigalpa/Managua (Nicaragua)
    13 Nicaragua
    14 Nicaragua
    15 Managua/San Jose (Costa Rica)
    16 Costa Rica
    17 Costa Rica
    18 (San Jose/
    19 (Panama
    20 Panama
    21 Depart Panama

*Allow two days for the journey from Merida to Belize.

Six weeks (42 days): Mexico City/Panama: $550/$600

Day 1 Arrive Mexico City
     2 Mexico City
     3 Mexico City (Teotihuacan)
     4 Mexico City/Taxco
     5 Taxco
     6 Taxco/Acapulco

21

Mexico and Central America

7 Acapulco
8 Acapulco
9 Acapulco
10 Acapulco/Mexico City
11 Mexico City
12 Mexico City/Oaxaca
13 Oaxaca (Mitla)
14 Oaxaca (Monte Alban)
15 (Oaxaca/Coatzacoalcos/
16 (Cuidad del Carmen
17 Cuidad del Carmen/Merida
18 Merida
19 Merida (Chichen Itza)
20 Merida (Uxmal)
21 (Merida/
22 (Belize
23 Belize/Guatemala
24 Guatemala
25 Guatemala
26 Guatemala
27 Guatemala/El Salvador
28 El Salvador
29 El Salvador/Tegucigalpa (Honduras)
30 Honduras
31 Honduras
32 Tegucigalpa/Managua (Nicaragua)
33 Nicaragua
34 Nicaragua
35 Managua/San Jose (Costa Rica)
36 Costa Rica
37 (San Jose/
38 (Panama
39 Panama
40 Panama
41 Panama
42 Depart Panama

Health

Don't forget the pills: This is not a part of the world affected by the worst infectious diseases, and in fact prides itself on its health record. You should however take certain precautions. You should avoid drinking the water unless you are in a good hotel where it is known to be safe. Certain low-lying, tropical areas are known to have an incidence of malaria, so you may wish to take some protection against it. The usually recommended drug for prevention of the disease is ICI's Paludrine (which is taken daily), whilst the quinine-based preparations are held to be best for curing the disease, and can also be taken for prevention (one weekly). You will probably contract 'Mexican tummy', caused by the change of diet or whatever, so it would be wise to take one of the preparations which rectify this. Many people travel with chlorine tablets.

Vaccinations: The vaccinations you will need depend very much on your actual travel plans. For Mexico you need only a smallpox vaccination (valid for three years). If you are going on through Central America, you will need more. To be sure, you should check with the embassies concerned, but here are some notes to help:

	Essential	Recommended
Mexico only	smallpox	tetanus
Mexico and non-tropical Central America	smallpox tetanus typhoid	poliomyelitis
Including some time in tropical Central America	smallpox tetanus typhoid poliomyelitis	paratyphoid

Visas and Tourist Cards

For entry into Mexico you need a tourist card, available free from the Mexican Consulates in most major cities in the United States (including

Mexico and Central America

Miami, New Orleans, San Antonio) and most European capitals. No photographs are required. Although tourist cards are granted normally with little fuss, do NOT leave your application until arrival at the Mexican border. If at all possible, get it shortly before your departure.

The chart below gives visa requirements for all the countries covered in this book. Further details on Central American visas are given in the text.

Country	Where to apply	When
Mexico	Your home state/country (or Miami, New Orleans, San Antonio)	Before or just after departure
Belize	Required by US citizens only: apply to British Consulates in US	Before departure
Guatemala	US citizens: USA (Miami or Mexico) Europeans: Paris, Miami or Mexico	Before departure or en route
El Salvador	Not normally required but check	
Honduras	Not normally required but check	
Nicaragua	Not required by British citizens Others apply to Nicaraguan Consulate	En route
Costa Rica	Not normally required but check	
Panama	Not normally required but check	
Colombia	Not normally required but check	
Venezuela	Panama or Colombia	En route
Barbados	Not normally required but check	
(United States	Your home country	Now)

I would like to stress that most of the countries above require tourists to be in possession of an air ticket out of the country before entry is permitted. This is the official policy. However, a bus ticket is sometimes acceptable; alternatively, if you are tidy, without long hair, and look respectable, a long-distance return ticket (eg Panama/USA, Miami/London, Barbados/Luxembourg) will often suffice.

Insurance

In spite of all travel agents' advice, and contrary to recommendations made in books like this, some travellers still neglect to take out insurance. Don't be one of them.

It is particularly important that you are covered against any medical expenses, which are likely to be very high in Mexico and Central America if incurred. As you are not travelling on a safari-type tour, you do not require expedition insurance and can insure your baggage against loss or theft. Your travel agent can advise you and issue the cover you require.

Luggage and clothing

Keep this to a minimum — remember that you have to carry it whilst travelling. Additional clothes, camera film, sunglasses, etc. are expensive in Mexico and Central America, so be sure you are well-equipped before departure. Sleeping bags, either sheet or padded, are not strictly necessary. All of the hotels in this handbook provide clean sheets, but often assume that one blanket is adequate (it usually is).

I don't believe in making clothing lists — some people may prefer heavy boots for walking, others may be more comfortable in moccasins: who is right? But in general, when deciding what to take, you should bear in mind three factors: weight, weather and appearance.

Weight: On a trip of this sort, a light bag seems to get lighter as the journey progresses, and a heavy bag heavier. If you are travelling in Mexico only, you may be happiest with a backpack. For Central America, you should avoid anything resembling a rucksack and take a large holdall.

Weather: Everywhere is warm or hot during the day, sometimes very hot. A folding plastic raincoat is a very good idea even if you are not travelling in the rainy season (summer). Take a sweater and a jacket for occasional forays into the mountains and the odd cool evening.

Appearance: It is always a good idea to look respectable: this should not just be a privilege of the border guards. Local people will generally be warmer towards you if you are tidily dressed, beardless, and with hair not too long. This doesn't mean you need to weigh yourself down with draggy clothes: jeans can be respectable if laundered regularly.

25

Student cards

If you have a student card, be sure to take it with you. Not only can it save you money on admission costs to archaeological sites, museums, etc., but in Mexico it can reduce your bus (and possibly train) fares.

Part 2
Mexico: Background Information

The Myth and the Reality

There are many myths concerning Mexico. One tends to think of the country in terms of the cowboy movies, with comic characters in big hats sleeping in the sun on the dusty street. True, most Mexicans wear sombreros, as they call them, but these are what we call 'Panama hats'. Unlike Spain the siesta is not a national institution here; the people are at least as industrious as their US counterparts. And far from the Mexicans all being quick with the switchblade, they are probably the friendliest, most honest and least aggressive people I have met. I have no figures, but I suspect crime rates are low. The Mexican does not seem to covet his neighbour's ox, or his ass, or anything that is his; such covetousness is usually the pre-requisite of theft. This does not mean you should leave your personal effects unattended; besides the fact that there are bad eggs in every nation, there is also the possibility that other travellers may seize the opportunity offered.

The least accurate myth of all is the talk of 'mañana' (pronounced manyana). Although Mexicans are very patient people, satisfied with their lot (as perhaps evidenced by the fact that they have elected the same government continuously since 1929), they understand that Americans and Europeans are less so. They may wait until tomorrow, but they do not expect you to.

But there is some truth in the image of Mexico. It is hot and dusty, and dirty. You should be careful where you eat and sometimes not drink the water. The country is becoming industrialized, but no steps are being taken to prevent or rectify the resulting industrial pollution. Some cities, such as Monterrey, have a smog problem. In many ways Mexico has more in common with Asia than with North America. The north, with its dust, high population density in the towns, poverty, even the bus system, reminds one very much of Turkey. Further south Mexico comes into its own, with less visible poverty, cheaper prices, and its rich pre-Columbian history, reaching a peak in the Yucatan.

Mexican history and archaeology

Mexican archaeology is still in its infancy, and has been hampered considerably by the Conquistadores' destruction of pre-Columbian cultures and buildings. The conclusions reached by archaeologists are therefore often speculative, especially in terms of chronology.

Assumptions are often made from flimsy evidence, new facts fitted into existing theories. Many readers may prefer the romantic explanations of the new breed of writers such as Erich von Daniken. In archaeology, perhaps more than in any other science, new evidence constantly invalidates officially held theories. With many hieroglyphics not yet translated, a proliferation of mysterious or ambiguous illustrations, and a system of chronology based on astronomical readings, we are still in the province of educated guesswork.

Many of the more important archaeological sites are described later in this book (Part 3: Mexican Itineraries) and most travellers are likely to have neither the time nor the inclination to visit more than this small representative sample. Nevertheless, these visits can add a new dimension to your trip. I hope that the notes below will act as an appetite-whetting (though necessarily brief) introduction to the subject.

Time span: The demise of the Indian cultures in Mexico is easily dated from the Spanish colonization in the sixteenth century. When the Conquistadores arrived, they found a thriving Aztec civilization with impressive, gleaming cities. They also found a lifestyle and culture which they were unable to understand, found repugnant and set about destroying. History since then is well documented in terms we can easily understand. But the development and time span of Mexico's indigenous cultures is something upon which we can only speculate. Fortunately, enough archaeological evidence has remained to enable us to trace back Mexico's history with a semblance of accuracy.

No one can be sure when the nomadic peoples of this area became civilized, in the sense of growing crops and manufacturing artifacts and implements. From evidence already sifted, archaeologists suggest that this happened about 3000 BC, although there is no evidence to deny that there were civilized peoples here before that date.

Geographical distribution: The richest areas in terms of their history and archaeology correspond to what are the most pleasant areas of Mexico today. The north is quite barren, whilst the central area around Mexico City and down to Oaxaca is densely populated with evidence of lost civilizations. And the Yucatan peninsula saw thriving cultures and splendid architecture, evidence of which continues into Central America. The jungles of this area must still hide other treasures of which we know nothing.

Early development: Evidence so far gathered seems to show that all of the people of this area were nomadic, hunting game and eating wild plants and fruit, until about 3000 years ago, when groups in the south and central areas began to settle down and cultivate crops. Both indigenous crops and imported plants were grown (maize seems to have come originally from South America). The beginnings of trade between different communities or tribes would have been generated at about this period. At this time, Mexico had the great disadvantage of having few of the domesticated animals instrumental in the development of European and Asian civilizations. Cattle, sheep, pigs and horses were unknown. The only meat was provided by poultry and game, which were therefore much favoured, as was hunting itself, right up to the Spanish colonization.

Although there was trade between these early settlements or villages, there seems to have been little long-distance travel. Presumably this was because the horse or mule was unknown, and also because the people were able to produce ample food for their needs. The development of the great cities started about 2000 years ago, and appears to have been simultaneous in different parts of Mexico, mâinly on the central plateau, the Gulf coast, and in the region of what is now Guatemala and the Yucatan. Evidence suggests that the people migrated inland from the Gulf and Caribbean coasts. There is speculatión therefore that the main architectural and cultural influences originated either from Egypt (the only other civilization to build in the pyramid style) or – more spectacularly – from Atlantis, which if it existed was in the area of what is now the Bahamas.

Teotihuacan: This is believed to be one of the first classical cities – it is in many ways the most spectacular and certainly the most famous. According to legend, the two great pyramids – the Pyramid of the Sun and the Pyramid of the Moon – were built by the gods, at a time when the world was overcast. When they had built the two pyramids, the gods ascended from the top of each in a ball of fire. The skies subseque.tly cleared and the sun and moon appeared.

Little is known about the Teotihuàcan civilization, apart from indications that its people came from the coast and moved inland – specifically to Tula – after the city's decline. Much has been restored, however, and we do know that the Pyramid of the Sun has greater similarities to the Egyptian pyramids that has any other construction in Mexico. Later developments seem to have moved away from the pure pyramid form, rather than towards it.

However, it is reasonable to deduce that any similarities may be coincidental. Most religious buildings throughout the world thrust heavenwards, and the pyramid is perhaps the most primitive method of building a tall structure. It is really a man-made hill, surmounted by a temple. It is more likely that its inspiration derived from a desire to show the contemporary political/religious system in concrete form. Even quite small villages were modelled politically on the 'pyramid' system. The mass of the people formed the base of the pyramid, while those more fortunate, either through merit or birth, were accorded greater privileges and responsibilities. The numbers of each group in the hierarchy were reduced in inverse proportion to the rights given and duties required.

Many of the Mexican cultures, particularly the Toltecs and Aztecs, were warlike and imperialist, where others placed greater emphasis on worship and production. The builders of Teotihuacan were in the latter category. They worshipped Quetzalcoatl, 'The Feathered Serpent', sometimes god, sometimes great leader, legendary inventor of writing and the arts. About 1000 years ago, Quetzalcoatl features as the last great priest-king of Tula, the city founded by the Toltecs on the central plateau. The Toltecs were the first great colonizers, travelling down from the north, adapting the cultures they found yet retaining their military outlook.

Other early civilizations: Around the time Teotihuacan was founded, perhaps slightly before, the Olmecs founded a civilization on the Gulf Coast. Their influence spread to Monte Alban, the city built on a mountain outside Oaxaca.

The Maya civilization has lasted for the greatest time. Tikal in Guatemala was founded about 1700 years ago, and was thus flourishing at the same time as Teotihuacan. Yet Mayan cities were built successively down the centuries, and there are today many Mayan communities in the Yucatan peninsula.

The Classic Period: The early civilizations of what is termed the 'Classic Period' flourished and died. Military conquest was hardly the reason for this decline as the Toltecs were the only imperialist power at this time, and their influence was limited to the central plateau and the north until much later. The reasons for the decline seem instead to have been flaws inherent in the political, social and economic order.

Any hierarchical system is susceptible to challenge from the most articulate of the underprivileged, unless the ambitious are able to enjoy the fruits of power and privilege. Building great cities over a long time period would involve a large workforce of labourers and artisans who would be unproductive in the sense of contributing towards the material welfare of

The remains of a Mayan fresco in the Ball Court at Chichen Itza, in the Yucatan peninsula. This is a predominantly Toltec city, although the frescoes and artifacts are of Mayan origin.

The quaint town of Taxco, now designated a Mexican-Baroque monument, and famed for its silver smiths.

A fresco at Teotihuacan. Thirty miles north of Mexico City, this is believed to be one of the first 'classical' cities.

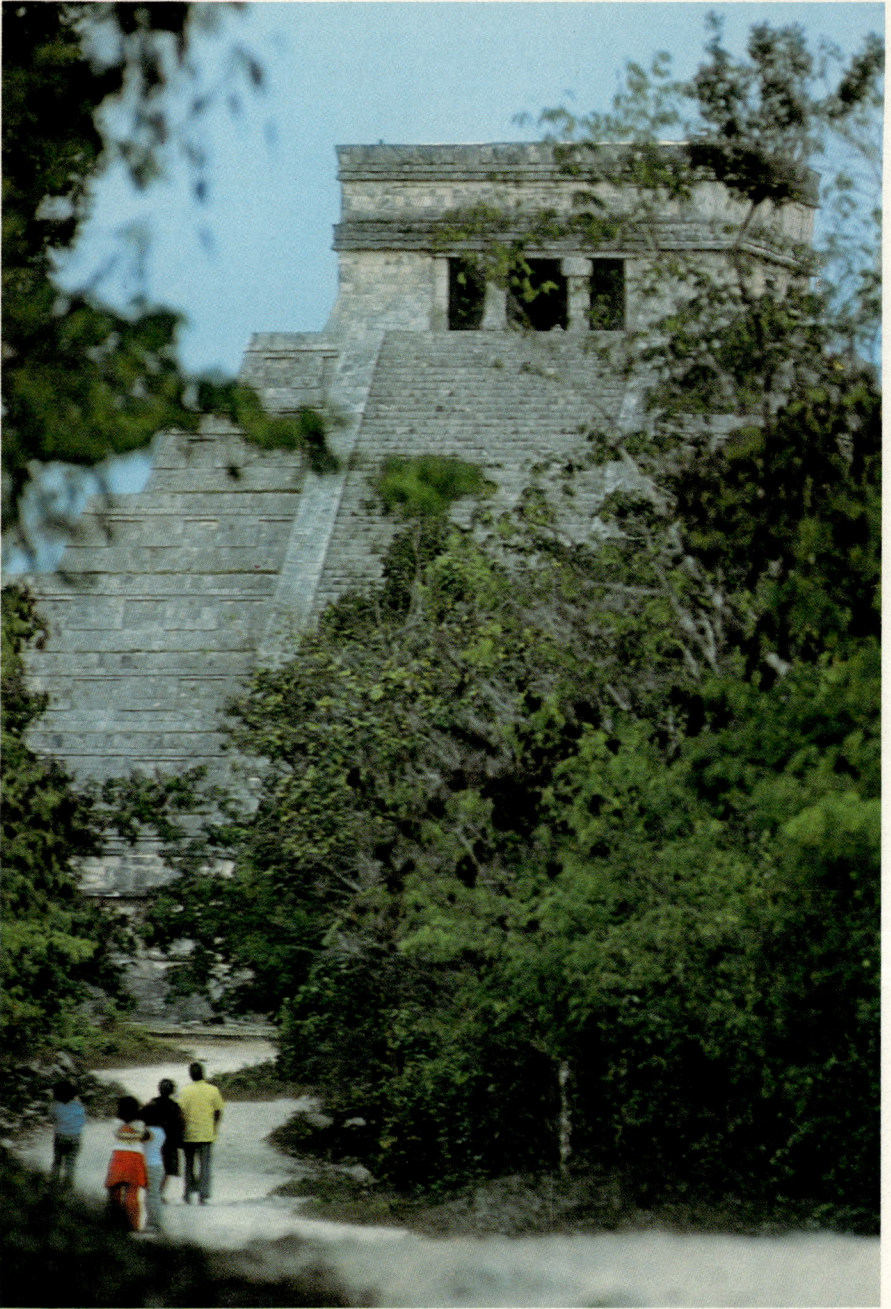

The great Toltec pyramid of Quetzalcoatl, Chichen Itza. The temples with which most of Mexico's pyramids were crowned were largely destroyed by the Conquistadores: Quetzalcoatl's remains.

the community. Over a period measured in hundreds of years, this labour force would increase as the cultural ambitions of the city's rulers became more demanding. Simultaneously, the harvests would become less plentiful as the land became increasingly barren, worked for the highest yields yet inefficiently fertilized. It is reasonable to assume that the cultural gap between an unproductive ruling élite and an illiterate servile class would widen. Respect between the extremes of the pyramid, and between each layer, would deteriorate progressively, causing domestic instability and leaving the city open to outside attack (though this seems to have been a rare occurrence). The first group to suffer would be the peasantry; probably they would be blamed for poor harvests. Logically, the labouring class would be the next to suffer. Thus the base of the political pyramid would make the whole structure unstable.

In many cases general undernourishment or starvation would force the people to desert their cities and seek greener pastures elsewhere – remember that the cities were provided for by a village economy, and that without cattle and horses the importation of food was not a practical proposition. In other cases, the mass of the people, if provided with articulate leadership, would blame their rulers, causing mass emigration or revolution.

Yet all this is speculation. What we do know is that the Classic Period ended in all areas between 1300 and 900 years ago. The Olmecs moved inland from the Gulf of Mexico, the Toltecs trekked south, and the Mayas travelled into the Yucatan. Yet even at this time, a new cycle was beginning.

The Toltec Empire: This is the first civilization, as far as we know, to attach as much importance to military prowess as to religion. Breaking free from the theocratic influences of the Teotihuacan culture, the Toltecs built splendid assembly halls and palaces for secular purposes, as well as pyramids and temples for worship. For a time, the beneficial influence of Quetzalcoatl prevented human sacrifice, but war, colonization and killing for its own sake gradually increased. For example, a sacrificial well would traditionally have received valuable treasures – ornaments, vases, plate, etc. – in return for the god's pleasure. Now a taste for human sacrifice developed.

The pervasion of this bloody mood was accompanied by a great spread in Toltec influence. On the one hand, armies would set out specifically to colonize, building new cities or taking over exisiting cities, even sacking and looting them. (It is reasonable to suppose that if the Toltecs conquered a territory without bloodshed, its cities would have been left largely

33

intact.) On the other hand, refugees would flee the new order, taking their skills and culture with them. Thus we now see a phase where an individual culture extended beyond the boundaries of a city to envelop a loosely knit state.

It is at this stage that archaeology is unable to account for legend, that is, the written and verbal history of the pre-Columbian people. Quetzalcoatl is recorded in history and sculpture as the god of Teotihuacan. Yet hundreds of years later, he appears as the last great priest-ruler of Tula, exercising benevolent and wise leadership. Despite these qualities, it is recorded that he was driven out of Tula – possibly his doctrine of peace was no longer welcome amongst the warlike Toltecs, or possibly he was held responsible for some calamity. Between 15 and 30 years later, Quetzalcoatl appears to have joined the Mayas with a group of Toltec followers; with a Mayan tribe, known as the Itza, he conquered part of the Yucatan and founded Chichen Itza.

Chichen Itza: There are of course several explanations accounting for Quetzalcoatl's extraordinary life span. He could have been a god, although it is then unlikely that the people of Tula would have been sufficiently strong to expel him – even if they had, he would have been more likely to return in strength than to found a new civilization elsewhere. Alternatively, the name Quetzalcoatl could refer to a ruling élite, who perpetuated the demi-god myth so that the people would accord them full respect, simply replacing the figurehead on his death or after a term of office. Another possibility is that Quetzalcoatl was a dynasty, respected enough, and strong enough, to last for several hundred years. We do know that throughout all pre-Columbian cultures, power was kept in the hands of a very few initiates. This latter theory is supprted by the recorded fact that Quetzalcoatl's methods of government had changed considerably by the time he founded Chichen Itza. Surely a god would preach a consistent philosophy? Not only did Quetzalcoatl conquer a relatively peace-loving people in the Yucatan, but he established there the principle of human sacrifice. At the back of the town, a well used for human sacrifice can still be seen.

Architecturally, Chichen Itza is identical to Tula. The first building one sees on entering the site is the Great Pyramid. In many ways, it is one of the best preserved pyramids in Mexico, as it still retains the temple with which it was crowned. Today, it dominates the site of Chichen Itza because so much of it remains, but this would not have been so in the city's heyday. In size and majesty it cannot be compared with Teotihuacan. Symptomatic of the new emphasis on secular matters, the remains of a large hall featuring numerous rows of colonnades and a large, raised, stepped platform surmounted by another secular building can be seen near the Great Pyramid. This could conceivably have been a palace with ground-floor living quarters for the palace staff and/or guard.

After the Toltecs: Tula was to fall before Chichen Itza reached its zenith. About 800 years ago, the new rulers who had replaced Quetzalcoatl were driven out, either by revolution or by invasion, and the city was sacked. Many buildings were destroyed and the Temple of the Morning Star was damaged. The golden age of Quetzalcoatl was recalled, and Cholula on the central plateau became a cult centre for the demi-god.

War had come to stay. The Toltec and Mayan cities of the Yucatan showed increasing emphasis on fortification as their civilizations become more decadent and more vulnerable to outside attack. Toltec influence, either from refugees or from colonizers, was felt along the Gulf coast and reflected in a Mixtec blend at Monte Alban.

Built on a hill, the compact site of Monte Alban reflects the insular and defensive nature of a people pre-occupied with repelling hostile forces. Thus, it is likely that here the Toltec influence was exerted by refugees rather than conquerors. There is evidence of early pyramids being used as the foundations for later structures.

With the fall of Tula, Mexico saw another invasion from the north. Nomadic tribes, still hunting with bow and arrow and clothed in animal skins, learned of its fall and moved southwards to the more fertile lands. They moved among the existing communities, sometimes hostile, sometimes peaceable, and learned to adapt their way of life to the agrarian economy they found. Utilizing their newly learnt skills, the majority of these invaders became sedentary and began to rebuild the cities of the central plateau.

The Valley of Mexico: Throughout history, the valley of Mexico has remained the focal point of the country. In the centre of this area lay a great lake (now dried up). Teotihuacan was built at the head of the river leading to it, Tula to the north, and Tenochtitlan or Mexico City was founded on an island within it.

The political life of the country was now centred around the city state, rather like ancient Greece. These traded with and sometimes fought each other. Each town was built around religious buildings — pyramids and temples — and grand secular buildings — palaces and halls of assembly, etc. The more temporary living quarters of the general populace spread outwards from this nucleus. The Toltec culture was still the most influential, though modified to greater or lesser degree. Long-distance travel, though hampered by a lack of transport, became more established, and only the north and the Yucatan retained a different culture.

The Aztecs (also known as the Mexico or Azteca) arrived fairly late and found the best land taken. They thus established Tenochtitlan (or Mexico City) on an island in the lagoon. In their early days, the Aztecs were denied full independence and were subjected to the rule of various other states. Presumably by skilful political manoeuvering, judicious alliances and some military prowess, the Aztecs were able to emerge from obscurity to become the major force in Mexico in the space of some 200 to 250 years. They formed a triple alliance with the cities of Texcoco and Tlacopan and were able to form an empire from the Gulf to the Pacific which was of a fairly homogeneous political nature, with centralized authority in Mexico City. This authority was somewhat limited, however, as one would expect in a country with Mexico's transportation problems, and it would perhaps be more accurate to regard Mexico City as the centre of a confederation of autonomous states.

Trade now developed apace, and a bourgeoisie began to take advantage of the business opportunities. The exchange of goods was accompanied by an exchange of ideas and skills. The Aztec civilization flourished, giving Mexico a greater homogeneity than it had hitherto experienced. This is not to suggest that there was an infertile standardization, but rather the opposite: clothing styles reflected the diversity of all the tribes of this central area; religious freedom (especially in Mexico City) was encouraged. In fact, the atmosphere of Mexico City must have been akin to that of any capital city in the Western world today.

Recent Mexican history: It was thus a well-developed civilization that the Spanish encountered, yet one which had not invented the wheel, gunpowder or other sophistications developed by the greater cross-fertilization of ideas in Europe and Asia. The inevitable result was an extensive Spanish-American colonization which included Mexico.

During the Viceroyal period a rich culture was produced by the fusion of the colonists and the natives, which was expressed in Mexican-Baroque architecture, rich, colourful and imposing. Yet the Spanish Empire was to crumble very soon. Increasingly harassed in the Caribbean and Europe by England, and faced by nationalist movements in its vast colonial territories, something had to give. The Mexican War of Liberation began in 1810 and reached a successful conclusion in 1821.

At this time, parts of what is now the United States of America belonged to Mexico, notably the state of Texas. Thus there was to be further conflict before the boundaries of present-day Mexico were settled. As with many a newly independent state, Mexico's new rulers did not always have the best interests of the populace at heart. There was a great deal of poverty among the mass of people, particularly in the rural areas, and exploitation by the ruling élite. Peasant revolts were frequent and were generally put down with the utmost severity.

At the beginning of the twentieth century, these uprisings developed into a revolution led by Francisco (Pancho) Villa, and after the revolution of 1910 Mexico settled down as a free, independent country.

The present structure of government is similar to that of the United States of America, with a president, senate, house of representatives and supreme court. There is no vice-president. There are 29 states, two federal territories and one federal district. Each state has a governor elected by popular vote, a house of local representatives and a superior court of justice.

Resumé of archaeological sites in Mexico

Page numbers refer to route directions given in the text.

Teotihuacan (page 77): I have already mentioned the two great pyramids and the temple dedicated to Quetzalcoatl. Recent excavations have unearthed another building, probably a palace, and as yet the only secular building to be discovered. There is a small museum here, featuring fresco paintings.

Tula: This Toltec city is situated fairly near Mexico City, approx. 40 miles to the north. Although showing evidence of deliberate destruction, the city still retains a wealth of remains, dominated by its pyramid surmounted by the giant Atlantes.

Sites in Mexico City: Tlaltelolco was discovered recently when a new residential area was being built in the centre of the capital. As more and more discoveries were made, the architect revised his plans to preserve as much as he could. He named the district "The Place of the Three Cultures" because in addition to its Aztec ruins and modern apartments, the site features a seventeenth-century Baroque church.

At Tenayuca in Mexico's suburbs are Aztec remains in a fine state of preservation. A double pyramid dedicated to Quetzalcoatl is guarded by his effigies. The small pyramid of Santa Cecilia (perhaps its name gives the

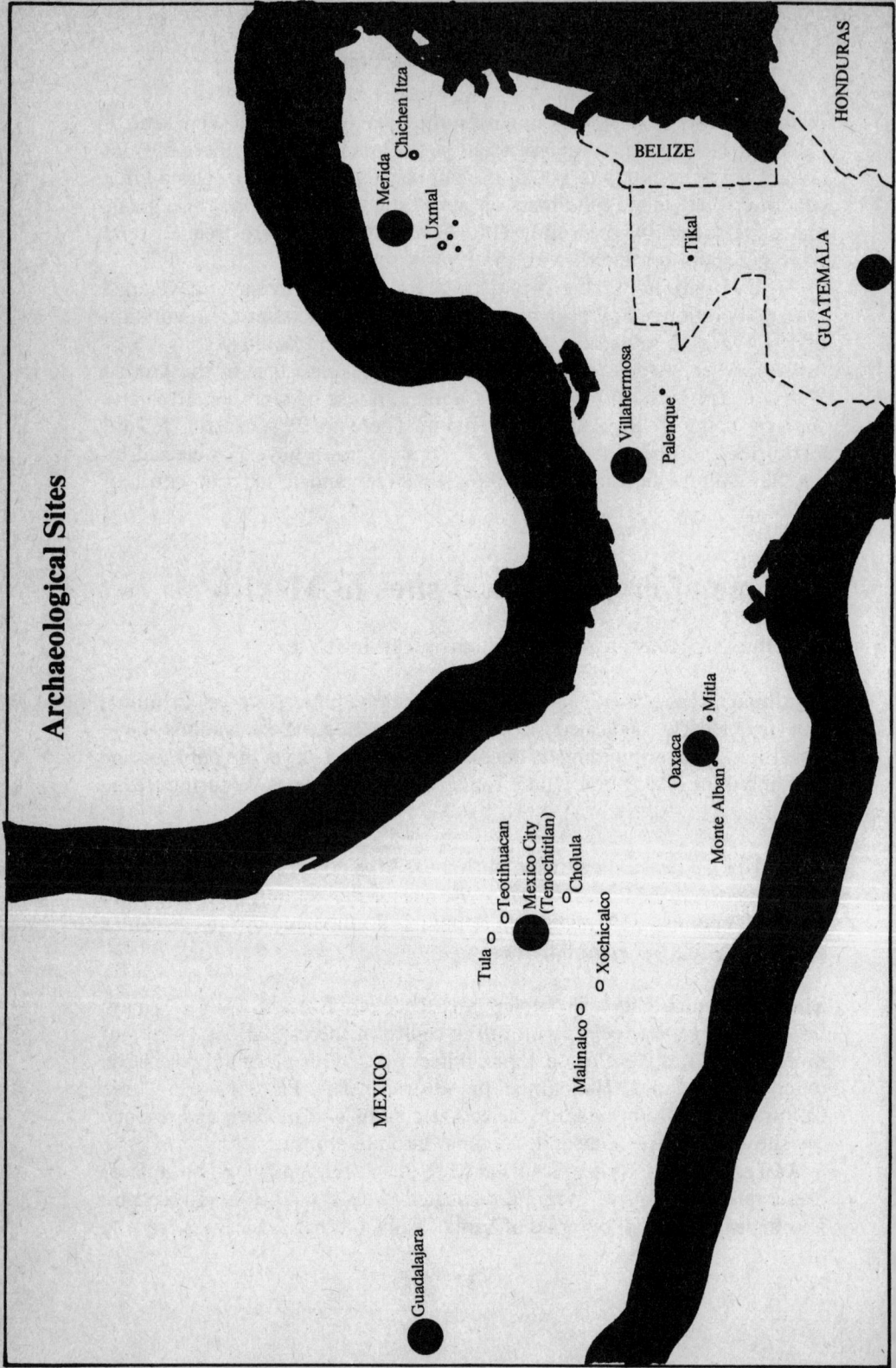

Archaeological Sites

MEXICO

Guadalajara

Tula o
Mexico City
(Tenochtitlan)
o Teotihuacan
Malinalco o
o Xochicalco
o Cholula

Oaxaca
Monte Alban
• Mitla

Villahermosa
Palenque •

BELIZE

• Tikal

GUATEMALA

HONDURAS

Merida
Uxmal
o Chichen Itza

clue as to why it was spared by the Conquistadores) is in almost pristine condition, complete with its temple in its original state.

Other sites around Mexico City: Xochicalco is situated 120 km (75 miles) south of Mexico City, past Cuernavaca on the road to Acapulco. Here there is a sacred citadel of pyramids, temples and ball courts, its finest building being a sanctuary dedicated to Questzalcoatl. Calixtlahuaca, near Toluca, 75 km (47 miles) from Mexico City, is an Aztec city. It shows how the Aztecs were responsive to outside influences, and includes a circular pyramid, one of the few examples to be found in Mexico. Malinalco, further south, is deliberately inaccessible. Its sanctuary dedicated to the eagle and jaguar is one of the wonders of Aztec building. Carved out of the rock, this was the last refuge of the priests hunted by the Conquistadores.

Monte Alban and Mitla (page 84ff): Monte Alban is built 1300 feet above the town of Oaxaca. The Zapotec first built this great yet compact city, levelling off the top of the mountain. Unable to expand the city horizontally, later generations constructed new pyramids over the original buildings. All the buildings lie in an exactly north-south direction with the exception of Building J (as it is unromantically known) which was built specifically as an observatory. Many treasures from the tombs built inside and outside the pyramids have been excavated and can now be seen in the museum in Oaxaca. These prove that during the decline of Monte Alban, the Mixtecs became predominant, deciding that this was a fit place to bury their rulers.

The few remains to be seen at Mitla are of secular origin. These palaces were still inhabited by the Mixtecs in the seventeenth century, when the Spanish arrived. Unfortunately, Mixtec art was very delicate and the Conquistadores had little difficulty in destroying what they found. A Mexican-Baroque church on the site was built on the foundations of one of the palaces and incorporates stone from the ancient city.

Palenque (page 91): One of the first great Mayan cities, Palenque today stands in the middle of nowhere. Its pyramids and palace, built in the foothills of the Usumacinta Mountains, rise out of the jungle. The Pyramid of the Inscriptions, its primary building, was used as a tomb. Here also is the observatory tower used by the Mayas to take the readings which created a calendar more exact than that which we use today.

Uxmal (page 94): In many ways, Uxmal represents the apogee of Mayan architecture. The Pyramid of the Soothsayer is the best known building, perhaps because of its unusually steep staircase. The Palace of the Governor and the Nunnery Quadrangle are both particularly impressive.

Chichen Itza (page 93): Although situated in the Yucatan, Chichen Itza is predominantly a Toltec city. The architecture is certainly Toltec, whilst the sculpture, frescoes and artifacts are of Mayan origin. Whether the Mayas worked as slaves or partners is not known, although written and verbal records support the latter theory.

Physical setting

Mexico considers itself a part of the North American continent. There are four natural regions: the peninsula of Baja California, the Yucatan peninsula, the isthmus of Tehuantepec and a vast plateau, the greatest area of Mexico, bordered by mountains along the Pacific and Gulf coasts.

Climate: Perfect. Somewhere in Mexico the climate is perfect always. But you are strongly advised to travel in autumn, winter or spring because summer is the rainy season. Coastal and low-lying areas are tropical, with an attendant possible malarial risk. The highlands are generally very warm during the day, with cool, sometimes cold, winter evenings.

ALTITUDE (ft) AND DAYTIME TEMPERATURES

City	Altitude	Minimum		Maximum		Average	
		°F	°C	°F	°C	°F	°C
Chihuahua	4667	36	2	102	39	65	18
Mazatlan	23	54	12	94	34	75	24
Mexico City	7349	34	1	88	31	60	16
Oaxaca	5071	37	3	102	39	68	20
Merida	30	50	10	108	42	79	26

Time zones: Mexico has three time zones, two of which concern you. After crossing the border from El Paso, you should put your watch forward one hour, from Mountain to Central Time. During your Copper Canyon train ride before arrival in Los Mochis, it should go back to Mountain time again. There it should stay until you leave the state of Nayarit shortly before Guadalajara on your bus to Mexico City, where it should go forward again into Central Time. You stay in Central Time until you board your aeroplane from Merida. They do make life difficult.

Currency

The Mexican unit is the peso, which like the US dollar is shown as $. In the Mexico sections we always refer to pesos not dollars, but to differentiate we show the peso as $M.

In practice you will probably be converting dollars into pesos from your traveller's cheques. In the north you can use US dollars but if the change is given to you in pesos the conversion rate will be unfavourable to you.

The peso is divided into 100 centavos. The most common notes are $M1, 5, 10, 20, 50 and 100, all of different colour and design. Coins are issued in 5, 10, 20, 25, 50 centavos and 1 and 5 pesos.

You will need to visit banks to change your traveller's cheques. Some of the bigger banks in the bigger towns have assumed all the trappings of bureaucracy, which may mean a long wait and a trial of your patience. Where possible find a smaller bank with a short queue at the money change counter. Always check that the bank does change foreign currency (avoid 'commercial' banks) and make sure you are queuing at the right counter.

Language

Spanish. Surprisingly easily recognizable as such, even though some words differ (bus in Spanish is 'camion', yet due to its invention being subsequent to the War of Independence Mexicans usually use the term 'autobus'; 'tortillas' means omelette in Spanish, yet here it refers to the small, heavy-consistency maize pancakes: 'huevos' is the term for omelette). Regional dialects blur the Spanish towards the end of the trip, and in the Yucatan much Mayan is spoken. There is less English spoken than you might expect. If you've been to Spain you should be able to find your way around and get what you want.

Mexico and Central America

Some Spanish Words:

Please	Por favor
Thank you	Gracias
Where is ... ?	Donde esta ... ?
Today	Hoy
Tomorrow	Mañana
Do you speak English?	Habla usted ingles?
I speak no Spanish	No hablo español
I do not understand	No entiendo
Yes/No	Sí/No
Your name?	Su nombre?
I/you/he/she	Yo/usted/el/ella
Good morning	Buenos dias
Good evening	Buenas noches
Goodbye	Adios
How are you?	Como esta usted?
How far?	Hasta donde?
How much is it?	Cuanto vale?
Too much	Demasiado
Very well	Muy bien
Don't mention it	De nada
I want	Yo quiero
Airport	Aeropuerto
Automobile/car	Automovil/coche
Bank	Banco
Change (money)	Cambiar
Check (bill)	Cuenta
Church	Iglesia
Information	Informacion
Toilets	Servicios
Gents	Caballeros/señores
Ladies	Damas
Occupied	Ocupado
Pharmacy	Farmacia
Post Office	Oficina de correos
Hotel room	Habitacion
Station	Estacion
Ticket	Billete (boleto)
Time	Hora
What time ... ?	Que hora ... ?

Stop	Alto
Beach	Playa
Entrance	Entrada
Exit	Salida
One	Uno, un
Two	Dos
Three	Tres
Four	Cuatro
Five	Cinco
Six	Seis
Seven	Siete
Eight	Ocho
Nine	Nueve
Ten	Diez
Fifty	Cincuenta
One hundred	Ciento
Monday	Lunes
Tuesday	Martes
Wednesday	Miercoles
Thursday	Jueves
Friday	Viernes
Saturday	Sabado
Sunday	Domingo
Breakfast	Desayuno
Lunch	Almuerzo
Dinner	Cena
Water (drinking)	Agua potable
Black coffee	Cafe solo
White coffee	Cafe con leche
Beer	Cerveza
Soft drinks	Refrescos
Pork	Puerco
Chicken	Pollo
Meat	Carne
Rice	Arroz
Bread	Pan
Creme Caramel	Flan
Dessert	Postre

Pronunciation is important. In the text on the Mexican part of the trip we give pronunciation details after place names, italicizing the syllable to be stressed. The most important mistake English-speaking people make is concerning the letters 'll'. This is pronounced more like the English 'y'. An example is the Spanish island of Mallorca. Pronounced 'Mayorca', its English spelling is 'Majorca'. 'Caballeros' is thus pronounced 'cabayeros'. The 'y' sound is also inserted after an 'n' with an accent; 'mañana' is thus 'manyana' and 'Español' is 'Espanyol'. Other pronunciation peculiarities you will pick up as you go along.

Food and Drink

Let's start with what tourist guides and some travellers call Mexican Food. From what these people say you would think all Mexicans eat it all the time.

Tortillas (tortiyas) are the small, flat, heavy maize pancakes traditionally eaten as bread. When filled with meat or chicken, rolled and sometimes fried, these become tacos. When filled with meat or chicken in a hot, tasty sauce these become enchiladas. In cheap eating places and when offered on buses, etc. tacos cost about $M1. Enchiladas are more expensive. Tamales are made from soft dough and filled, and often served in the maize husk. You can try turkey or chicken in a spicy 'mole' sauce, but you may wish to avoid chicarones, pork fat fried until crisp. Frijoles (friholes), called refried beans in Texas, are perhaps the most common vegetable, often mashed into a brown mound. Remember arroz means rice. The above is what is generally referred to as Mexican Food. But as you can see, if you eat this all the time you will not have the advantage of a balanced and varied diet.

Salads are usually dressed and very good. Seafood can be recommended in coastal areas, but shrimps are expensive nowadays.

You will find that whereas most restaurants include enchiladas, etc. somewhere in their bill of fare, this is only one of the many items on the menu. Unless you speak Spanish, or there is an English translation, you are likely to find out about most Mexican food the interesting way. There are many delicious local specialities, particularly in the Yucatan. In Mexico's larger towns the restaurants provide a set menu with anything from two to five dishes per course to choose from. Thus in Mexico City you can buy a very varied and filling meal, often containing fillet steak and/or oysters, of five or six courses for between $M15/$M25.

Many Mexicans believe that they drink a lot as a nation. It is not noticeably the case. The beer (cerveza) is very good, but the national drink is of course tequila, taken with salt or dried worms. Beer is normally from $M5 to $M12.

Accommodation

We want to keep you off Skid Row. Unfortunately good accommodation is not always available at a fair price, and you should be prepared for lower standards in Mexico. It is conceivable you may start a war with the plumbing, as the Mexicans (like the Spanish) traditionally leave their used toilet paper in a waste bin by the toilet. You don't have to follow suit however.

Most of the suggested accommodation will cost $M45/$M50 for a single, $M50/$M90 for a double. Others of our suggestions are cheaper – the prices above include bathroom. As a general rule you get what you pay for if you look for the listed prices. By law all Mexican hotels are required to display their official documentation showing room rates, which are set by the government. This doesn't mean they all do, but it does help you to identify an honest hotel. We have recommended these hotels where possible. Except for Chihuahua where it is impossible, and Mexico City where it is unadvisable, we have selected accommodation near to arrival and departure points.

Shops and services

Shopping and cleaning: Shops are open from 10am to 6pm with late nights until 8pm. Laundromats are a rarity in Mexico, only to be found in big towns. Some of the hotels will do your laundry for you.

Post Offices and telephones: Unless you speak Spanish, there is not much chance of your using the phone. Post Offices can be rare.

Electricity: Sometimes 125 and 220 volts AC 50 cycles. Sometimes 125 and 220 volts AC 60 cycles.

Tipping: Taxi drivers do not expect tips. Waiters expect and deserve 10/15 per cent for good service and chambermaids deserve something if service is good.

Cigarettes: Cheaper than in the States. Capri and Del Prado are two cheap brands that should cost $M3/$M5. In practice you will be charged more in the north because you are a foreign tourist. There are no tiresome anti-smoking regulations.

Prices: Mexico is less economically independent than the United States and inflation is more marked (approx. 15 per cent in 1976). Although cheaper than the States, it is not as cheap as you may think. However the Mexican government does everything it can to protect the tourist with regard to prices and standards of service. This means that Mexico is probably the only country in the world where the capital city is cheaper than the other towns in the country. In the north particularly, the residents have become accustomed in the past to American tourists with money to burn, and price their goods accordingly. This syndrome (also evident in tourist towns such as Oaxaca) is so much a part of life that you probably won't notice it − until you become aware of its absence in Mexico City.

Transport

Mexico is a far larger country than you may expect. Although by international standards it has good roads and bus services, travel is far more difficult than in the USA. General transportation problems are not eased by some of the most spectactular and beautiful scenery you could wish to see. We have chosen a route that includes the famous Copper Canyon Railway, opportunities to see and visit the sea (both the Pacific and the Gulf of Mexico) and splendid twisting mountain roads. Although your travel in Mexico will probably be quite tiring, it should always be enjoyable.

Bus: Don't expect drivers or conductors to speak English, even in El Paso, although some may have a smattering. Buses in Mexico generally travel very full, with people standing. And with people babbling away in Spanish you are very conscious of being in a foreign country.

There are two classes on the buses and trains, 'primera' and 'secunda'. There is usually little difference in the fares and standards. Do not expect to find both classes on the same bus; the primera is generally quicker and usually comfortable, stopping less often with tickets pre-paid and seats reserved. Look for the seat number on your ticket. Your ticket will only be valid for the particular departure reserved, so if you miss the bus you will have to book and pay again. Secunda buses vary very greatly in standard and booking procedure. Some are as good as primera vehicles, with reserved seats. Often they make no more stops than would a primera vehicle, and consequently the fare difference is slight. Other secunda buses can be old and dilapidated, no seats are reserved and you pay on the bus. Fares, standard of vehicle and booking procedures vary with the bus company, and there are very many of these, none of which covers the whole country.

There is one complication which may cause you frustration and difficulty. If a bus has begun its journey before the point at which you wish to board, you will usually not be able to book until the bus pulls in, and the ticketing staff ascertain how much space it has. For example the bus you take from Los Mochis may be operating from Mexicali to Guadalajara. You may have to wait before anyone will take your money. There is no queueing – it is every man for himself. If you are able to book in advance it is always advisable to do so.

Always keep your luggage in sight, making sure it is loaded and unloaded when you are. This is not so much to prevent theft as to stop it going astray. You will often be able to check in your baggage shortly before the departure of your bus. In these cases you receive a baggage check which you produce to reclaim your luggage.

Train: Although Mexico has an extensive rail system the only section suitable to this journey and recommended in this handbook is that from Chihuahua to Los Mochis.

Most trains have primera and secunda class sections. On the one we use, Chihuahua Pacifico, primera is at the back. The primera fare is $M205, secunda $M170. The difference between the classes is greater than these fares would suggest, although secunda is comfortable enough. I travelled in secunda, the only foreigner amongst the natives. Primera class is really designed for the American tourists, with motor-coach type seats, an observation car, and a restaurant car. Oddly enough when I travelled primera was full, yet there were empty seats in secunda – perhaps due to a recent price rise. Drinks served by stewards with trolleys are relatively expensive and they will try to rip you off. When they get to the primera section the prices increase still further! The class you choose is up to you, as the price difference is justified. If you take the evening train I recommend primera so that you can sleep (remember you will miss much of the scenery). Otherwise the choice is: do you want to travel with the tourists or the natives?

Taxis: Most taxis outside Mexico City do not have meters. Therefore you should always agree the fare before boarding. A useful tip is to ascertain what the fare should be from a neutral source, then bargain down to this fare, or as near as you can get. There is nothing to stop you walking along a line of taxis until you get a reasonable offer. Taxis and other transportation within Mexico City are dealt with in detail later in the book.

Suggested transport schedules

The summary below is intended as a rough guide only. Full details are in the text. You will find the 24-hour clock used for all transport schedules throughout Mexico and Central America, and we have therefore adopted the system in this book.

Carriers	From	to	Departure Times	Arrival Times	Cost
Omnibus de Mexico	El Paso	Chihuahua	About 9 per day	Journey takes about 6 hours	$4.80
Chihuahua-Pacifico	Chihuahua	Los Mochis	08.00 08.20 21.00	18.00 20.00 12.00	$M170
Many: Pacifico	Los Mochis	Acaponeta	23.00 to 02.00	07.00 to 10.00 (next day)	$M90
Local buses	Acaponeta	Tecuala/Playas de Novilleros	hourly	1-3 hours	$M5
Local	P. Novilleros	Tecuala/Tepic	varies	4 hours	$M26
Estrella Blanca	Tepic	Mexico City	About 8 per day	12 hours	$M122
Cristobal	Mexico City	Oaxaca	7 per day	9 hours	$M90
Local	Oaxaca	Mitla	¹/₂ hourly	1 hour	$M5

Mexico: Background Information

Headboard:					
'Tuxtla'	Oaxaca	Juchitan	6 per day	4 hours	$M37
or ADO	Oaxaca	Merida	3 per day	24 hours	$M200
Golfo P	Juchitan	Coatzacoalcos	6 per day	6 hours	$M39
ADO	Coatza.	Cuidad del Carmen	6 per day	6 hours	$M58
or	Coatza.	Villahermosa	12 per day	3 hours	
Autobus	Coatza.	Merida	3 per day	11 hours	$M142
de Sur	C. Carmen	Merida	6 per day	8 hours	$M72
Pan AM	Merida	Miami	10.10	13.30	$82

Part 3
Mexico Itineraries

El Paso

There is nothing special about El Paso except its aspect as a frontier town. The flavour of this, and the excitement of being on the threshold of Mexico, will probably strike you when you arrive. The mountains of Mexico are visible in the distance.

If you intend to travel to Chihuahua by bus, as described in the following section, go to the Trailways terminal and book your seat. Note that neither Trailways nor Greyhound operates scheduled services into Mexico, although both are agents for Mexican bus companies providing regular services (Trailways handle Omnibus de Mexico, one of the bigger and better companies). Alternatively, if you wish to go direct to Acaponeta by train, as described on page 59, cross the bridge to Juarez in Mexico (cost 2 cents) and buy your train ticket at the railway station. The tourist office in El Paso (near the Trailways terminal) will give you information on departure times, etc.

Although there is little to see in El Paso, you may wish to stay overnight. A cheap hotel is the McCoy, 100 yards from the Greyhound

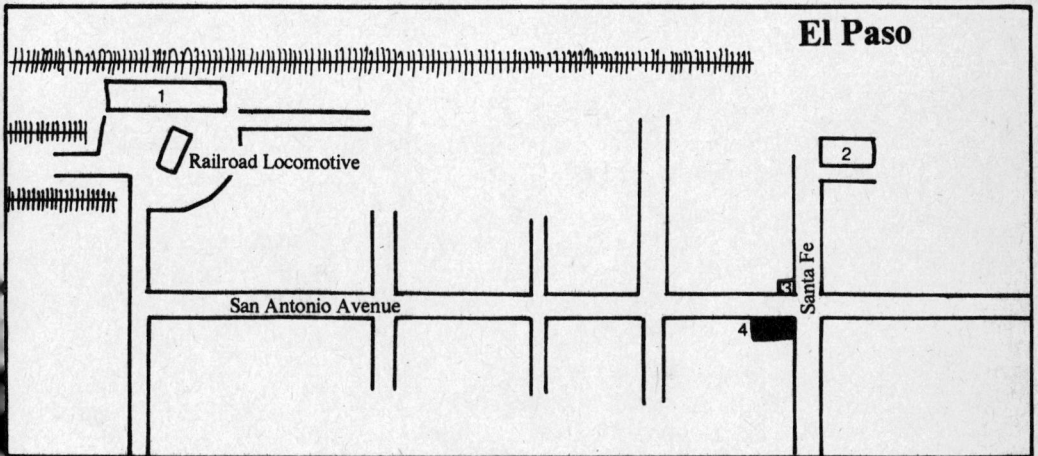

El Paso

1 Railroad Locomotive

San Antonio Avenue

Santa Fe

2

3

4

El Paso: Key

1	Amtrak	3	Tourist Office
2	Greyhound Terminal	4	Trailways Terminal

$10 double

terminal on San Francisco. Cost US$4 for a single. If staying over, you should certainly visit Juarez. Spanish only is spoken here by the locals. Don't forget to take some form of identification with you as you will need to show it on your return (non-US citizens will be required to show their passports).

El Paso to Acaponeta

Although a point of major interest – the Copper Canyon or Barranco del Cobra – is featured during this part of the journey, this stage is best taken rather quickly. The north has been accustomed to tourists from the USA for some time and has adapted itself to the situation. Prices are higher and standards lower than further south.

Customs and Immigration: You are allowed to bring the following into Mexico:
>   200 cigarettes or 50 cigars
>   one bottle of wine, a quart of spirits
>   up to six gifts of no more than US$80 total value
>   all the personal effects, camera, baggage, etc. which you are likely to need on the trip.

Immigration formalities are very straightforward. Your Mexican Tourist Card allows you up to six months' stay (see page 23). US citizens will be asked to show some form of identification, not necessarily a passport. Non-US citizens must show their passports.

El Paso to Chihuahua: The bus gets you into Chihuahua about six hours after leaving El Paso. (The actual journey time is five hours, but you have to put your watch back one hour on crossing the border.) So either leave at 05.00 to get a good night's sleep in Chihuahua, or as late as midnight or 01.00 to arrive in the early morning, thus saving on accommodation. The fare is US$4.80 – a student reduction may be available.

$ 4.60

Be sure to catch your Chihuahua-bound bus from the Trailways station. As often as not, it is likely to pull up in the street outside the Trailways offices, so stay alert (it is *normally* announced!). The company is Omnibus de Mexico. The bus takes you over the bridge to Mexican immigration formalities (those on the US side are usually skipped). It then continues to the main terminal in Juarez, where your baggage is checked by customs officials in your presence, before it and you are loaded aboard the bus for Chihuahua. All this is confusing for the first-timer, so the

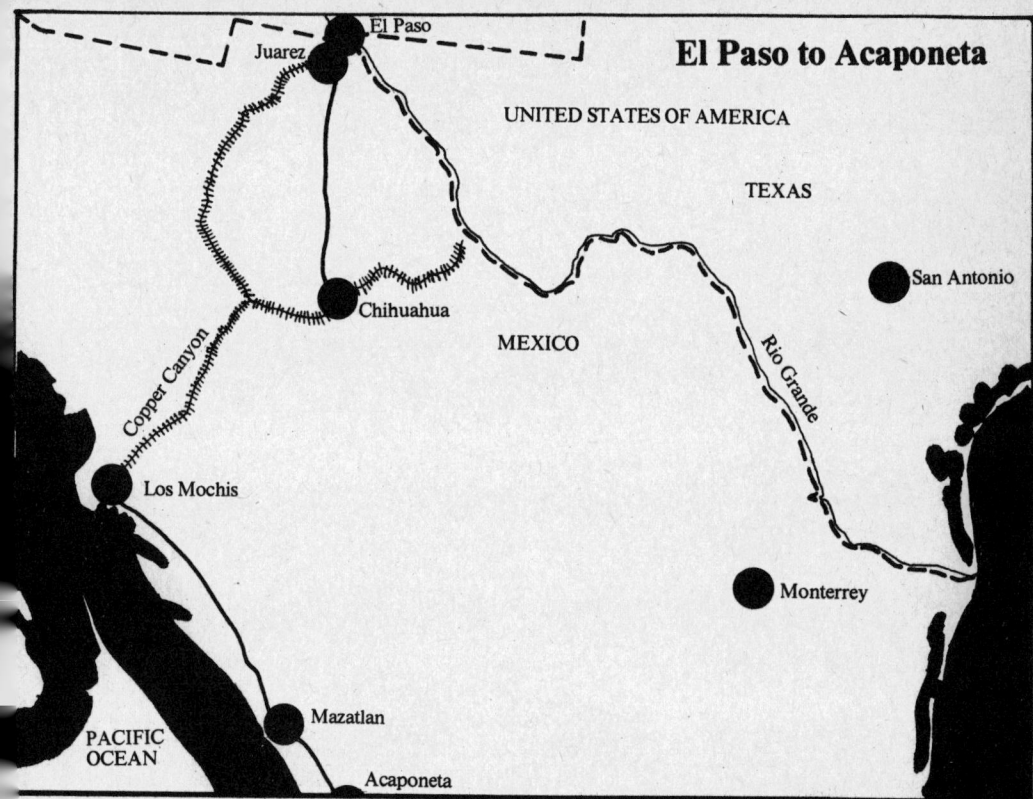

El Paso
Juarez
UNITED STATES OF AMERICA

El Paso to Acaponeta

TEXAS

San Antonio

Chihuahua

MEXICO

Copper Canyon

Rio Grande

Los Mochis

Monterrey

PACIFIC
OCEAN

Mazatlan

Acaponeta

conductor usually keeps your ticket, guiding you through the formalities and placing you in the correct seat on the correct bus. Don't expect him to speak English.

This bus will normally be the Mexico City service, and as good a vehicle as you will have experienced in the USA, except that smoking and spitting are allowed.

Chihuahua: Note that although US dollars are accepted in northern Mexico, change is usually given in pesos, at a rate unfavourable to you. Early location of a bank is therefore advisable.

Your movements on arrival in Chihuahua will be dictated by your arrival time, and by the train schedules to Los Mochis. The early morning train is the best one to take, leaving at 08.00 or 08.20. Trains run every day except Sunday and Wednesday.

Should you arrive early in the morning, say between 04.00 and 07.00,

Chihuahua

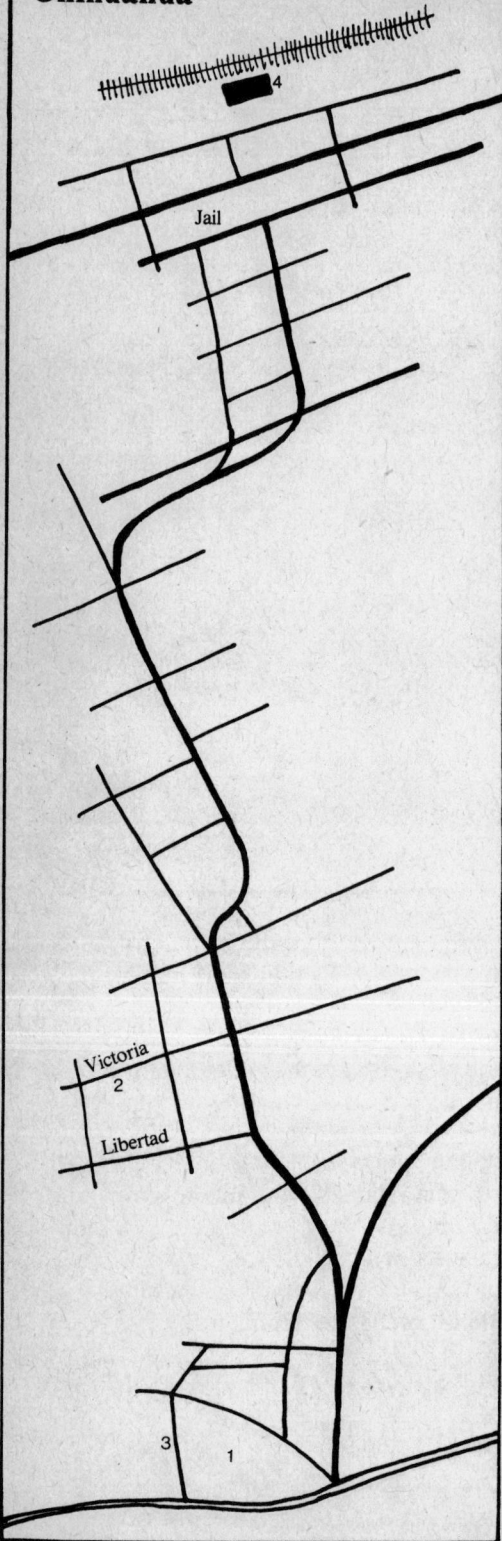

you may prefer to go straight to the railway station. Ask for estacion. It is perhaps a mile from the bus station, so a taxi is suggested. The fare should be $M14. If you arrive at any other time you will need hotel accommodation. You will probably be tired.

Hotels generally in north Mexico are poor value, either expensive if acceptable or dirty if cheap – and then not always as cheap as you may think. Fortunately there is a hotel in Chihuahua between the bus and train stations in Victoria Street. This is the San Juan. Rooms with bathroom cost $M50 for a single and $M70 for a double. Very highly recommended. Their restaurant can also be recommended. All the other hotels we inspected were either dirty or expensive.

If going straight to the railway station arrive early enough to buy a ticket, as this is a popular activity among the locals shortly before departure. Note that there are two morning trains, 08.00 and 08.20. The 08.00 is a more touristy affair, two cars only and faster. The 08.20 is the local, stopping train. The evening train leaves at 21.00.

On arrival in Chihuahua, your best plan is probably to spend a day in the town, in which to purchase your ticket and familiarize yourself with the town's layout, rising early the next morning to catch your train. The hotel staff can be relied upon to wake you at 06.30 if you ask them (all rooms have a telephone).

Chihuahua is one of Mexico's biggest towns and not very nice. You may be disappointed. Of interest, theoretically, is Pancho Villa's (pronounced Viya) house. You will be reverently shown the exhibits, with commentary in Spanish, before being led to the great man's widow. So they say, and she is old. She expects American dollars for her trouble. Apart from that, there is little of interest, save the Cathedral on Plaza Constitution and a good Sunday market. There are few Chihuahua dogs.

Chihuahua to Los Mochis: The train journey takes 13 hours through what is a very interesting route in its middle stages. Though for obvious reasons the railway is not built in the canyon itself, there is a photo-stop at Divisadero Barrancas where the view is spectacular. You'll get about 20 minutes before the train's whistle imperiously summons your return. Here you will see Tarahumara Indians clad in native dress, selling souvenirs and other goodies. The canyon is their home.

After the photo-stop the train climbs and drops among splendid scenery, twisting in all directions over 39 bridges and through 86 tunnels, sometimes crossing above or below its own tracks. It is a journey little known outside North America, but I feel it is the best way of crossing northern Mexico.

Additionally, your journey ends at Los Mochis, a little way from the Pacific coast. This means you then take the coastal road southwards, which, in addition to being intrinsically preferable to the central route, brings you to a beach devoid of tourist comforts and therefore tourists – Playas de Novilleros.

Los Mochis to Acaponeta: On arrival at Los Mochis you will find the railway station a long way out of town. The taxis are a rip-off, having grown fat on the tourist trade. Ignore them, and follow the locals out of the station to the bus stop (see map). The bus fare into town is $M1. Ask for 'Central Camionera por Mazatlan' and keep

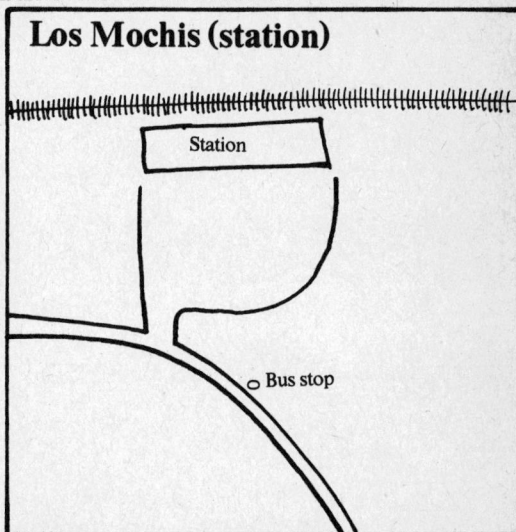

Los Mochis (station)

Station

Bus stop

The map labels (left figure):

o Bus for Tecuala

Bank

Plaza

Bus Depot

Acaponeta

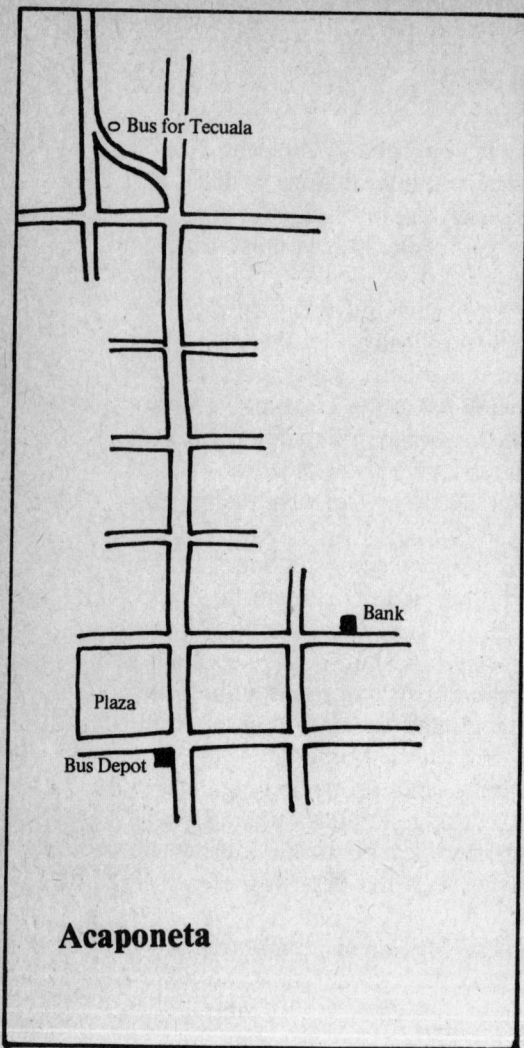

your eyes skinned as the bus passes at least one bus station.

Los Mochis has learned to cater for the tourists from the train, and so the best idea is to get out quick. But if you do want to stay, ask for the hotels Santa Anita, Lorena or Obregon, which should charge you about $M30/$M40 for basic accommodation.

For the journey to Acaponeta a secunda bus via Mazatlan is best. The fare should be about $M90 (the fare to Mazatlan is about $M67). The companies have individual depots in Los Mochis, and there is little to choose between them. Expect a wait in Mazatlan, although you will probably continue in the same bus, arriving in Acaponeta between 07.00 and 10.00. There is a bank here where you can change money.

If you want to spend a fair amount of time on Mexico's Pacific coast, you should stop off at Mazatlan and continue on the leisurely trip to Mexico City (see pages 63–70).

Primer 143

Alternative Routes: El Paso to Acaponeta

The following is secondhand information, gleaned from Edward Reed Matlack (who lives in Tecuala) and fellow travellers. It features a greater utilization of the railway system to Acaponeta. Note that the Copper Canyon railway is expensive because it is a tourist route; railway fares are generally competitive with the buses, although trains tend to be slow and crowded.

1. Continue as before to Chihuahua, then purchase a train ticket to San

Blas (note that San Blas is a common name: do not confuse this town with the better-known resort near Tepic). Here, after a few hours' wait, you can transfer to the southbound Ferrocarril del Pacifico train to Acaponeta. The cost is about $M115: it may be less. You would thus miss Los Mochis completely.

Alternatively, you may be able to buy a train ticket straight through from Chihuahua to Acaponeta – ask at the station.

2.   Train all the way from Juarez to Acaponeta. It is possible to pick up the Copper Canyon train at Juarez, El Paso's twin town, and connect at San Blas as described above. I would estimate your fare at $M265/$M285. You would thus eliminate your Chihuahua stop with a consequent saving of time and money. The tourist office in El Paso (near the Trailways terminal) will give you further details.

Acaponeta to Mexico City

Leaving Acaponeta: Follow the main road out of the plaza to where the bus for Tecuala will pick you up (see map opposite). The fare is $M3.

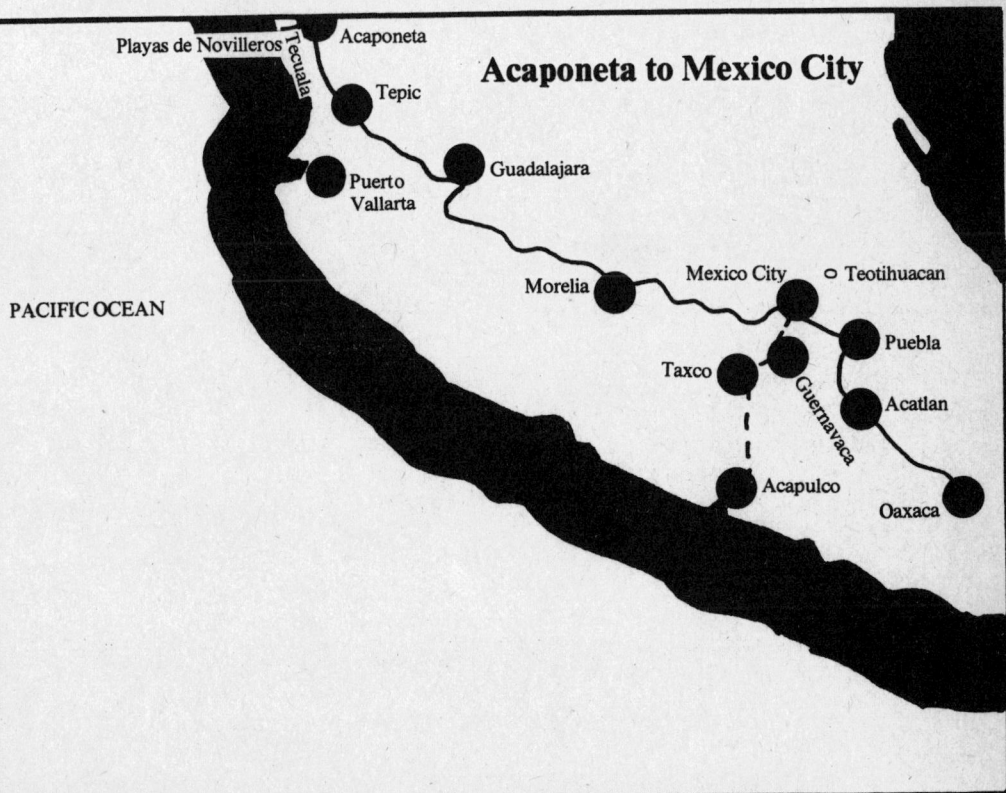

Acaponeta to Mexico City

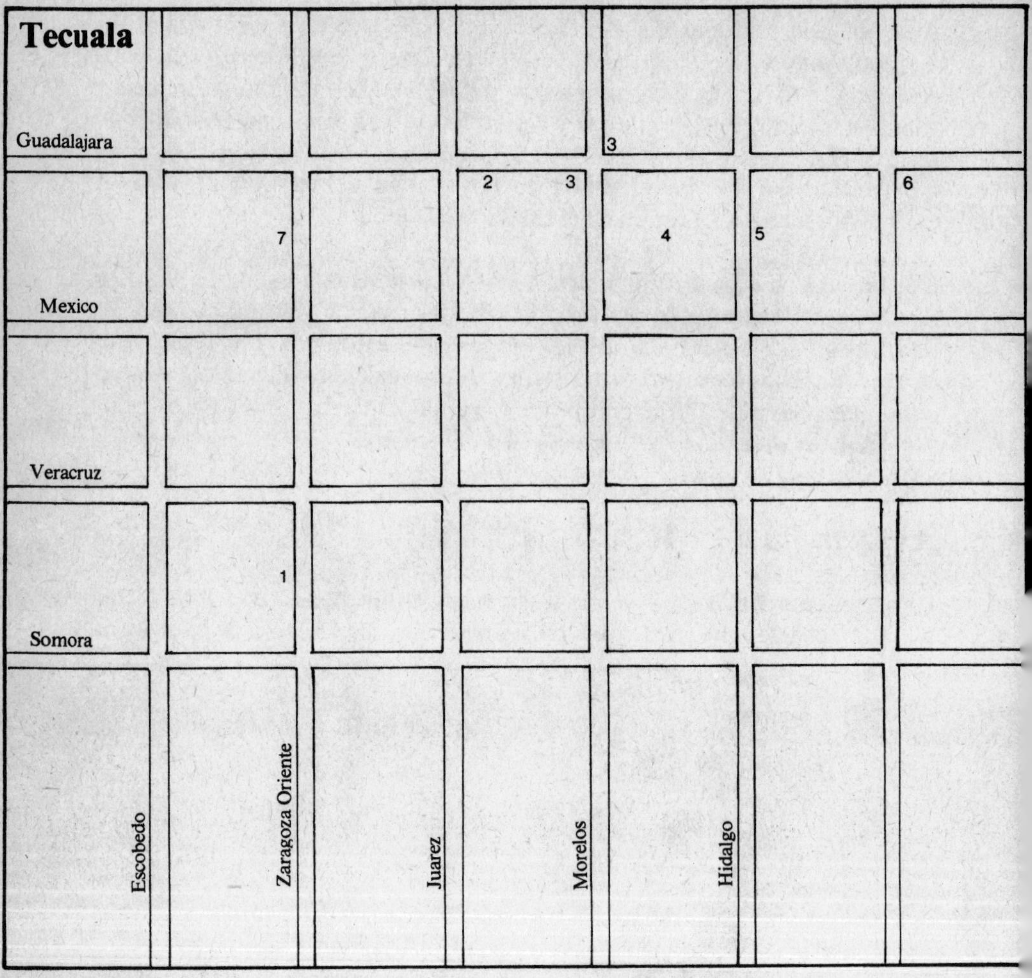

Tecuala

Guadalajara

3

Mexico

7

2 3

4 5

6

Veracruz

1

Somora

Escobedo

Zaragoza Oriente

Juarez

Morelos

Hidalgo

Tecuala: Key

1	80 Zaragoza Oriente (Edward Reed Matlack)	4	Market
2	Los Arcos restaurant	5	Bus depot
3	Banks	6	Church
		7	Taxi rank

Tecuala (pronounced Te*ku*ala): Either before or after you go to the beach

60

from Tecuala, you may wish to visit the local mine of information –
Edward Reed Matlack, an American living here. His address is Zaragoza
Oriente 80 (see map). It is through a letter this gent sent to Trail Finders in
1975 that I first became aware of the beach. He is always glad to dispense
advice and help any travellers who pass through. Amongst the
information he can give you are details of the bus timetables. He also
knows the location of many traditional Indian villages: one of these is set
on an island in a lake. It is circular, and its canals and streets radiate from
the centre.

Playas de Novilleros (pronounced Pliers de Noviy*e*ros): This is a beach,
50 miles long, on what is effectively an island. Rarely visited before
September 1975 when a bridge connecting it with the mainland was
opened (a hazardous ferry, dependent on tides, had hitherto been the only
means of communication), the island has a population of only 4000, in
small communities. Situated in what is perhaps Mexico's poorest state,
Nayarit, there is no evidence yet that development is going to make this
another of the world's famous beaches. If the bright lights and tourist
attractions entice you, then you have Mazatlan, San Blas and Puerto
Vallarta on this part of the coast, and Acapulco further south.

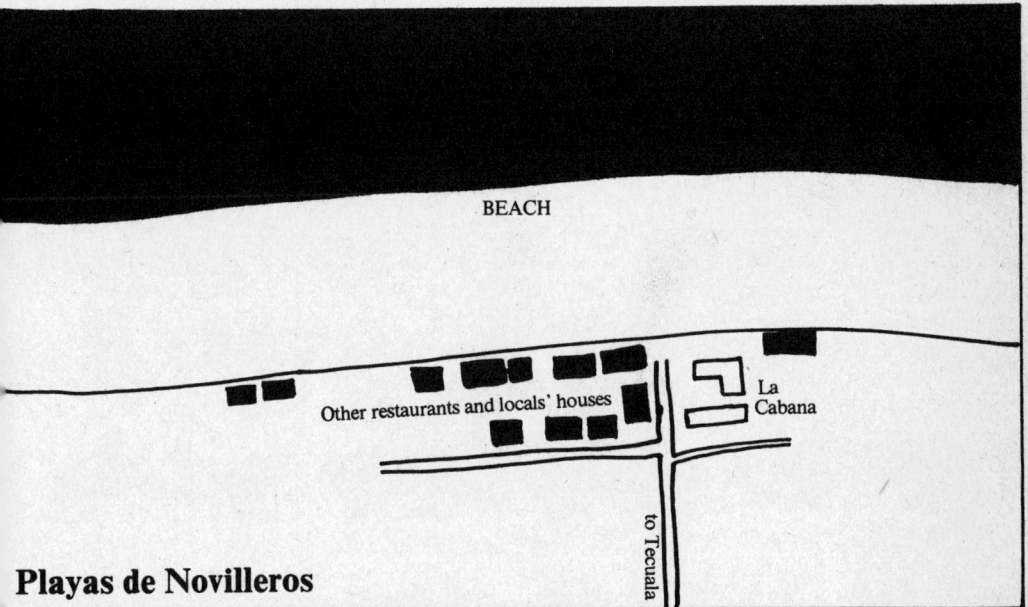

BEACH

Other restaurants and locals' houses

La
Cabana

to Tecuala

Playas de Novilleros

On my visit there were about 100 Mexican tourists (it was during the Christmas/New Year holidays) and 12 foreigners, of whom 8 were American. You can expect few tourists here, with the exception of Easter when it is packed with Mexicans and prices hit the roof.

If you like tourist-free, flat golden sands, enough fresh food to fill your belly and somewhere cheap to rest your weary head, then come here. I wasn't knocked out by it, having experienced miles of deserted sands elsewhere in the world, and the Mexicans have a propensity for scattering litter which scars the most used beach area. Walk a quarter of a mile down the beach however and you have it to yourself. Although not expensive I didn't find the food cheap either, and the available accommodation, though cheap, is spartan with what I feel are inadequate toilet facilities. But perhaps I am hyper-critical; it is only fair to state that the other 11 foreigners thought of it as a paradise, and most of the Mexicans had made a long journey here. In any event at this stage of the journey a beach like this is probably just what you need.

Accommodation is available at La Cabana, as you enter the beach on the right. The facilities are very spartan but as each twin-bedded cabin is only $M17 a night this is all one can expect. There is a good little restaurant here too, under the same management. Other restaurants are also within easy reach.

Tecuala to Acaponeta or Tepic: You can take a bus from Tecuala back to Acaponeta, from where services run to Guadalajara. Here you could link up with the leisurely trip to Mexico City (see page 68).

You may prefer the 06.00 (very much secunda) bus from Tecuala to Tepic for $M26. This can be booked in advance and it is advisable to do so.

Tepic to Mexico City: If you have a few hours to spare in Tepic, it is possible to leave your baggage with the bus company and take a stroll in the hills. Tepic is an interesting little town insofar as it could be described as 'typically Mexican'. On the fringes of the town the horse is still a major means of transport, with excellent riders from the age of six upwards. Many of these people still wear the traditional costume.

There is one bus terminal here, which makes life easy. And as buses for Mexico City start here you can book a ticket on your arrival. Estrella Blanca (White Star) charges $M122 for the journey. They have perhaps the smallest representation in Tepic, and relatively few services, yet their reservations and handling are of a high standard, their secunda buses as good as many primera vehicles, and they have good drivers. Omnibus de

Mexico are much bigger and again tend to have the better buses. Pacifico and TNS have many buses of a poor standard.

After a 12-hour drive you will arrive at the northern bus terminal in Mexico City. Information on Mexico City continues on page 70.

Taking it Easy: Mazatlan to Mexico City

If you want to see the coast, and are in no hurry, you could take the more leisurely itinerary described below. Details on the route from El Paso to Mazatlan are provided on pages 54–8.

Mazatlan: Our recommended hotel is the Fiesta, opposite the bus station: single with bath, $M55.

'There are food stalls outside the hotel. The beach is 300 yards walk, and the bus stop for the town centre 100 yards. There is an interesting town centre jammed with shops, markets and high thrones on which wide-brimmed straw-hatted Mexicans were sitting, enjoying shoe shines. Processions and fireworks were in progress around the main plaza. There are no end of eating places (reasonable) and fruit and groceries available at the nearby market. There is a local tourist office on the main plaza, and a national tourist office ten minutes' walk away on the promenade. Here they are very helpful with route details of Mexican public transport and advice on the most interesting towns to see.

'Mazatlan's coastline is about four miles long. The fishing harbour at the southern end is lively, and by walking past these tied-up boats you can get a close look at the way these deep-sea fishermen live. You can also join them at the food stalls and perhaps take a photograph of these tough characters. A little way along the waterfront I saw heaps of sharks being gutted. The ferry terminal is the departure point for La Paz in Baja California. I considered the possibility of crossing to La Paz, looking around this coastline, and returning to the west coast of Mexico by ferry to Acapulco; but I decided against it.

'North of the terminal is the sports fishing jetty where I saw catches being landed between 3 and 4pm. Sailfish and marlin turned the scales at 150lb, measuring 10ft or more. I spoke to a fisherman who thought Mazatlan offered the best fishing in all the Americas. In fact, as I walked by the beaches fish were leaping into the air positively asking to be caught!

'Continuing along the jetty I met a lighthouse keeper who invited me up to the lighthouse the next day. However, it was so hot that I merely waved to him in his 500ft-high eerie from the jetty. For the more energetic, the view is splendid and well worth the climb. The beaches get better for swimming the further north you go, and about two miles past the town's centre the luxury hotels are sited on good sandy stretches. Here also is the Handicraft Centre and Zoo which for the size of Mazatlan is small by comparison with the other attractions. The animals were missing at the time of my visit.

'Mazatlan's local bus service is frequent and cheap. Most buses stop outside the entrance to the covered market, but the local bus station is five miles from the long-distance bus station.'

Mazatlan to San Blas (this is the better known San Blas, near Tepic): 'Take the Tepic bus ($M39) and get off at the San Blas cross roads and change to a Tepic/San Blas bus. I got a lift in a jeep (distance 65 kilometres (40 miles) from cross roads). The scenery gets more and more tropical as you go along. In San Blas I stayed at Hotel Bucanero ($M46), then moved to Hotel San Blas which had big rooms with double and single beds, kitchenette, bathroom but no hot water ($M52). Spotless, but I discovered lizards had rendezvoused in my hanging towel. Popular with Americans for long stays.

'San Blas is a small typical Mexican coastal village, with a plaza surrounded by shops and cafés and hotels, all within five minutes' walk. Restaurants: El Pescadito; steak and potatoes, $M20. Large turtle steak, beans, rice, $M17 (super!), especially at McDonalds. Coffee and milk, $M3.50; 7-Up, $M2.50; small loaf $M5. The bar opposite the Bucanero has six very large live alligators in the room. On the beach 500 yards away you can buy fish grilled on sticks for $M6. The market has all the necessities for self-catering. The Iron Washerwoman is a laundrette where one can also borrow books. All these amenities have developed to cater for the artists and writers who shack up here cheaply during the winter months. I met an American watercolour artist, a RWS exhibitor spending four months painting local scenes to be put on show in Los Angeles. Still San Blas has retained very much the atmosphere of old Mexico and the locals lend lots of colour to the small plaza. They also lent some noise in the form of fireworks, music by emergent maricias bands and children singing at café tables, whilst small processions threaded their way through the narrow cobbled streets. The adjacent beach, although long, wide and sandy, is not very inviting to swimmers, who go a few miles away to Matanchen Beach. The quiet port area at San Blas is being reconstructed to take the car ferry from Baja California and sugar shipments. A general air of lassitude prevails, possibly due to heat and humidity. There is no

Fishing boats on one of Mexico's many inland lakes—Lake Patzcuaro.

A Mayan temple at Palenque—one of the most remote archaeological sites in Mexico, its palace and temples rising out of the jungle.

The magnificent turquoise domes of Acatlan—a delightful lunch-time stop on the bus from Mexico City to Oaxaca.

One of the many giant stone heads of the Olmec culture found during geological surveys for oil in the Gulf of Mexico, and now displayed outside Mexico City's Museum of Anthropology.

lassitude, however, on the part of mosquitoes and their allies in the insect world, who mount sustained and penetrating attacks on humans. Take plenty of repellent unless your tequila-impregnated tissues are immune from bites. This is a very friendly place – I received invites back to hotels and help from all living there. It's uncommercialized.

'I walked one mile back along the Tepic road to the river bridge for the Jungle River Trip, which is arranged on the spot. I joined seven others for a four-hour trip, $M30, passing mangroves, dense foliage with orchids on branches. I saw turtles, crabs, racoons, iguanas, huge butterflies, white herons, flocks of black and yellow parrot-like birds and others. To see maximum wild life you should start early in the morning. I was told there were jaguar hereabouts. It smelt like the jungle and sounded deafening with chattering and twittering and honkings. At the far end we steered into a clear lake and landed ($M2) for lunch and a swim. Drinks and food were available but we brought our own as prices were high. It is a lovely spot where water is drawn for use in San Blas. The chap in charge of the water supply equipment had erected a trapeze from a branch and gave demonstrations of how to swing out over the water and then dive in. A few of our party tried to copy this veritable Tarzan ... their animal calls were fine, but the dive was a complete and utter failure.'

Matanchen: 'I caught the 09.00 bus ($M3) from San Blas market which leaves each morning for Matanchen Beach, passing on the way Matanchen Village. The collection of huts is made from bamboo and palm leaves and accommodation here costs $M35 double. There is a landing stage on the river for small boats. The walk from here to Matanchen beach takes about half an hour. The beach is wide, sandy and several miles long; ideal for surfing as it is possible to obtain one of the longest rides in the world. Along the edge of the beach were some trees containing huge iguanas; at first I had difficulty in distinguishing them from the broad green leaves but their moving tails gave them away. There are palm leaf shelters on the beach where you can get fish and chips for $M20, but my favourite snack was available in a shack on the promontory – a shrimp taco, $M2.50. They were heaped high with jumbo shrimps and three made a satisfying lunch. Another local bite worth trying is banana bread baked each morning in a small beach hut. I thought San Blas and the adjacent Matanchen Beach ideal for a spell of quiet relaxation and fully understood why writers and artists settled here for a spell of creativity ... but don't forget the insect repellent.'

San Blas to Puerto Vallarta (pronounced Puerto Vay*ar*ta): 'The bus leaves San Blas at 08.30, arriving Tepic 10.15; cost $M12. Change. Depart Tepic 10.16, arrive Puerto Vallarta 14.30; $M30. Watches should go forward one hour. Guest houses are plentiful in the streets opposite the bus station, $M45 double. The restaurant nearest the bus station serves three-course dinners for $M20, excellent value. A meal from the food stalls costs 10 pesos with tortillas.

'Puerto Vallarta is a built-up resort with some large hotels adjacent to the beach, but although the central beach is crowded I found it attractive and unsophisticated. If you like grilled fish then this is the place for you; a score of stalls grill freshly caught fish, non-stop, on the sands, at prices from $M5 upwards. They are handed to you on a smouldering stick straight from the hot ashes. Continuing past the broken-back pier with its thatched roof, there is an area where the parachute hangers take off. For $M140 you can be towed round the bay, two to three hundred feet above the waves, suspended below a brightly coloured parachute. I spoke to a fellow who had just landed and thought it sensational. Taking off is easy enough, as the chute quickly fills with air as you walk towards the water, but landing is a tricky job. You have to spill air at the right time to miss the fringe of coconut trees and touch down before hitting the water. He

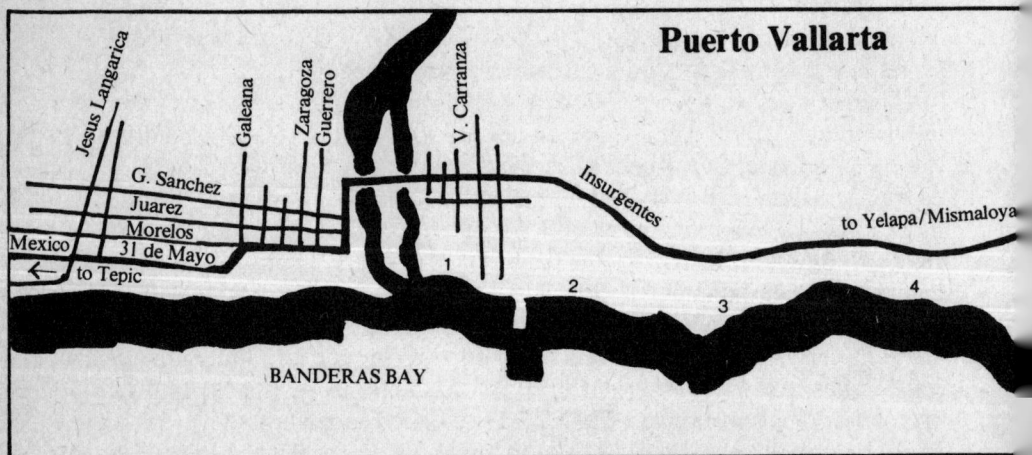

Puerto Vallarta: Key

1	Playa de los Muntas	3	Las Amapas
2	Playa del Sol	4	Playa Macumba

overshot twice.

'Behind the beach I saw a car parked with what looked like a very large tabby cat sitting in the back seat; when I looked through the window it snarled at me and I saw it wore a leather harness with a carrying handle above its back. The owner appeared and I asked him what sort of animal it was. He held up the handle and said it was an ocelot which he had captured two days' horse ride from Puerto Vallarta. He had trained it to act as a guard cat.

'The country round Puerto Vallarta is very picturesque but camping can be risky. From the pier (or rather jetty) an excursion boat leaves for the south-sea-island-style village of Yelapa, $M85 return. I did not go on this trip. In the centre of Puerto Vallarta a bridge crosses the river and I walked upstream where I was intrigued to see the women washing clothes on the river banks. The shallow waters divide here and the central island is a good point to take in the local scene. It is very colourful and lively although some tourist development has begun to take shape.'

Puerto Vallarta to Guadalajara (pronounced Gwadalahara): 'The bus leaves at 15.30 and arrives at 22.00. Fare $M53. During my four or five weeks in Mexico the weather was practically always bright and sunny and this turned even a mundane scene into a scintillating picture. After a while I accepted this as the natural order of things until, on the way to Guadalajara, I saw the sunset. This surpassed any combinations of colour and shapes I had ever before seen in the sky, although, later on, the evening scene on Lake Chapala was a good runner-up.

'Guadalajara bus station is vast and confusing, noisy and crowded. I tried seven hotels but they were all full. I ended up at the Hotel Pacifico, cost $M28. It is pretty basic, 200 yards from the station. Later I had a night at the Hotel Terminal opposite the bus station. $M58 with bath and helpful manager. A restaurant opposite serves eggs, bacon, and other European dishes at reasonable prices. The proprietor gave me a half-hour Spanish lesson free each time I went in. Meals and all food are obtainable at rock-bottom prices in the market (Calzada Independencia and Juarez). This market is definitely worth a visit if you want to buy anything at all. Local dishes are obtainable on the floor above. Local buses stop at the corner of every street (no signs) and frequently a couple of guitarists play music on the way and collect as you get off. The bus service is excellent.

'A few hundred yards from the bus station is the park and Handicraft Centre, possibly the largest in Mexico with prices as low as one can find in any gift shop, with an unequalled variety of man-made goods. Half an hour in here will make you price-wise to gift shops all over Mexico. I liked the fados on show which replace neckties – a wrought silver brooch sliding on a plaited leather tie with silver ends was offered for $M57.

'For a quick look round the main sights of Guadalajara go to Plaza Mayor, which is central for viewing the main buildings and contains the tourist office. It was very hot during my stay but this city has many attractive plazas with trees and fountains which provide welcome resting places during sightseeing. I thought this city had the amenities, cultural interest and Mexican atmosphere to make it well worth a visit. All the residents I spoke to were very helpful.'

Guadalajara to Ajijic: 'Buses leave hourly and take 45 minutes. Having heard this was an artists' colony, I made this short side trip to the mainly Indian village on the edge of Lake Chapala. Accommodation was scarce, a motel on the plaza charging $M80. I stayed at the Pension Playetta ($M35) which was old with a courtyard and in the process of decoration. I found the nights extremely cold. Some cafés round the plaza had limited menus.

'Ajijic borders the lake. Access to the water is limited to the width of streets leading to the lake, except for the 100-yard foreshore used by fishermen. There is very little activity on the lake which is backed by mountains. I searched for signs of the artists' colony and saw a couple of small galleries which were closed and no other evidence of artists at work. I met an American who was writing an article on the local bakery. I accompanied him to the primitive bakery with its mud-packed floor and watched him taking pictures of the baker at work. The locals can be seen in the morning, queuing outside the shop with buckets of maize which have been soaked overnight. For a small charge the shop pounds the maize into a dough from which tortillas are made. In various towns in Mexico I watched tortillas being made on machines which converted the dough into flat pancakes. Their whirring wheels, slipping chains, gears and crank levers moved in fits and starts, with squeaks, grinding and clattering that threatened imminent breakdown. But no, the tortillas appeared with amazing regularity in their finished state, after their ordeal by rack, pinion and fire, to be sold immediately by the kilo to the waiting shoppers. Mostly I found these pancakes to be heavy and indigestible; just in a few places were they baked sufficiently to make them enjoyable eating rather than a necessary filler.

'I found few tourists in the village, which was a quiet place. The milkman rode his rounds on horseback with a churn slung across the saddle. From this he dispensed the milk into small cans which he deftly passed through the doors of houses without dismounting. In the evening the lighted plaza is the only bright spot. I told someone that the following day I intended to take a walk up in the surrounding hills, but was advised against this; among the reasons given was the presence of rattlesnakes.

Ajijic to Chapala: 'From Ajijic I took the bus ($M2) to Chapala town. I stayed at Pension El Palmatos, $M46, at the back of the market. Other accommodation is available, which is probably better value.

'Food is very plentiful in Chapala. Around the market, a local dinner costs $M12. The corner restaurant provides 2 eggs, ham, salad, beans, coffee for $M14. A supermarket and stalls make shopping easy. Chapala is a lively resort along the water's edge and although I was there at Christmas it was not crowded. Quite a long promenade is partly taken up by stalls selling food and gifts. The fruit venders make wonderful salads from a large variety of fruit and are kept very busy all day in the hot sunshine. Many other tempting snacks are sold by the venders here.

'The American Community Centre is two hundred yards to the left of the fountain, if you are facing the waterfront, and caters for the large numbers of Americans who are having long stays in Chapala. The Secretary to whom I was introduced made me very welcome, invited me along for the Christmas dinner, and indicated that the Centre extended its amenities to travellers such as myself. A few hundred yards further on are two lakeside restaurants which specialize in serving whitefish caught in the lake, a local delicacy much cherished by visitors, most of whom appeared to be expert gourmets. It is rare to see anyone in Chapala town who is not eating something or other in a café or on the street; this is no place for dieters who would quickly succumb to the tasty temptations displayed every few yards.

'Just past the restaurants there are horses for hire. Youths gallop these smallish steeds at a furious pace along the front, returning the animals, drenched in perspiration, at the end of half an hour to the anxious owner. At the other end of the promenade are more restaurants where mariachi bands play for the benefit of diners and passers by. One in particular, nearest the fountain, is composed of excellent musicians whose performance is well nigh faultless. Eight in number, the three violinists double as vocalists whilst the remainder are equally at home playing saxes, trumpets or guitars. The musical arrangements are expertly designed to make the most of each composition and this, combined with the very professional rendering, produced the best Mexican outdoor music I encountered anywhere. Take a seat near this band, taste the juicy ripples of flavour in a fruit salad, watch the sun setting behind the mountains across the lake, and then you will experience the quintessence of Chapala town.'

Chapala to San Miguel de Allende (pronounced San Migel de Ayende): 'The bus from Chapala to Guadalajara costs $M6 and takes 1 hour 15 minutes. Change buses at Guadalajara for departure to San Miguel de Allende at 12.30, arriving at 21.00. Hotel San Miguel is clean and quiet; $M28 with bath. Meals are expensive around the plaza but very reasonable in the market area; for example, steak and potatoes, $M10; big coffee, $M1; oranges 3 for $M1. Whilst I was there (December), the weather was fine, but cold in the mornings (37°F/3°C): people were standing around wearing blankets and gloves.

'San Miguel has the appearance of an old Gothic-style town and is an art centre. I visited the institute where short courses in languages and the arts may be taken – they will also help with accommodation if required. I met both professional and amateur artists on courses. In the plaza I was approached by a young man from Chile who asked me to criticize the sketches he was carrying with him. I had nothing about me to indicate that I was interested in sketching, but it appears that in this town one is automatically classified as being allied to that subject. Before long I was having advice given to me about drawing and painting by whoever happened to be sitting next to me in the plaza or, on the other hand, was being asked for my opinion about some arty matter.

'I joined a number of artists at mealtimes, saw them painting outdoors and was invited to their lodgings. The whole atmosphere of San Miguel is permeated with art and merely to be there for a few days will, I am sure, encourage to the full anyone's most modest artistic leanings.

'After dark the plaza is the scene of a passeo which tightly packs the square with boys and girls, counter-marching with a verve and precision that leaves little opportunity for the courtship and flirtation which the passeo is there to promote. This is definitely worth seeing. One of the best set meals may be had at Quinto Loretta Hotel, roast beef, potatoes, vegetables, dessert, coffee, for around $M20. There are scorpions in the surrounding country, so "knock out" your shoes in the morning.'

San Miguel de Allende to Mexico City: 'The bus takes 4 hours, costing $M36. I took the 10.30 bus, arriving at 14.30.'

Mexico City

The northern bus terminal of Mexico City is the most impressive bus terminal of the entire trip. Besides the normal facilities and good signposting, it has a bank where you can change money and an information desk (the girl speaks Spanish only, but you should have picked up enough by now to communicate). The taxi system here is the most efficient I have seen anywhere in the world. You will see large maps displayed by desks with the legend 'Boletos por taxis'. The maps are marked with coloured circles radiating from the bus terminal and display the taxi fare for each zone. The Tourist Office is just within Zone 2, but Avenida Uruguay – where you will find the recommended hotels – comes into Zone 3. Find out where you want to go and then purchase your ticket from one of the desks. A taxi will be called over for you, just outside the terminal. You do not pay the driver anything, and none of the people involved expects a tip. If you prefer to take a bus, modern, uncrowded services operate through Mexico City and depart from the terminal, but it is a long journey.

Nearly all the hotels display their rates, as they are required to do by law, so you don't have that uneasy feeling of being taken for a ride. The Hotel Ontario, 87 Avenida Uruguay, is cheap, shabby but clean, with a daily maid service. A single with bath costs $M46 per night, the same room with double occupancy $M52. The only cheaper hotels are of markedly inferior standard and outside the downtown area. Mexico is one of those few towns where our recommended hotel is not situated near the bus terminal; it would be pointless to stay near your arrival point in the north, or near one of the southbound terminals for that matter. As you will spend at least three days in Mexico City the Ontario is ideally situated. If you want to pay more the Monte Carlo at Uruguay 69 will have a double for $M80 and the Capital for about the same price (the rates are not displayed here).

The Tourist Office will give you maps and information booklets, but you have to ask for them as they are hidden under the counter in the manner of moonshine tequila. They speak English here, but don't expect such a luxury at our recommended hotels and restaurants.

You will find food far better value here than anywhere else on the trip. Prices are government-regulated and many restaurants display them prominently in their windows. Two meals a day, breakfast and a late lunch, should be sufficient, with perhaps coffee and a pastry in the evening. These habits can be very economical as the restaurants offer 4, 5, or 6 course lunch menus – good food at prices which suggest they knew we were coming.

A recommended area for dining is Indepencia, which runs parallel with Avenida Juarez. At N16 Indepencia you will find the Palma de Mallorca Spanish-Mexican (Mallorquine?) restaurant. Their 'Lonch' menu costs $M23. The six courses include fruit juice, soup or consommé with fresh

Downtown Mexico City
(main streets only)

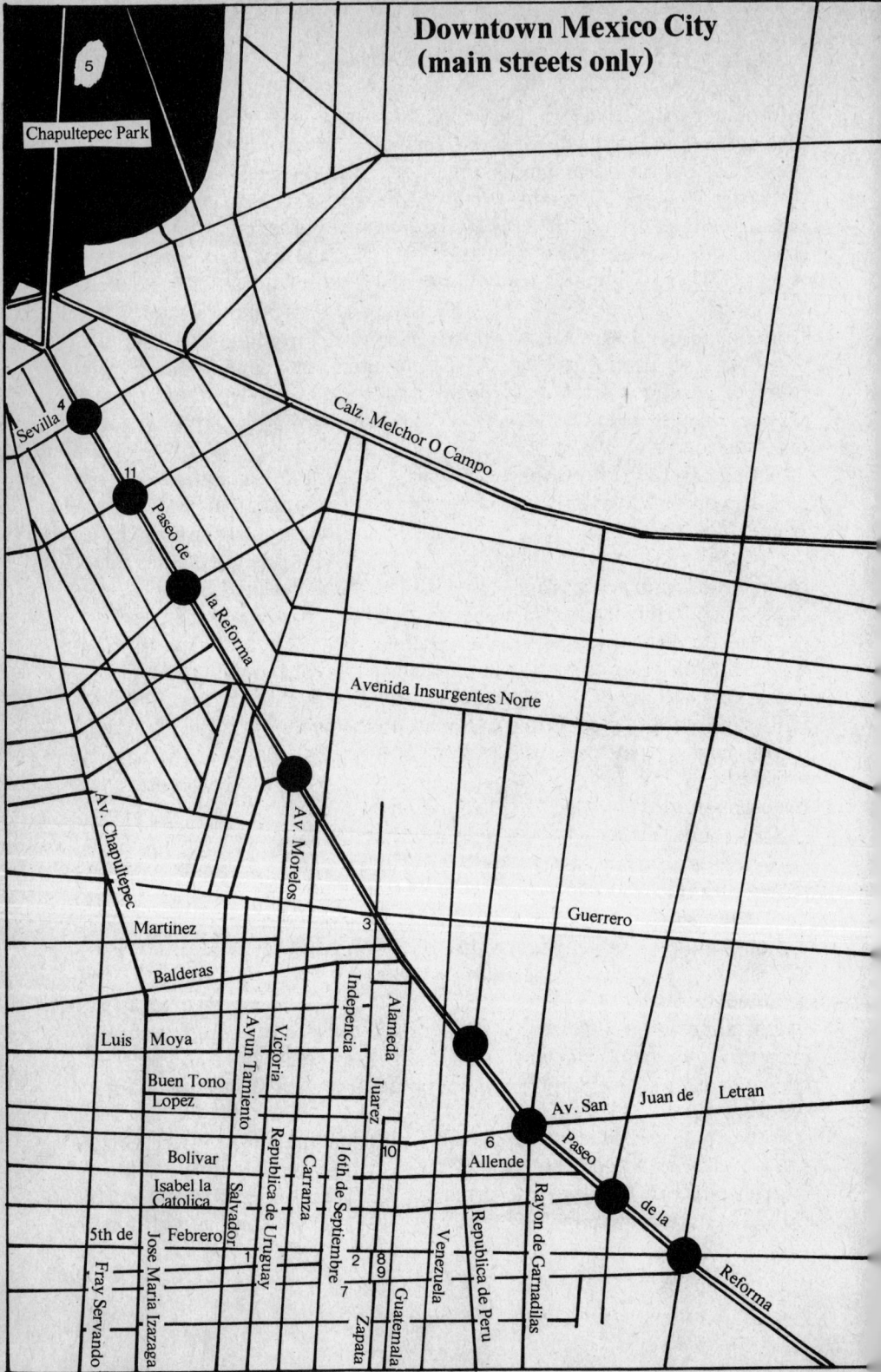

5

Chapultepec Park

Sevilla

11

Paseo de

la Reforma

Calz. Melchor O Campo

Avenida Insurgentes Norte

Av. Chapultepec

Av. Morelos

Martinez

Guerrero

Balderas

3

Luis Moya

Buen Tono

Lopez

Indepencia

Victoria

Ayun Tamiento

Alameda

Av. San   Juan de   Letran

10

6

Allende

Paseo

Bolivar

Republica de Uruguay

Carranza

16th de Septiembre

Juarez

Venezuela

Republica de Peru

Rayon de Garnadilas

de la

Isabel la
Catolica

Salvador

1

2   8 9

7

Reforma

5th de   Febrero

Jose Maria Izazaga

Zapata

Guatemala

Fray Servando

Downtown Mexico City, main streets only: Key

1	Hotel Ontario	7	Palace
2	Zocalo	8	Cathedral
3	Tourist Office	9	Aztec ruins
4	La Carreta Rosa	10	Post office
5	Museum of Anthropology	11	Monument of Independence
6	Plaza de Garibaldi		

---

bread rolls, a rice dish, a main course, dessert and coffee. They claim 'The Best Food And The Best Service'. Food and service are very good. Nevertheless there are many other similar restaurants that you may wish to investigate. Incidentally, do not be put off by the credit card signs in the window or the smart appearance of the place. Although in these places à la carte can be relatively expensive, the tables d'hôte (always with a choice for every course) are tremendous value. Many young travellers eat in the markets among the filth, completely unaware they can have a six-course meal for $M25 or less.

If you walk back from Chapultepec Park along Paseo de la Reforma, you will be in need of refreshment. On the corner of Reforma and Sevilla (see map) you will find La Carreta. Wow! Again do not be put off by the credit card signs. Their table d'hôte for $M30 includes a 'first course' of draught beer (normally $M9 in itself here, à la carte) or fruit juice, soup, macaroni, a main course (the steak with champignons is delicious), dessert and coffee. Very strongly recommended, but you should note that the à la carte menu is expensive. Ask for the special menu (it is displayed in the window). In all these restaurants more conventional Mexican food is of course included on the tables d'hôte.

Another fine eating place, perhaps the best I found, is a restaurant with no name at 64 Isabella Catolica, close to the hotel. Very unprepossessing from the outside, no better inside, they offer a table d'hôte with a wide choice for $M25. An example is pollo consommé with pollo in it (lots), a yellow rice course with meat and tomato, oyster cocktail, chicken in sauce, choice of three desserts and coffee or tea. Probably better value than the other two restaurants and the best meal you're ever likely to get for the price.

At most of these places the menu is in Spanish only, so when ordering you will be involved in a fair amount of guesswork!

Mexico City really hits you first with its hustle and bustle. Traffic, both vehicular and pedestrian, is anarchic. The sidewalks are choked with

---

Mexico City, The Central Downtown area: Key

1	Hotel Ontario	6	Palma de Mallorca
2	Hotel Monte Carlo		restaurant
3	Hotel Capital	7	La Carreta Rosa
4	Tourist Office	8	64 Isabella Catolica
5	Zocalo		restaurant

---

crowds ambling or rushing along. But at night this becomes almost magical. There is no reduction or regulation of the anarchy, quite the opposite. The street marketeers bring out their wares. Avenida San Juan de Letran becomes one long street market. Pavement venders sell bags of peanuts, jewellery, clothing, food, literature — just about anything you care to name.

For a cheap and extremely interesting night out walk northwards along Avenida San Juan de Letran to Avenida Peru. Continue past and on your right is Plaza de Garibaldi. This is an incredible place. The evening's fun really gets under way after 9 pm, when the traditionally dressed bands of musicians start to play. On the corner are stalls selling heart, liver, testicles, etc, steaming hot. Running into the square from the corner are western-style bars. But the real treat lies just off the main square proper. Built like a giant covered market is what can only be described as a gargantuan eating hall. Inside are scores of stalls, each with a counter area and stools; not all the stalls sell the same food. You can buy thin steaks served with raw spring onions, seafood, desserts and cakes, drinks and so on. But the most common are the head stalls, where half a pig's head will grin wickedly at you, cooked sheep's heads smoulder, and a cow bares its teeth as its skull is picked for all that's digestible.

The night also brings out the beggars and the very poor. In any other city you would be fearful for your life.

If you had a late lunch and are wandering in the evening, try the pastry shops. You can buy cakes to take away, or find one where you can sit down with a cup of coffee. It is also worth noting that Mexicans are fond of tortas, crusty rolls with various fillings — ham, cheese, etc.

A visit to Chapultepec Park will use up a very long morning. The park

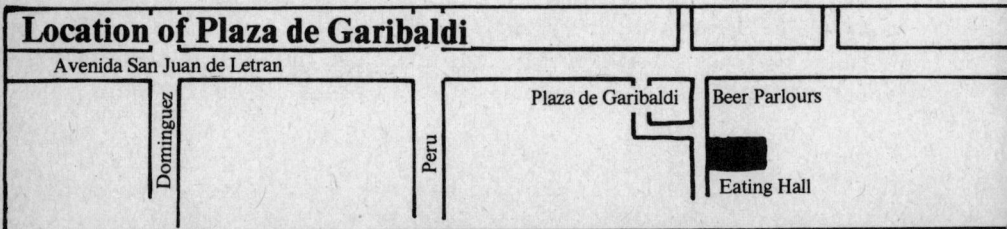

Location of Plaza de Garibaldi

Avenida San Juan de Letran

Dominguez

Peru

Plaza de Garibaldi

Beer Parlours

Eating Hall

Mexico City:
Central Downtown Area

Balderas

Humbolt

Morelos

Guerrero

Alvarado

Violeta

evillagigedo

Moya

Paseo de la

Reforma

Ayun

Luis

Moya

Articulo

Indepencia

Alameda Central

Avenida Hidalgo

Avenida Juarez

Tamiento

Victoria

123

Trujano

Lerdo

Buen

Tono

Lopez

6

Mina

5th de

Mayo

San

Juan

de Letran

3

Belizario

Plaza de
Garibaldi

Bolivar

16th de

Venustiano

Allende

Septiembre

2

Republica

Tacuba

Dominguez

Republica

bel la

Catolica

de Uruguay

Carranza

Republica

de Chile

de Peru

h de

Febrero

1

Republica

del Brasil

20th de Noviembre

5

ino

Suarez

Cathedral

Republica de

Argentina

Palace
Corregi

Moneda

Venezuela

Apartado

Republica de Guatemala

Correo

Mayor

Carmen

Dora

E. Zapata

Pena y Pena

Jesus

Maria

itself is nothing spectacular, although there is a free zoo. But even if you are not a culture vulture you should visit the Museum of Anthropology, described by many as The World's Finest Museum. Entrance is $M15; according to some guidebooks there is a further charge of $M20 for taking photographs, but I was not charged for this, and neither were others entering with cameras at the same time. If you are taking photographs with flash a polarizing filter will be useful. This museum is a must for every visitor to Mexico City. Although there is not a word in English, it is laid out so well with exhibits, models and drawings that unlike most museums it fails to be boring. It may be exhausting. There is a restaurant, expensive as you would expect. The whole is housed in a very modern, open building, two storeys, with fountains and plenty of provision for resting. It deserves its reputation.

Walk either to or from Chapultepec Park along Paseo de la Reforma, the Regent Street or Fifth Avenue of Mexico City. Here are many of the airline offices, including Pan American at the upper end (Paseo de la Reforma 35; telephones (5) 662600 and 464670). If you intend to return to the USA from Merida, you can book or reconfirm your flight here (see Appendix 1: Homeward Bound, page 161). You will see the Monument of Independence (El Angel), and statues to Cuauhtemoc, Christopher Columbus and El Caballito.

Mexico City has an excellent, though limited, subway system. The flat fare is $M1.40. If changing trains be careful that you don't wander out of the station, or you will have to pay again. The trains, which run on rubber wheels, are quick and quiet. The afternoon rush hour is around 4pm; I was assaulted by the crowds as the train pulled into 'Insurgentes', a station which for me has earned its name.

'Fifteen miles south of the city are the Floating Gardens of Xochimilco which is popular for local outings. I joined a Mexican family party of twelve and we were punted through the canals for about two hours for $M28. I did not see many gardens floating by; on the other hand a great number of venders floated by on their boats, offering all kinds of wares and services, food, drinks, flowers, zarapes; photographers, musicians all glided along, politely enquiring as they passed whether we required anything. On one boat was a long wooden xylophone played by two musicians who would, for a few pesos, hitch their boat to ours so that we would float across the waters in tandem to the accompaniment of Mexican Water Music. Mariachi bands were also pouring out melodies whilst the boatman leisurely punted them on their way.

'One of our party hailed a group who were seated at a table in their boat, dining and drinking beer; they returned the greeting by lobbing several full cans of beer into our boat with which we speedily drank their health before they were hidden from view by the foliage along the water's edge. There are not many places in the world where one can sit in a gaudily decorated boat and enjoy scenes such as these. Although it is fundamentally a rendezvous for families at weekends, when it gets very crowded, I think it is worth the tram ride for a change. One man I met intended to spend several weeks at Xochimilco to study the rare plants which are grown by nurseries at the side of the water. I walked through the nurseries but one cannot go very far before requiring the use of a boat. And it's the boats which convert these inland waterways into an ever-changing kaleidoscope of colour which is fascinating to watch.'

Teotihuacan (pronounced Teoti*waca*n): Maybe the best thing about Mexico City is the old city of Teotihuacan about 30 miles north. To get the bus walk to Calle Alarcon (see map) where you should see the buses parked. The company with the most regular services is Autobuses Teotihuacan, with buses leaving every 15 minutes. Ask the driver for 'Piramides' as not all the buses go there. The buses are very good, of primero standard. The fare is $M8 each way. Not all the buses use the

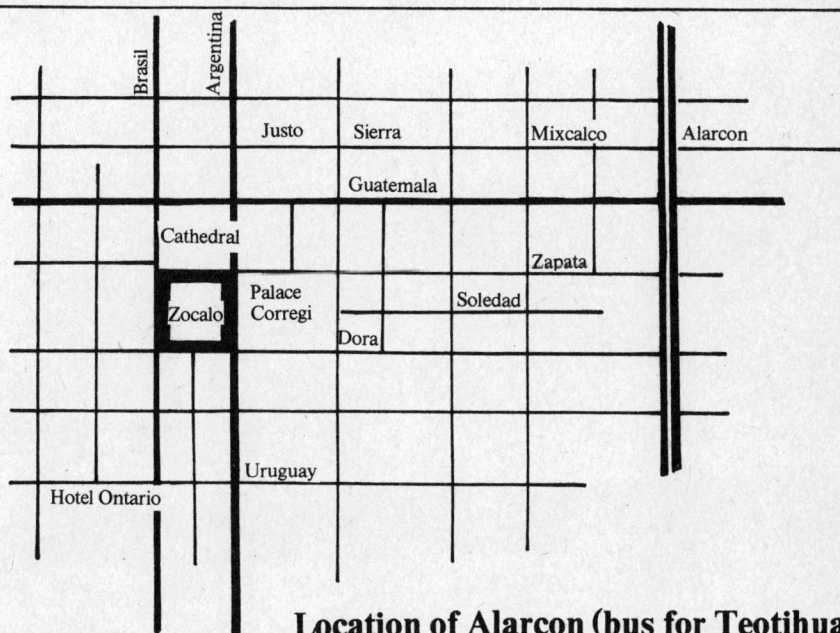

Location of Alarcon (bus for Teotihuacan)

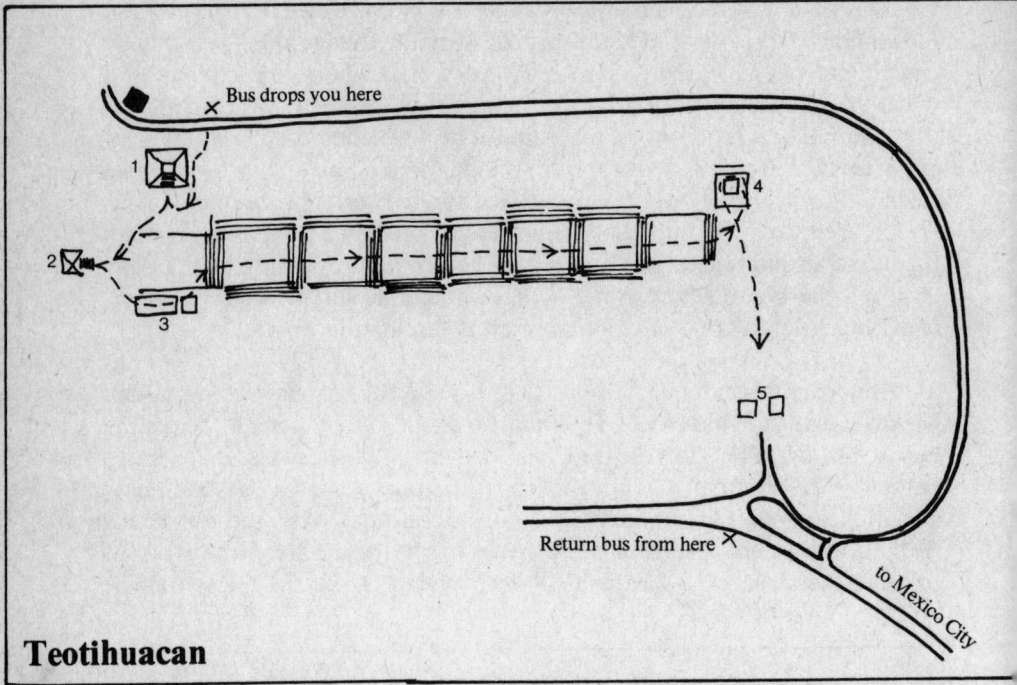

Teotihuacan

Teotihuacan: Key

1 Pyramid of the Sun
2 Pyramid of the Moon
3 Palace

4 Temple of Quetzalcoatl
5 Museum and restaurant

autopista. Normally the standard roads are used, with the bus making regular stops to pick up passengers. Once outside Mexico it is a very interesting ride, passing through villages with their own Mexican-Baroque churches. You will often feel an urge to get off and look around. Ever seen a garden fence made of cacti (the long, phallic kind)?

Usually the bus will drop you off at the Pyramid of the Sun, the perfect place to start your tour. Entrance is $M15. No tripods or professional movie cameras are allowed. Walk around and up the pyramids, then to the Temple of Quetzalcoatl, finishing up at the restaurant and museum (see map). Cross the road for the bus back.

Having invented the step, they built the whole city round the principle.

Walking from the Pyramid of the Moon to Quetzalcoatl you are faced on every side with innumerable banks of steps, perhaps having reference to some hierarchial order. Although it is a walk of only a quarter mile, the constant ascent and descent of steps in the hot sun can be tiring. This city, which was eclipsed with the advent of the Conquistadores, is even today perhaps the finest part of Mexico.

Mexico City to Taxco and Acapulco

Before you continue your journey to Merida, you may have the time and inclination to visit Acapulco and/or Taxco. This is best taken as a side excursion (if you can describe a round trip of almost 2,000 kilometres/1,250 miles as such).

Mexico City to Taxco (pronounced Tasco): 'The bus for Taxco leaves from the Tesquena bus station and takes $4^1/_2$ hours. I caught the 13.40 bus, arriving at 18.00 ($M24 secunda class). The road passes through splendid mountain scenery.

'The Jardin Hotel is adjacent to Taxco cathedral, with a panoramic view from its balcony. A single costs $M52.

'Taxco is a beautiful town with no modern buildings. (It is a designated national Mexican-Baroque monument with no new building allowed by government decree.) The steep streets are cobbled with patterned stones of black and white and at every few steps another enchanting view is presented of this quaint old Mexican town. The market extends beyond the covered area along narrow twisting streets which lead past fountains, up balustraded staircases and through ancient stone arches draped with foliage, each turning making a pictorial setting for the mural of Indians squatting by their piles of fruit and vegetables. Oranges were four for one peso and food generally was varied and cheap in and around the market. Not so the goods in the silver souvenir shops of which there are some 250. (Taxco is most famous for its exquisite silver working and attracts many tourists who go mainly for this purpose. The prices reflect this.)

'The silver is mined nearby. The works siren sounds off at 6am and if you sleep through that a nearby carillion of bells will five minutes later be sure to arouse you. At one silversmith's I saw some brooches made from silver with inlaid turkey feathers dyed bright colours. Apparently no other place in the world employs this method of decoration which was extremely attractive. The Taxco residents are very friendly and will make you welcome as you sit in the small plaza, listening to the mariachi bands playing from the surrounding balconies. A short stroll to the outskirts of Taxco will be rewarded by splendid views of the high mountains which surround this silver town.'

Taxco to Acapulco: 'This bus trip takes 6 hours. I took the 14.30 bus, arriving at 20.30 ($M55 first class). The bus carried a hostess who served coffee without charge, after each stop as well as on request.

'Hotel Acapulco is central, 100 yards from the Sports fishing quay. $M40 with bathroom. Fairly basic accommodation but excellent value considering the enormous tariffs some hotels charge. Eight miles away on the Pied de la Questa beach it is possible to rent a thatched hut with a palmetto bed for $M23 per day.

'There are many restaurants surrounding the Hotel Acapulco which is not far from the Zocalo. Several of them offer tables d'hôte for $M20 which would include fruit cocktail, vegetable soup with pasta, a plate of flavoured rice with peas, $^{1}/_{2}$lb of meat, potatoes, vegetables, rolls, tortillas, ice cream or coffee. Cheaper meals of excellent quality are also available in this area.

'Acapulco has 20 different sandy beaches and is surrounded by mountains. In between the sand and the sierra is an area filled to overflowing with luxuriant foliage and brilliantly coloured tropical flowers. The sea also extends a warm welcome to visitors; 80°F (27°C) make long immersions a delight. Local buses maintain a frequent service along the front and this is the best way to travel economically around the town. Some of the high-priced hotels are sited on the Condesa Beach, the cheapest single in the Hotel Fiesta Americana being $M800 per night. There are however much more expensive hotels than this one.

'From the Zocalo a bus runs to Caletta Beach ($M1 fare) which is a sheltered inlet ideal for swimming. Glass-bottomed boats will take you on an underwater sightseeing tour, and for game fishing there are boats for hire equipped with four swivel armchairs from which one can "play" the monsters of the deep. At 10 am a small boat crosses to Roquetta Island ($M7 return). The passengers on arriving have to walk through shallow surf up to the shore. This is a tiny island for picnics and swimming. If you want to stretch your legs, take the path through the woods which in twenty minutes or so of steep climbing leads you to the lighthouse. The lighthouse keeper's wife will sell you a drink and offer a seat from which you can take in the views along a truly marvellous scenic coastline. Below, the ultramarine blue sea edges along coves, lagoons, inlets and shore until in the distance the heat haze makes definition difficult. Up here by the lighthouse one can wander round the small plateau and look out in all directions, or enjoy nearby the homely scene of donkeys and a few other domestic animals sheltering under shady trees.

'Another interesting beach can be reached by a $M3.50 bus ride from the Zocalo to Puertos Marques. About half a mile of the beach is taken up by restaurants which sell local and fish dishes cheaply, mainly to the local populace who come out here for a day's excursion. Coconut drinks are very plentiful hereabouts. I partook of one under the palm tree roof of a beach restaurant; looking along the line of eating places I saw some of the owners swinging in their hammocks whilst awaiting the next customer. Life appears to be taken very easily in Puertos Marques. Pigs wander about the main road behind the beach and children sell stuffed animals at ridiculously low prices. One young girl was parading about carrying a stuffed armadillo on her head and clutching several iguanos by their tails; she was followed by a handful of laughing youngsters who helped her to find potential purchasers.

'The divers of Quedabra should not be missed. Quedabra is a mile and a half from the Zocalo, up a steep road which leads to a high pavilion set in the vertical rock cliffs, above a small inlet where the sea surges and foams. The adjacent hotel displays a notice of diving times which vary each day. I saw the Torch Dive at 9 pm. At the top of the steps leading to the pavilion, a diver appeared holding a flaming torch aloft. In Olympic fashion he advanced to the cliff edge and dived into the dark waters below. He then swam to the foot of the cliffs on the opposite side of the inlet, and barefoot commenced the 130 foot climb up the sheer cliff face to the diving station. This act is no mean mountaineering feat and is one which would usually call for the use of ropes and pitons by the average rock scrambler. The small crowd of onlookers applauded as he reached the flat ledge from which he would make his dive, and then remained silent as he prepared himself for the plunge. Holding two torches in his outstretched hands, he swallow-dived through the darkness to within a few feet of the glistening waters before he released the flares to bring his arms together for a perfect entry.

'On the next day at noon I returned to see the daylight performance and to attempt a sketch of the general scene with watchers grouped round the bronze statue of "The diver". Although the same dangerous dive was undertaken by three different men, I thought the evening Torch Dive more spectacular to watch.

'The Indian Pottery Market is situated on the waterfront where some very ingenious work is on display; in particular the designs embellishing the clay vessels are worth close examination. They embody most original patterns drawn in vivid colours. Further along the beach is the landing stage for the game fishermen, who return about 3 in the afternoon with their catches of marlin and sailfish which are strung up on gantries for photographers. Further along still is a permanent open-air art exhibition arranged by the local painting club. A member is usually present to help those seeking information on art matters.

'After dark, the Zocalo becomes very lively and crowded. It is a popular trading area for the smaller type of open-air vender, very prominent amongst whom are the balloon sellers, each proclaiming his presence by blowing a loud squeaker at frequent intervals. The weather in Acapulco is well-nigh perfect and it seemed to me that the varied amenities offered to every class of holidaymaker were on a par with the weather.'

Acapulco to Mexico City: The 10.30 bus from Acapulco will get you in to Mexico City by 18.00. Fare: $M55 secunda, or $M83 primero.

Mexico City to Merida

Mexico City to Oaxaca: The best bus company to use for your journey to Oaxaca is Cristobal Colon, because their terminal is nearest to the hotel, on the railway line (subway). Of the two stations nearest the Hotel Ontario, Zocalo is closer, but you will have to change trains. It is better to walk a little further in the other direction to Isabella Catolica. You want a Zaragoza-bound train. Get off at San Lazaro (the fourth stop). The terminal is at 38 Zaragoza (see map).

This is a really mickey mouse terminal, dirty, overcrowded, with spartan eating facilities. However. Buses leave for Oaxaca at 07.15, 10.15, 12.15, 15.15, 20.15, 22.30 (local services) and 21.45 (express). The fare is $M90. Arrive an hour before the bus is due to leave to be sure of getting a seat. The local services take 9 hours for the trip.

You are very strongly recommended to take the 07.15 or 10.15 service and to stay awake, as this is possibly the finest day's journey of the trip. Once clear of Mexico and its environs, the journey is a pleasure as the bus rockets like a roller coaster, up, down, through hairpin bends as if glued to the roads. You can see splendidly decorated Mexican-Baroque churches both in the villages and towns you pass through, and from afar, in the valleys, as you swing through the hills. The half-way lunch stop town of Acatlan is a delight (10.15 bus). There is a 20/30 minute stop here by a restaurant where you can eat. Or you may prefer to walk into the square where there is a splendid church with turquoise domes, almost Persian in

Mexico City to Merida

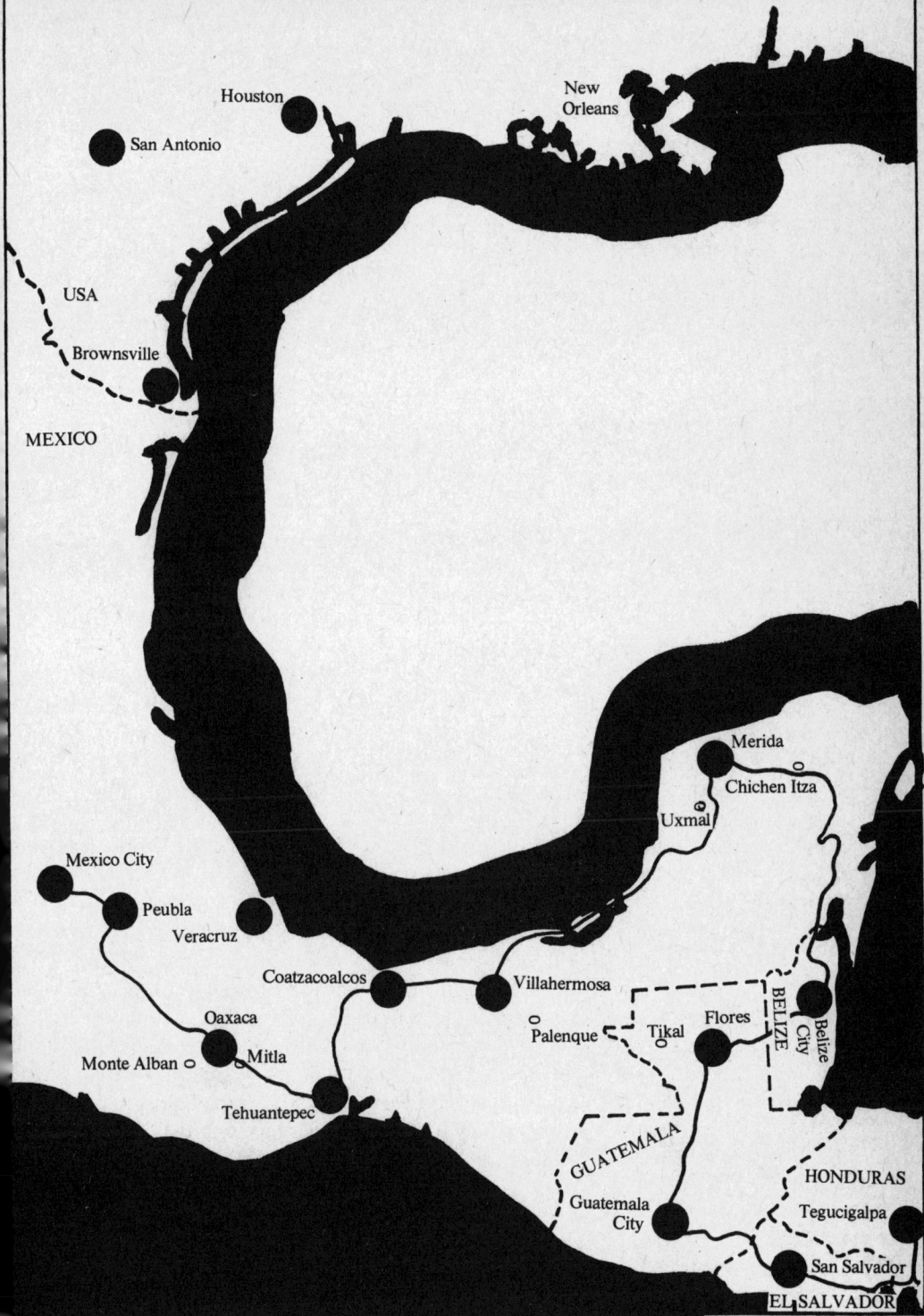

their magnificence. From the unrolling mountain vistas literally peppered with cacti to the traditional Indian dwellings, the sights are too numerous to detail here. It is worth $M90 just for the trip! Cristobal Colon use their best equipment for this run, vehicles as good as Trailways', dressed in a smart livery.

Oaxaca (pronounced W*aha*ca): Oaxaca is full of tourists and travellers, especially in the Zocalo, and prices are generally higher than elsewhere in Mexico, to make them feel at home.

Around the Zocalo you will find restaurants offering a table d'hôte for $M30/$M40. The value is not as good as in Mexico City, but probably the best in Oaxaca. Three restaurants grouped together in one corner of the square, the Café Guelatao, Mesonde Tostada and Monte Carlo, are probably your best bet. Salesmen (and women) of Mexican artifacts and apparel proliferate here, as do beggars, attracted by the tourists. Just grin and bear it. Remember that these are Special Tourist Prices – anything you want to buy will be cheaper elsewhere.

The hotels near the Cristobal Colon terminal are expensive – $M75/$M90 per night. There are many hotels of varying standard near the Mitla bus terminal, though few display their prices. The Hotel de Valle (see map) does: rooms start at $M30 for a single, $M45 for a double. These are basic, however. If you want something better, there are hotels of a higher standard in the same area.

On arrival in Oaxaca, you would be advised to eat, if you did not do so in Acatlan. If you have come in from Mexico City on the 07.15 bus (or, at a pinch, the 10.15 bus) you may prefer to go straight on to Mitla. Take a taxi from outside the bus depot 'por terminale autobus Mitla'. The fare should be about $M12: agree this beforehand. Buses leave from this terminal every 30 minutes – fare $M5, pay on the bus. Just ask for Mitla, where the bus terminates.

Note: before you visit Mitla and/or Monte Alban, it is a good idea to reserve your seat on the ADO Oaxaca/Merida bus (see page 87).

Mitla: Mitla may appear closed if you arrive late, and you may find it impossible to get a meal. The cheapest accommodation is at the 'Hotel and Restaurant Mitla', $M30 for a single. It is very spartan with strange regulations concerning the toilet, but clean. Beware of the dogs. If it seems closed, knock at the main door, loud, and they will let you in. They may be induced to prepare some food for you, for example tortas. Most of the tourists stay at 'The Museo Hotel and Restaurant' over the road, $M65 for

Oaxaca (departure bus terminals)

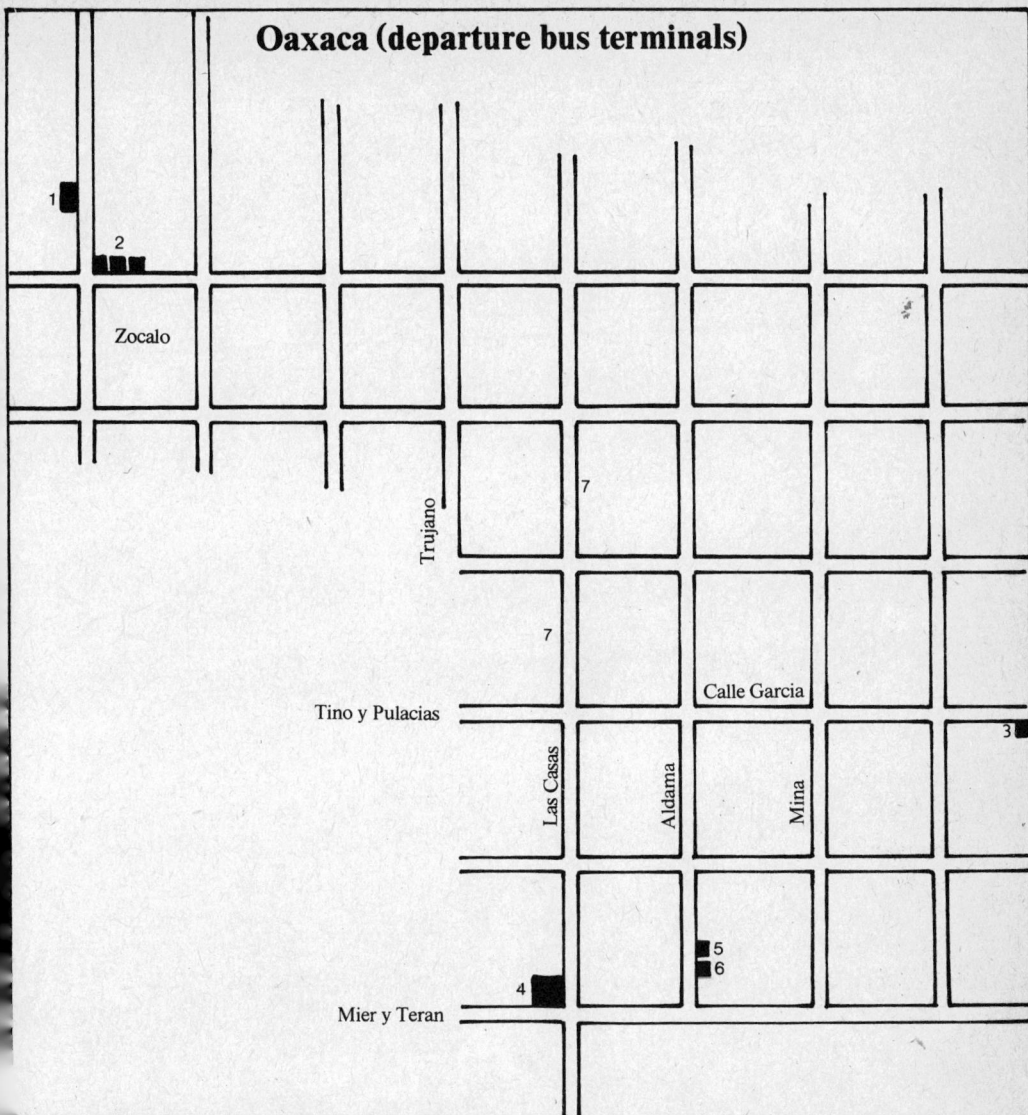

Zocalo

1

2

Trujano

7

7

Tino y Pulacias

Calle Garcia

Las Casas

Aldama

Mina

3

4

5

6

Mier y Teran

Oaxaca (departure bus terminals): Key

1   Bank
2   Restaurants
3   Bus for Monte Alban
4   Bus for Mitla

5   America Hotel
6   Hotel de Valle
7   Market

Mitla

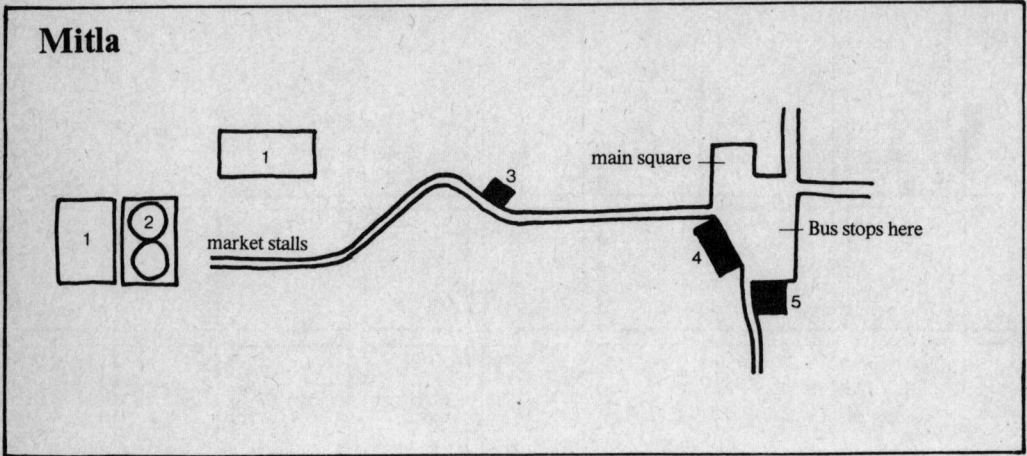

Mitla: Key

1	Ruins	4	Museo Hotel and Restaurant
2	Church	5	Hotel and Restaurant Mitla
3	Motel		

---

a single. The motel on the road to the ruins charges $M60 for a single with bath..

The greatest interest in the ruins at Mitla lies in their difference to other pre-Columbian remains in Mexico. There are no pyramids here, but instead the partly excavated remains of palace buildings, one of which is fairly well preserved. The Spanish found pyramids difficult to destroy because of the intrinsic strength and size of the structures, although they were usually able to destroy the temples atop them. But conventional buildings such as these were more susceptible. Perhaps the most interesting aspect here is the way the Mexican-Baroque church is built into the ruins. Admission is $M3. You will probably find a handful of foreigners here, but no Mexican tourists.

From the square you can take the bus back to Oaxaca, to the same terminal you left from.

Monte Alban: The bus station for Monte Alban is in Calle Garcia (although street signs are rare here) – see map of Oaxaca. Buses (Autobuses Turisticos) leave at 10.30, 11.30, 12.30 and 16.00, returning at

01.00, 14.00 and 17.30. The fare is $M10 return.

Monte Alban must have been spectacular in its day. Less impressive than Teotihuacan in its size, the pyramids are smaller and less complete. The differences are that while Teotihuacan has been carefully restored and covers a large area, excavations are less advanced at Monte Alban, and the site more compact, atop a mountain. Excavations currently being undertaken seem to show there is another city below the present one. On careful examination you can see that the ground is not quite flat, and shows signs of remains underneath. Underground tunnels, possibly utilizing the work of previous civilizations, can be seen. These may connect the various structures. There is also evidence here that there are other, older, pyramids inside the most recent buildings. The city is built, like most planned towns, on a rectangular plan with most angles at 90°. Building J breaks this rule, much to the pleasure of those who prefer variety to uniformity. While the city as a whole could be built very much with the accepted aesthetics in mind, Building J was constructed with a functional purpose − to be used for taking astronomical readings.

Building J's positioning at an angle at variance to the whole, and its unique design, in which aesthetics only play a part at the unimportant, southernmost end, suggest it was the last structure to be built. Many peculiarities about its design, including intricate and minute passageways, suggest that knowledge of astronomy was fairly well advanced, enabling an observatory to be built to a specific design dictated by the requirements of its function.

The short ride up and down to Monte Alban is quite fun too; admission is $M10.

Oaxaca to Merida: For this journey there are numerous possibilities. You could take a direct bus, for which you will have to return to the Cristobal Colon terminal and pick up an ADO (Autobuses de Oriente) bus. You could take two, three or four days over the journey, with stopovers. Or you could do the journey in about 30 hours changing bus lines along the way. What you decide to do will depend upon your remaining funds, time and appetite. If still unsatiated this is the best time to branch out.

ADO runs two buses daily from Oaxaca to Merida. Expect to pay $M180 to $M200. This is if you want a straight-through, one-bus, journey. It will be your longest journey of the trip, taking 24 hours approximately.

If you are taking time over this part of the journey, the most often recommended sights are the ruins of Palenque in the jungle, reached by train from Villahermosa (see page 91), and the Indian-influenced town of

Tehuantepec in the isthmus. Tehuantepec is often quoted as one of the few towns left with a strongly Indian personality, yet there are many towns and villages in this region with these characteristics.

The third way is the compromise. By almost continuous travelling you reach Merida in two days and one night (about 30 hours), yet by changing buses you break the monotony, and the short stops along the way enable you to rest and walk about. This is the route I took.

Oaxaca to Juchitan: Buses leave your friendly 'Autobuses por Mitla' terminal approximately every two hours. Usually the bus is destined for Tuxtla Gutierrez and its headboard will read TUXTLA. The fare to Tehuantepec or Juchitan is $M37 – pay on the bus. You will probably get a better idea of the Indians by studying your fellow travellers. These are very much secunda buses, very crowded, not air-conditioned, and they make many stops. Juchitan is the last stop before the junction of the roads, east to Tuxtla Gutierrez and north to Coatzacoalcos and the Gulf route to Merida. Juchitan is a main transfer point for the natives, so it is best for you to dismount here. If you are lucky there will be a bus (probably Autobuses Gulfo Pacifico) bound for Coatzacoalcos waiting at the same terminal. Just transfer your baggage and person.

Juchitan to Coatzacoalcos: You pay your fare of $M39 on the bus. Usually this will be a better vehicle, of primero standard. Although still crowded with people standing, you should be able to sleep.

When dropped in Coatzacoalcos make your way to the ADO/Cristobal

Coatzacoalcos (bus terminals)

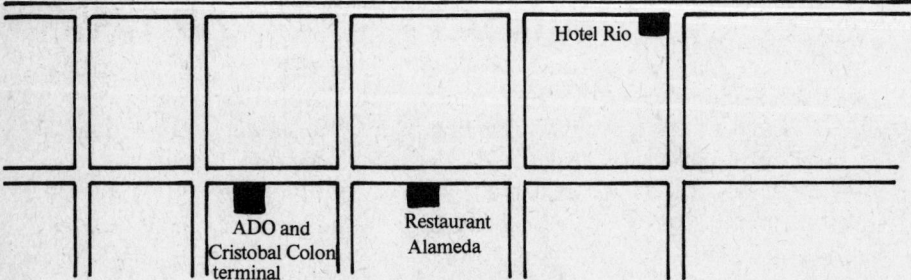

AGP bus stops here

Hotel Rio

ADO and Cristobal Colon terminal

Restaurant Alameda

Colon terminal as shown on the map below. There are hotels if you need them (eg, the Rio, $M85/$M90 double with bath, negotiable; or Hotel Pallas, $M55 single). ADO have two services daily for Merida, taking about 11 hours, in the morning or 21.15 at night; fare $M142. If you cannot connect with one of these services take a bus to an intermediate point, for example Cuidad del Carmen, Villahermosa or Campeche. I took the Carmen bus, fare $M58. Book in advance.

You will probably have time to eat. The restaurant Alameda is ideally situated for this purpose. It offers a reasonable range of cooked meals and pastries at reasonable prices. If you have time to kill and square eyes there is a television.

Coatzacoalcos to Cuidad del Carmen: The ADO bus is a primero vehicle and worthy of the name. If you are travelling overnight you should have no trouble sleeping. Between Coatzacoalcos and Cuidad del Carmen there are five ferries to be taken; I was asleep for the first four but required to get off with the other passengers for the fifth.

Cuidad del Carmen (bus terminals)

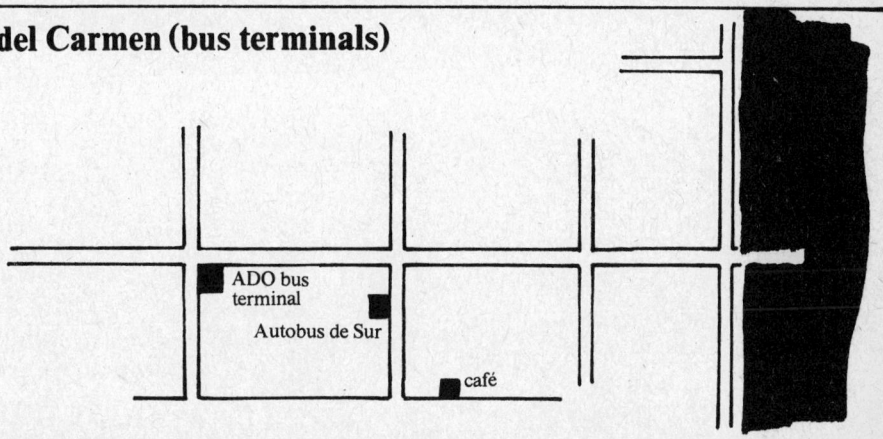

ADO bus
terminal

Autobus de Sur

café

Cuidad del Carmen is said to be the world's largest producer of shrimp, though I haven't checked the veracity of the statement. By Mexican standards the town is fairly cosmopolitan and gives the impression that it would like a tourist industry.

Cuidad del Carmen to Merida: This bus journey is very pleasant, a large part of it running along the Gulf (Bahia de Campeche). Autobuses de Sur has regular secunda services at $M72 for the trip into Merida. From Campeche the road turns inland and meanders through fairly flat country to Merida, passing the ruins of Uxmal on the way. Shortly after you start this journey there is one more ferry (the most interesting). The 09.30 bus gets you into Merida at about 17.00/17.30. For information on Merida, see page 91.

Alternative Route: Mexico City to Merida

Mexico City to Veracruz: 'The 09.00 bus from Mexico City arrives in Veracruz at 16.00. Fare $M75.

'Hotel Leita is cheap but very basic – $M17 a night. Hotel Santillana, opposite the fish market, charges $M60 for a room with bath. Food is cheap in the cafés adjacent to the market; local fish specialities are obtainable in restaurants by the harbour front. Veracruz is fundamentally a port, although it has the atmosphere of a holiday resort. The land ties act as a promenade with seats equipped with loud speakers relaying light music during the day and evening. At breakfast the guitarists wander around the tables in the cafés and in the early morning groups begin playing in the streets. Restaurants have their own bands. Huge xylophones, harps, violins and percussion augment the sounds which make this place a musical Vera Cruz.

'Swimming is not good near at hand so a $M2 ride to Boca del Rio is necessary to indulge in a spot of aquatics. As the name suggests, this is situated at the mouth of a river where there is a tiny plaza, some few huts and cafés. Continuing on the bus for another $M2 brought me to Mandanga – a picturesque native settlement by the shores of a river. Thatched-roof huts and shelters are there in small numbers to cater for residents and local visitors who spend a day boating across the waters and dining off freshly caught fish. Dugout canoes rest by the water's edge or are slowly poled through what appear to be oyster beds. Native musicians play by the shore, alternately directing their efforts towards the diners and the boats setting off for the short ride to the Isle d'Amour. I saw no one swimming or indeed no one exerting himself greatly in any manner ... Mandanga almost seemed to say "mañana".

'When I returned to Veracruz it was nearly dark, the main street (Indepencia) was crowded and a slow-moving cavalcade of cars packed with musicians added mobile music to the scene. Open-air dancing was due to start in the Plaza d'Amee, whilst near at hand marimbas, guitars and harps were still being played with as much gusto as when they started nearly twelve hours ago.'

Veracruz to Villahermosa (pronounced V*i*yahermosa): 'The bus departs at 22.00 and arrives at 06.00 next day. The fare is $M82. I had difficulty in finding accommodation in Villahermosa and after six refusals was accepted at the Hotel Provincial, $M58 with bath. This town appeared to be a stopover for people visiting the ruins at Palenque. There is not a great deal to see or do in Villahermosa, apart from an indoor and open-air museum, the latter being set in woods near a lake. Not far from the bus station is the market where I saw live iguanas on sale; they are supposed to taste like chicken. In the high street there were a number of leather workers offering saddles embossed with much ornamental work; I had not seen saddles so covered with decoration anywhere else.'

Villahermosa to Merida: 'Take the scenic coast road and not the new inland route. Depart 09.20; arrive 18.00.'

Merida

The Hotel El Alamo, close to the bus station in Merida (see map), can be recommended. Singles start at $M40 ($M63 double) and for $M46 you can have a nice little single with bathroom. The building is old and fairly small, but the fittings are modern. The desk clerk has his official price list to hand, so you can just point to the room you require.

Although a tourist town, Merida is not dominated by the genre, who rarely venture outside their own part of town. Restaurant prices seem to be fairly standardized, so it's a question of going for quality. In the hotel/ bus station area there are a number of restaurants. The bus station itself, though expensive, may be worth a try. Avoid the Merida restaurant opposite unless you are starving. A walk down to the main road and along (about a mile) will bring you to the Playa restaurant. Over the road is another restaurant. At each the clientele is Mexican. Food and service are both good at the Playa and there are two Mexican table d'hôte menus: $M20 and $M25. Next to, and belonging to, the Hotel Caribe in the centre of town is a small restaurant with two table d'hôte menus plus an à la carte menu. This can be recommended. Otherwise the other restaurants I found had little to recommend them, so maybe you should just compare prices and avoid the obvious tourist traps.

The Yucatan is justifiably regarded as the finest part of Mexico, and the

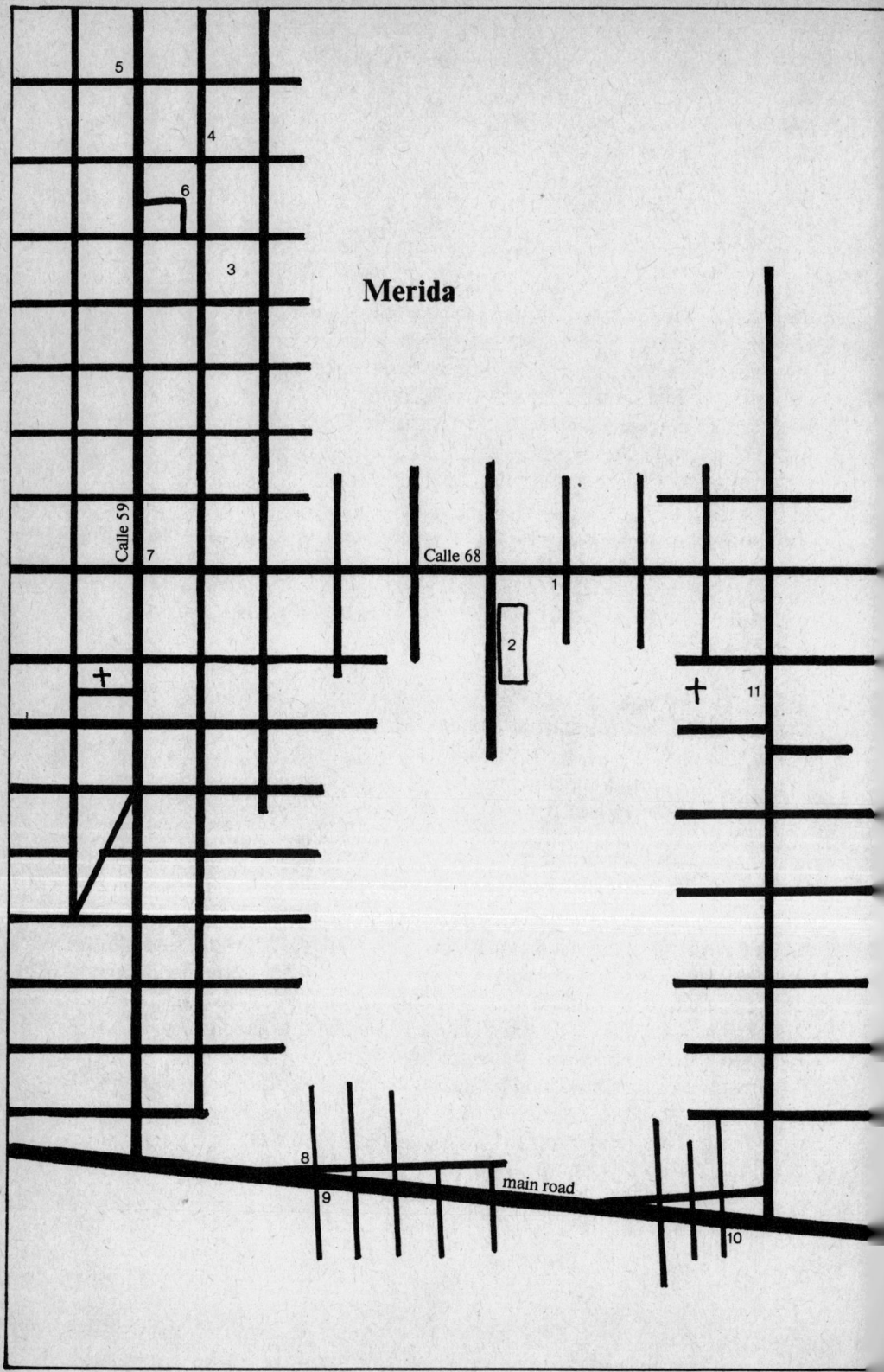

Merida

Calle 59

Calle 68

main road

Merida: Key

1	Hotel Alamo	6	Hotel Caribe
2	Bus terminal	7	Autel
3	Zocalo	8	La Playa
4	Pan American airline office	9	Other restaurant
		10	Hotel/Restaurant
5	Bank	11	Baseball ground

Mayan influence here is strong. This is evident in the food and there are many local specialities here worth trying. Many of them are often included on the tables d'hôte.

'Buses leave Merida about every twenty minutes for Progresso, the port; fare $M5. I found the long sandy beach practically deserted with few shops open, giving the place an "out of season" appearance. I met some people who had rented a beach bungalow a mile or so from the town and seemed happy with the arrangement.'

Important: If you do not intend to go on to Central America, you should book or confirm your flight back to Mexico City or Miami at the earliest opportunity – before visiting Chichen Itza or Uxmal. Details on flights and fares from Merida are given in Appendix 1: Homeward Bound, page 161.

Chichen Itza: Chichen Itza is probably the most interesting of the pre-Columbian sites. The most important and best preserved remains straddle the main road.

Buses (secunda class normally) passing through Chichen Itza leave the central bus station (the one near the Alamo) every hour in the morning, taking about two hours for the trip: $M18 each way. It is about 120 km (75 miles) from Merida. Alternatively, if you are going on through Belize and Central America, following the route in this book, you may prefer to leave your visit to Chichen Itza until your departure from Merida; the bus from Merida to Chetumal passes through Chichen, and it is possible to get off if you wish (see page 94).

Chichen Itza's remains are from the Toltec civilization, usurpers of the Mayas in this part of the Yucatan. As the bus stops, and on entering the main area of the ruins, you will see the Great Pyramid. According to the tourist literature this has 91 steps on each of its four sides, and one around the top, making 365, the number of days in a year. However when I

93

climbed them it seemed more than 91, and anyway 'the one round the top' is cheating! Two sides of the pyramid have crumbled badly, leaving two stairways climbable by tourists. Though not as big by any means as the Pyramid of the Sun, this one seems to have more severe effects on sufferers of vertigo. There is much else of interest among the remains here, in various states of preservation, and a sacrificial well at the back of the city. Do not forget to cross the road for the other buildings. As the pre-Columbians used soft rock, time and weather have taken their toll with the resulting deterioration that can be seen at most sites. This is especially noticeable in the case of carvings. Although erosion has left its mark, you can see how the stonework was carved here, and although much faded by time, there are examples of the paintwork that once adorned these buildings.

Uxmal: (pronounced Ooshmal): This lies in the opposite direction, southwest of Merida. You pass it on your way in. The bus fare is $M13 each way. The greatest interest here lies in the Pyramid of the Soothsayer with its steep stairway. Much of the sanctuary at the top remains, as is the case with the temple atop Chichen's Great Pyramid. The Indian buildings and civilizations in the Yucatan peninsula were relatively untouched by the Spanish arrival.

Merida to Chetumal

Chetumal lies on the Mexican border with Belize, and so this is really the first stage in the Central American itinerary.

'The ruins of Chichen Itza are 120 kms (75 miles) out from Merida on the way to Chetumal. Although the normal arrangement is to make a separate excursion (see page 93), it is possible to stop off at the ruins and then continue to Chetumal without returning to Merida.

'I left Merida bus station at 06.30 and made the following changes: Chichen Itza, Valladolid, Carillo Puerto. Buses pass Chichen hourly, so the time allowed for visiting the ruins can be adjusted to suit your required arrival time in Chetumal. Allow eight hours total travelling time and on arrival at each changing point check departure times for your next destination. For the last section of the journey I travelled on an unscheduled freelance bus. The total fare came to $M77.

'In Chetumal, the border town, the Hotel American ($35) is fifteen minutes' walk from the bus station. There is a small sea front with a few holiday resort facilities, but the main attraction for visitors in this town are the shops offering duty-free goods. This being a free port, all imported articles are considerably cheaper than in other Mexican towns. I did not see a plaza, or indeed any of the usual features which characterize Mexico. Although the frontier to Belize was still a few miles away, I had the feeling that I had already left Mexico behind me. Many of the residents spoke English as they would in Belize, and in several other ways I was not to experience the sharp contrast between countries as I did on crossing the bridge at El Paso when I started my journey across Mexico.'

Part 4
Central America

Central American History

Why should Central America consist of six republics when in total size the area is smaller than Texas and half the size of Mexico? Why is there not a United States of Central America, as there is further north (USA and United States of Mexico)?

The answer is to be found in its history, both pre-Columbian and colonial. Like all the Americas, this area was inhabited by many different Indian cultures, most nomadic yet some sedentary. The Maya civilization was established in Guatemala and parts of Honduras before moving north into what is now Mexico. Other cultures, with economies based on fishing, agriculture (even these were nomadic) or hunting, were isolated from each other. When the Spanish began to arrive, Central America was spared the full brunt of their 'civilizing' influence for two reasons: there were few precious metals to be mined or melted down from Indian artifacts, and few sedentary farmers on whom an exploitative agricultural economy could be based. This meant that very few Spanish colonists came to settle in this area. The pickings were richer in South America and Mexico, both centres of Spanish administration.

Communications across the Central American isthmus were far from satisfactory (the Pan American Highway not having been built). So although Mexico pulled from the north, and Columbia from the southeast, the colonists and natives of Central America were largely left alone by Spain. They therefore established smallish communities with a high degree of self-sufficiency.

The Viceroyalty at Mexico City established Guatemala City as an Audiencia or seat of law for the area. With independence from Spain in 1821, the Central American provinces were invited to join the Mexican Empire. This was temporarily enforced, but soon collapsed. Then followed the first of many attempts to unite these countries, with the exception of Chiapas which seceded to Mexico and has remained Mexican ever since. Many bloody attempts at federation were made between 1821 and 1842, when the idea seems finally to have died. Between 1960 and 1968 an attempt was made at close economic co-operation, in the form of the Central American Common Market. Jealousies and nationalism have weakened the effect of this, although it made a very good start.

This post-Columbian history, allied with the varying resources and climates of each country, has tended to diversify the racial mix. The predominant strain, everywhere except Cost Rica, is 'Ladino', the result of free inter-marrying between the few settlers and indigenous natives.

The Indian population was decimated by disease rather than by force of arms. Guatemala was least affected by disease, so that today over half the population is pure Indian. On the other hand, the indigenous population of Costa Rica was all but eliminated by disease, so that today the population is mainly of European descent.

Climate

ALTITUDE (ft) AND DAYTIME TEMPERATURES

City	Altitude	Minimum		Maximum		Average	
		°F	°C	°F	°C	°F	°C
Belize City	Sea level	76	24	83	28	79	26
Guatemala City	4265	41	5	90	32	64	18
San Salvador (El Salvador)	2297	61	16	90	32	73	23
Tegucigalpa (Honduras)	3304	57	14	84	29	72	22
Managua (Nicaragua)	184	68	20	93	34	81	27
San Jose (Costa Rica)	3675	48	9	91	33	68	20
Balboa (Panama)	102	64	18	95	35	81	27
Cristobal/Colon (Panama)	39	64	18	99	37	81	27

Further notes on climates are included in the background information on each country.

Transport

As you will notice from the details given in the text, your travel through Central America will at times be considerably rougher than you have experienced so far. Although travelling mainly by bus or truck-bus, you

GULF OF MEX

JAMAICA

Grand Cayman
(to UK)

CARIBBEAN SEA

Barranquilla

Cartagena

COLOMBIA

Panama City

San Andres (to Colombia)

Canal Zone

PANAMA

Limon

COSTA RICA

San Jose

Managua

NICARAGUA

HONDURAS

Tegucigalpa

San Salvador

EL SALVADOR

Belize
City

BELIZE

Merida

MEXICO

Tikal

Flores

GUATEMALA

Guatemala City

will find yourself relying on your own resources and initiative. Although the distance is not great, you will be passing through seven countries. Besides changes in currency, continual meetings with customs and immigration, etc, there are obviously transportation differences.

This is not as difficult as it seems. Between Guatemala City and Panama, Central America is united by the Pan American highway. TICA Bus is a Costa Rican company operating regular scheduled bus services between these points. We reproduce their timetable below.

TICA Bus has a very good reputation, particularly in respect of the company's efficiency and the speed and comfort of its buses. The one-way adult fare from Guatemala to Panama is US$37.50. Children under ten accompanied by an adult qualify for a half-price fare, and infants under two years pay 10 per cent of the full fare. Addresses of TICA Bus offices in Central America are as follows:

GUATEMALA: 14 Calle 4–10 Zona 1. Telephone: 8-43-25.

EL SALVADOR: La Calle Oriente No. 531. Telephone: 21-95-56.

HONDURAS: Frente Parque La Libertad Calle Real. Telephone: 22-75-75.

NICARAGUA: Frente Fundicion 'La Perla'. Telephone: 23031-26094.

COSTA RICA: Oficinas Generales Costado Norte de la Iglecia La Soledad, Aparto No. 10167. Telephones: Terminal 21-89-54; Cont. 21-92-29.

PANAMA: Bajos Hotel Ideal. Telephone: 62-20-84.

SOUTHBOUND		NORTHBOUND
Depart 13.00	Guatemala	Arrive 12.00
Arrive 18.00	San Salvador	Depart 06.00
Depart 06.00		Arrive 18.00
Arrive 15.00	Tegucigalpa	Depart 09.00
Depart 09.00		Arrive 15.00
Arrive 16.45	Leon	Depart 07.30
Depart 17.00		Arrive 07.15
Arrive 18.00		Depart 06.00

Depart 07.00	Managua	Arrive 17.00
Depart 09.00		Arrive 16.00
Arrive 08.30	Granada	Depart 15.45
Arrive 08.45		Depart 14.45
Depart 10.30		Arrive 15.30
Depart 10.45		Arrive 14.30
Arrive 14.30	San Jose	Depart 08.30
Arrive 16.00		Depart 07.30
Depart 08.45		Arrive 05.00
Depart 22.00		Arrive 21.00
Arrive 18.30	David	Depart 18.30
Arrive 09.30		Depart 15.30
Depart 19.00		Arrive 18.00
Depart 10.00		Arrive 15.00
Arrive 02.00	Panama	Depart 12.00
Arrive 16.00		Depart 07.00

BELIZE (BELICE): Background information

Bordering Mexico, Guatemala and the Caribbean is one of Britain's last remaining far-flung colonial territories. In 1964 British Honduras, as it was then called, became internally self-governing. The name was changed to Belize — or Belice in its Spanish-American spelling — in 1973, at about which time it was hoped Belize could be given full independence. This has been prevented however because Guatemala has claims upon the territory, and makes little secret of the fact that it would back up its words with military force if and when Belize is given independence. There are subsequently few residents of Belize hankering for independence. Unfortunately most countries in the immediate area support Guatemala's claim. Brief historical details will explain how this position arose.

The modern borders of this area are only a relatively modern innovation, a result of European colonization and subsequent independence movements. As is testified by ancient remains found in the Central America area, and particularly in this, the Yucatan peninsula, this was the centre of the flourishing Mayan empire. With the emigration of the Mayas into the Yucatan proper, these jungle areas became as empty as they are now. Largely ignored by the Spanish, the rich forests attracted woodcutters from Jamaica. Often driven away by the Spanish, the settlers, without the backing of the British Government, persisted and inflicted a resounding defeat on the Spanish at the end of the eighteenth century. Both Guatemala and Mexico threw out the Spanish in 1821, and both placed claims on Belize. These appeared to have been resolved by treaties, Anglo-Guatemalan in 1859, and Anglo-Mexican in 1893. Belize became a Crown Colony in 1871. Guatemala resuscitated its claim, and renews it from time to time — the present being one such. This has caused the recent positioning of British troops in the colony.

In a sense Belize is not a part of Central America at all. Historically, politically and economically it is quite apart from the six republics; it is only in a geographic sense part of Central America.

Belize is mainly comprised of thick forest which renders communications difficult and largely explains the underpopulation. The population is in the region of 140,000, of which half is Creole, around 18 per cent Indian (mainly Mayas), 10 per cent black and another 10 per cent European, mainly Mennonite (a Swiss-originating Protestant sect). The remainder is a mixture of Arabs and Chinese.

Currency: The British Honduras dollar is linked to the pound sterling at a rate of $BH4 = £1. There are banks in both Belize and Belmopan (Barclays Bank International).

Customs and Immigration: US citizens need a visa, available from British consulates in the USA. British and Commonwealth visitors do not need a visa. There may be duty payable on such items as radios and cameras, but this is refunded when you leave the country. Although Guatemala has suspended diplomatic relations with Britain over the Belize affair, movement between Mexico, Belize and Guatemala is fairly free. BUT.

It is well known that border officials are very choosey about who they let in. If you are equipped with bulky backpack, beard and/or insufficient money there is little chance that you will be allowed entry.

Language: Officially English, but be prepared for 'Creole English'. To a minority Spanish is the mother tongue, and of course you may encounter Mayan speakers.

Climate: Being sheltered on its coast by the cays, the second longest barrier reef in the world, yet also experiencing cool trade winds from the Caribbean, Belize rarely experiences intolerably hot weather. Rainfall is abundant.

Belize City: This is the old capital, largest town and has the international airport, ten miles away. It is a smallish town, of the shanty variety, surrounded by swamps. The capital now is Belmopan, 50 miles inland to the west. This is a planned city, mainly consisting of government and administrative buildings.

Chetumal to Belize City

'At Chetumal bus station I encountered several disconsolate travellers who had been turned back from the Belize border, and who were now working out costs and schedules which would enable them to circumvent that country and enter Guatemala direct from Mexico. The reasons given for not being admitted to Belize varied, the main obstacles appearing to be rucksacks, beards, long hair, inadequate funds and appearance. So I was not surprised when on boarding the bus the ticket collector told passengers with rucksacks and beards that most of their fare would be refunded should they be refused entry to Belize – in fact he intimated that they were embarking on an unnecessary journey. As it turned out his dismal prophecies came true; all large rucksack bearers were turned back at the border, and it was rather a sorry sight to watch them tramping back across the bridge to return to Chetumal to reroute their journey. Those who had hidden their rucksacks in gigantic canvas bags or had dismembered the frame and stowed it in a holdall, and those who were clean shaven with well-brushed clothes, were finally given clearance and we were on our way to Britain's Caribbean colony. The bus left Chetumal at 10.00 and we arrived at Belize City six hours later (fare $BH5). The bus journey over unpaved roads goes through flat country, large areas being covered with forests, with mahogany trees prominent in the timbered landscape.

'Accommodation: Hotel Meserva, $BH5, provides a bare room but is clean. There are many others. Meserva is in the centre of town, fronting on to the river by the swing bridge. Opposite the hotel is "Moms" restaurant, which offers substantial meals – dinner about $BH3.50. There did not appear to be many low-priced eating places in the area. The mouth of the river provides a place to stroll along but in general Belize does not warrant a long stay. The main destination for travellers are the cays, a number of small offshore islands where people can relax for a few days. Arrangements for transport to the cays can be made at "Moms".'

GUATEMALA: background information

Half of Guatemala's thickly forested and mountainous area of over 100,000 square kilometres is unpopulated, although this hasn't stopped them trying to get their hands on Belize. The most recent population figures show that a sixth of the total live in Guatemala City. As has been seen continually in recent history, most recently in January 1976, the country is subject to very violent earthquakes. These earthquakes tend to run in a line through the centre of the country and out into the Caribbean. Movements along this fault destroyed the old capital of Antigua in 1773, causing the new capital of Guatemala to be founded in 1776, 45 kms (28 miles) distant; more recently Guatemala City itself was almost completely destroyed in 1917/1918, causing the city to be rebuilt with a mixture of modern buildings and copied colonial. The tragedy of 1976 again hit the capital. Many volcanoes, two of which are still active, attest to the volatile nature of the region.

The economy is largely based on agriculture, particularly with regard to exports. Coffee, cotton, bananas and sugar are the most important crops. Industrialization is growing, though mainly at the moment for domestic consumption. Much of Guatemala's trade is local. Resources such as nickel, petroleum and rubber are beginning to be exploited.

The Indian community still largely lives its traditional life, away from the towns (Guatemala is the only big city, ten times as big as any other), yet is becoming assimilated, for better or for worse. Although largely self-supporting, the Indians too have a money-based economy. The population is 63 per cent illiterate (everyone has the vote); they are subject to debilitating minor diseases and malaria.

Currency: The currency unit is the quetzal, named after an almost extinct bird of the trogon family and the national emblem. One quetzal (Q) = US$1. The quetzal is divided into 100 centavos. US dollars are accepted in many parts.

Customs and immigration: All nationalities need a visa or tourist card. A visa costs US$2.50 and is usually issued single entry. If you stay less than 30 days, an exit permit is not necessary. You can get your visa en route at the Guatemalan embassies in Miami or Mexico City. (British travellers who wish to obtain a visa in advance should apply to the Guatemalan Embassy in France – 73 Rue de Courcelles, Paris 8e – as Guatemala has suspended diplomatic relations with Britain).

There is reputed to be a Guatemalan Consulate in Belize but don't bank on it.

There can be some resentment towards travellers with long hair/beards/rucksacks, etc.

Language: Officially Spanish, though this is little used by the rural Indians of course.

Climate: The climate varies according to altitude. Most of the population live at altitude, and so enjoy a healthy and warm climate, although the nights can be cool. The low-lying coastlands are hot, humid and tropical.

General: Tourists may be subject to overcharging in hotels and on transport. Watch it. Hotel staff, restaurants and taxi drivers expect to be tipped.

Belize City to Guatemala City

Belize to Flores, Guatemala: 'Two buses leave Belize, one for San Ignacio Town and another one which goes nearer the frontier to Benque Viejo nine miles further on. I left Belize from Pound Yard at 14.00 and arrived at the frontier (Benque Viejo) at 16.30. Being Sunday, US$2 was charged by customs. There appeared to be little prospect of finding overnight accommodation at Benque Viejo, although I was told one could rent shelter for a hammock. Whilst contemplating my next move a small truck passed through customs and the customs man asked me if I would like a lift to Flores as a bus did not depart until next day. I thanked him for his kindness and climbed over the tailboard on to the iron floorboard of the open truck, there to endure three and a half hours of the bounciest ride I had so far experienced, as the vehicle careered from one gigantic pothole to the next.

'Leaving the frontier we passed dense forests with an occasional stick hut in a clearing. This northern area was indeed the remote backwoods of Guatemala where the natives live in a very basic fashion, just well spaced bamboo sticks supporting palm tree roofs protecting the residents from the elements. As the evening grew darker and cooler, blue smoke drifted up through the hut roofs as though the whole lot might be on fire. Later on I went inside one of these huts and found it contained just one room with a rough partition separating the sleeping area. The floor was made of compressed mud and in one corner a fire could be lit, the smoke filling the room and then finding its way through the palm leaf roof. The forests, with little sign of habitation, extend all the way to Flores.'

Flores: 'Near the causeway, 400 yards from the bus terminal, is the Hotel Aha Una Ulu. Costing 5 quetzal, it features a communal shower and electricity which is switched on for lighting between 6 pm and 10 pm. This is an excellent hotel which provides very satisfying meals for Q1. Indian-style food may also be obtained near the bus terminal.

'Hotel Aha Una Ulu is at one end of the causeway leading to the town of Flores which is built on an island (the hotel is actually in Saint Elinor). Photographers will find scores of subjects on this unique island; the town is built on a hill rising from the lakeside. The narrow, steep streets meet at the plaza from where entrancing views near and distant can be enjoyed. The descending rows of houses are enveloped in foliage which leads the eye to a mirror-surfaced lake, reflecting on the opposite shore the forests extending to the distant horizons. I timed my return to St. Elinor to coincide with the sunset and I waited to enjoy this remarkable spectacle from the middle of the causeway. As well as experiencing the tranquillity of this area, one can be a little more active – swimming can be quite good in the lake and it is possible to take a trip in a dugout canoe; fishing too could be profitable.

Tikal: 'The ruins of Tikal can be reached by bus from Flores. It departs at 06.45, and arrives at 10.00; fare $Q1^1/_2$. Take your passport as this must be shown at the entrance to the ruins. The journey is over a rough earth road passing through the jungle; here and there are a few native huts. It is possible to obtain expensive hotel or cheap hammock accommodation on the site, but take food, which is very expensive. I was told the bus would return at 13.00. As this does not give enough time to see the extensive ruins I arranged for a lift back at dusk with a jeep driver. Flying is the more usual way to see Tikal.

'I found a warm welcome at the Jaguar Hotel (they mainly cater for parties, but fitted me in for lunch) while the English manageress recounted meantime the circumstances surrounding their existence in the middle of the jungle. There are many wild animals in the area including jaguar and ocelot, also a great variety of birds; as we were talking a humming bird poised itself in mid-air just outside the window. The hotel is used a great deal by bird watchers, as well as those visiting the ruins.

'The Mayan ruins extend over a vast area which would require several days to cover on foot. Many of them are screened from view by foliage and can only be detected a short distance away. Shortly after starting my walk to the temples I encountered two men, one of them an Indian guide; the other, I learned, was a Professor of Antiquity at an American university, paying his fourth visit to Tikal. He suggested I join him and his guide for the next hour or so while he looked at some of the remains close by. Afterwards he was going further afield, hence the guide, who would lead him during his week's stay to more remote finds.

'Perhaps the Professor succeeded in transmitting some of his own enthusiasm to me, or it may have been that the jungle and the ruins themselves excited my imagination, but I became more and more absorbed by the atmosphere which pervaded the scene of the long past Mayan civilization. Here it was not easy to define where earth ended and building began. The temples were set upon rocky hillocks and the soaring edifices appeared as though they were fashioned from the very bedrock itself. The forest had sent vines and creepers growing up the steep sides of the hillocks to continue to envelop the lower parts of the building, so further enhancing the appearance of unity between man and nature which the original architects had striven to achieve so many centuries ago. The ruins of Tikal should not be missed.'

Flores to Guatemala City: 'The fare is approximately Q7. The bus was due to start from the terminus at 08.00, but we sat for 50 minutes while the passengers' belongings, including furniture, were loaded on to the roof. I had actually intended to go as far San Philip — about halfway to Guatemala City — and next morning complete the journey by river boat; but I changed my plan as the journey progressed. We eventually reached Guatemala City at 02.30 the next day.

'We left the Flores terminus and stopped 100 yards down the road to fill up with petrol; 300 yards further on we stopped at a garage to repair a puncture in the spare wheel. The coach was then driven on to a car lift, still with passengers inside and with the engine running; the lift hoisted us up into the air thus enabling the bus crew to switch front and spare wheels. After being lowered back on to the road the passengers waited expectantly for the driver to take his seat and drive away. However the engine, which had been firing smoothly on the hoist, stalled when the clutch was let in and refused to start up again until assisted by twenty passengers pushing from the rear. The time was now 10.00.

'The earth road was deeply rutted with potholes no more than two feet apart, giving the bus' suspension system a mighty buffeting which made the passengers hang on tightly to the seats in front of them. We stopped now and again to pick up more people, all very rural-looking, and each man carrying a large machete. If the machete had a sheath the owner was permitted to take it to his seat; unsheathed ones were stored by the entrance seat on which I sat. Soon my leg was brushing against some dozen blades with razor-sharp edges. Later on I was to see these tools put to good use.

'A little while after we had picked up a couple of natives, we were bouncing along at a fair speed when I heard, above all the noise of our ill-used bus, a tapping on the window by my side. I looked out but could not see anything to account for it, and assumed some stones had been thrown against the glass. A few moments later the tapping was repeated and I saw an arm hanging down from the roof of the bus. The arm was withdrawn and an upside-down face appeared level with mine, shouting in a most disturbing manner. I opened the window so that a native might hear and interpret what was being said. This action of mine was all that was required however by the man on the roof. He now had enough handholds to clamber down the side of the bus and get inside through the door. Apparently this was one of the three-man bus crew whose duty it was to stow the equipment on the roof, a job which he did not complete until the vehicle was well on its way. After this incident I was on the alert to assist this daredevil stuntsman whenever he was engaged in his spider-like performance.

'It had begun to rain at midday and by 16.00 the red clay surface of the road had become slippery and soft, so the sight of a vehicle ahead of us stuck fast in the mud came as no surprise. Our driver pulled out on to the side of the road to pass him, struck a very soft patch, then sunk up to the wheel hubs in the morass. All male passengers alighted, a rope was hitched on to the front of the vehicle and a thirty-man tug o' war team heaved it onto firmer ground. We took on board passengers from the other, stationary, bus, one of whom sat by me with her live chicken. This started a sustained pecking session on my left side until I threatened it with one of the machetes stored beside me.

'An hour later we again got bogged down trying to pass a truck held fast in the clay. We again floundered about in the soft red mud, often sinking down several feet, heaving and pushing, but all to no avail. The spinning wheels wore the smooth grooves deeper and deeper. Then the driver shouted a command. All the men returned to the bus and reappeared armed with their machetes which they wielded like demons as they cut vines and creepers and branches from the jungle bordering the road. Soon a mattress of these was laid around the wheels and this, combined with pushing and heaving, finally freed our bus.

'At 19.00 we pulled into the riverside town of San Philip where a half-hour stop was arranged for snacks. It was at this point that I had intended to transfer to a boat to complete the journey to Guatemala City. However after learning of the uncertainty of the boat passage, and having experienced several hours' delay already, I decided to stay on the bus for the remainder of the journey. After the ferry crossing the road was surfaced and our driver set about making up lost time. He careered along at breakneck speed like an expert racing driver. At 14.30 we pulled up in the centre of Guatemala City. The same driver had been at the wheel the whole time. When he was not driving he worked to repair or free the bus with gusto; the only meal he appeared to take was a packet of biscuits.'

Guatemala City: 'Accommodation: Hotel Capri, Q3, with hot showers. In this large city there are numerous eating places; Q1 will buy a satisfying main meal and as usual the precincts of the market near the cathedral offer cheap local dishes. The Tourist Office is near the main square which has several public buildings spaced around it. I found the National Palace of interest, and those interested in Mayan remains should enquire at the Tourist Office, who will provide details of weekly lectures in English. I found the people of Guatemala very friendly, often going out of their way to give directions.'

Guatemala City to Panajachel: 'Several buses go to Panajachel each day, taking $2^1/_2$ hours. The fare is Q4.50. Accommodation in Panajachel: the Panajachel Hotel, Maya Kunel. A single costs Q3, sharing bathroom with one other. It is comfortable and clean. The Restaurant Hamburgeisa provides a good meal for Q1.50 with liberal helpings of meat followed by desert; several other restaurants offer good value around this price. One has a notice announcing that all vegetables are washed in iodine – a necessary precaution in these areas.

'Panajachel is about fifteen minutes' walk from Lake Atitlan. It is a recognized holiday resort, where tourists make long stays to enjoy the relaxed atmosphere and beautiful mountain scenery; indeed one's first sight of the intense blue sheet of water with its backdrop of volcanoes is the memory that first returns at the mention of Guatemala. The Indians also provide pleasant reminders of this wonderful country. Their friendly greetings, colourful costumes and happy disposition evoke much goodwill among visitors who, after a short while, themselves become more pleasantly disposed towards others. Small dugout canoes are used for fishing and for transport across the lake to the other small villages and it is easy to arrange a trip in one of these at low cost.

'I walked one day to another lakeside village called San Katerina. This took about an hour and three-quarters on a scenic track high above the

First established on Costa Rica's Caribbean coast, banana plantations now provide one of Central America's most important crops. Bananas from Honduras plantations such as this make up over 50 per cent of the country's total exports.

Mayan children by Lake Atitlan, Guatemala. Their direct forbears founded Tikal in Guatemala 1700 years ago.

Tegucigalpa, the capital of Honduras, built at the foot of and up the sides of Mount El Picacho. An attractive city of low colonial buildings, with a lively market and an exciting, sometimes dangerous nightlife.

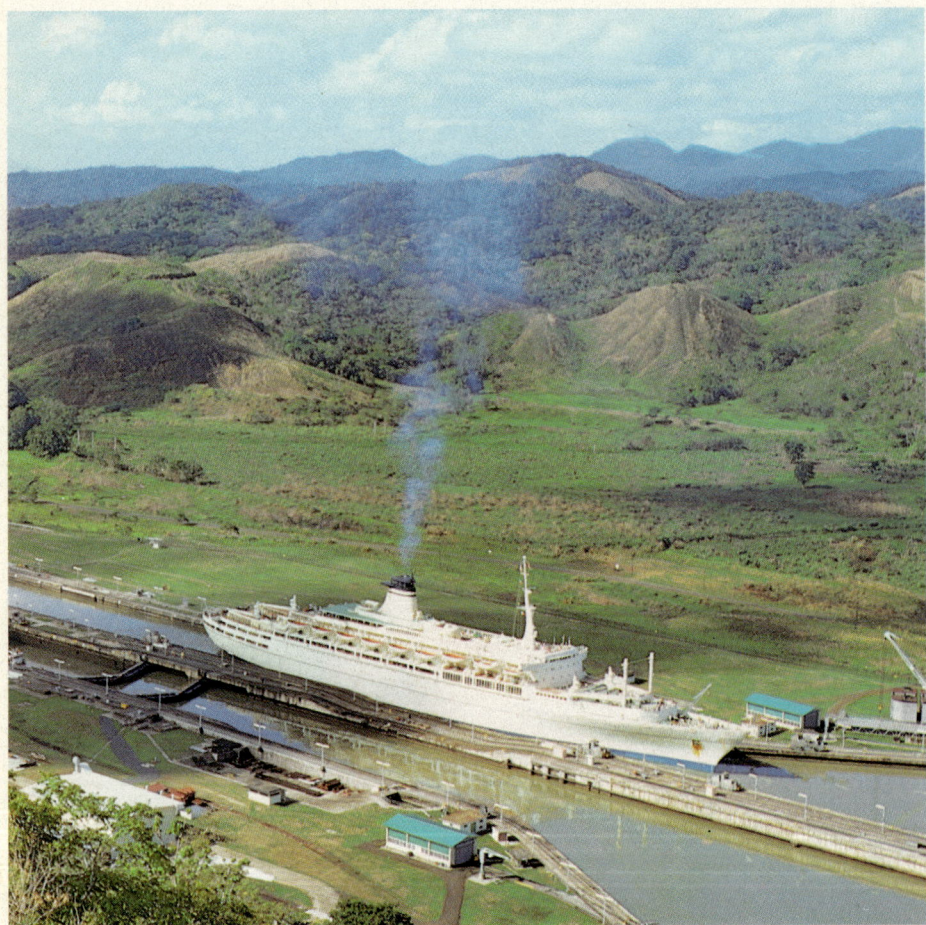

Panama's main source of income, the Panama Canal, which cuts a technological swathe through dense jungle from the Atlantic to the Pacific.

edge of the lake. Indians were the only inhabitants of this village. The water supply came from an ornate fountain, made more picturesque by coloured water containers and the brightly clothed girls who waited their turn, standing in small groups by the shadow of two huge bells suspended under a tiled and wooden structure. Other Indian girls were busy in front of their huts, kneeling whilst they wove many-hued cloths, wearing several strands of large coloured beads around their necks. No-one appeared to be selling the cloth, nor was any attempt made by the weavers to attract custom, just a nod and a friendly smile as I passed by.

'About 100 yards away on the lakeshore, fishermen were landing their catch of fish; it looked very much like bass. I was offered a ride in a dugout back to Panajachel. I did not accept and returned along the same track which had brought me here. The view across the water to the mountains was magnificent. Later I encountered some people who advised me that it was possible to obtain accommodation in a hut in San Katerina; they knew of one person who had stayed several weeks, studying the art of weaving.

'The other lakeside villages are also worth visiting but are accessible only by boat. Property is cheaper across the lake from Panajachel, where I discovered that retired foreigners were finding it more economical to purchase a house and a motor boat than just a house in Panajachel. They regarded the regular boat journeys they made for shopping as part of the novelty of retiring away from their large North American cities.

'On Friday I took the bus (25 cents) to Solala for the market. The bus climbs all the way to this 7000-foot-high village, revealing lovely views of the lake at every bend in the road. A brass band plays in the central square and around them seemingly thousands of Indians, all dressed very much alike, stand or squat shoulder to shoulder. Through this great press of people one nudges one's way to view the vast variety of produce and handicrafts on sale. Woven goods of every hue imaginable are prominent, the prices being comparable with other, even larger, markets held in other adjacent villages. Photographers will find much to interest them here, especially by the fruit market where two huge bells hang from a trestle. The Guatemalans adopt extremely photogenic poses as they quietly wait. For all the buying and selling going on, there is very little noise, no raised voices, no entreaties to buy; they just wait beside their piles of fruit, vegetables or fabrics until a customer comes. And come they do, probably just as quickly as if they had been exhorted to buy.'

Panajachel to Guatemala City: 'The bus fare for the return journey was Q1.50, less than on the outward journey; different companies have varying tariffs. The bus left Panajachel at 15.30. Whilst it was being loaded with a motley assortment of passengers, I watched the Indians loading the roof rack with bales of vegetable produce destined for the City market. Each bale was estimated to weigh 11 hundredweight and measured $4 \times 4 \times 4$ ft approximately. They were stacked on a low wall by the road, adjacent to the bus. Four men manoeuvered the load onto the back of the loader, who crouched in a bending position by the wall, then, balancing the bale on his now horizontal shoulderblades, lurched forward and grasped the steep handrails which led to the roof of the bus. Without losing momentum he mounted the iron rungs and when on a level with the roof bent and shrugged so that the load slipped from his back into its place on the rack. Then without a moment's pause he leapt down to repeat the performance. Several of the passengers were remarking on the amazing strength of these stocky people who, it was said, in their whole history had never resorted to using a horse to ease their physical effort.'

EL SALVADOR: background information

This is the smallest, in terms of area, of the Central American Republics. Largely neglected by the Conquistadores, few Spaniards settled here. There seemed little to come for. Most of El Salvador is volcanic and hilly, with two main volcanic ranges running from northwest to southeast. The few settlers intermarried freely (the term 'intermarried' should be regarded in the general sense; 68 per cent of the births are illegitimate) so that now 80 per cent of the population is Ladino, 10 per cent Indian and 10 per cent of European ancestry. The dominant religion is, as usual, Roman Catholicism. The total population is in the region of $3^1/_2$ million, making El Salvador the most densely populated country in Central America. El Salvador seceded from Guatemala in 1841 with a small population, and it is since then, and particularly in the twentieth century, that the country has developed to its current populous state.

Standards of living and health are improving, particularly with regard to the urban middle classes and skilled workmen, yet still leave something to be desired. In this respect however El Salvador is already ahead of many Latin countries. Universal suffrage is in force here (the illiteracy rate is 50 per cent); extremist political parties are outlawed.

The economy is still largely dependent on agriculture. The soil, comprised mainly of volcanic ash and lava, is ideally suited to coffee growing; this, with cotton, is the most important crop.

Sugar and maize are increasingly being cultivated with an eye to export earnings. The land is still owned by a few wealthy families, with the majority of workers still very poor. Industrialization continues apace, making El Salvador one of Central America's more industrialized nations. Textiles, furniture, shoes, chemicals, cement, cosmetics and rubber goods are some of the main industries. Exports of manufactured goods account for a quarter of foreign exchange earnings. Following the 'Football War' of 1969 Honduras not only ceased trading with El Salvador, but refused to allow passage through Honduras of El Salvadorean goods. This has increased trade with countries outside Central America, especially with the USA, West Germany and Japan. This industrialization has encouraged labour to drift to the towns.

San Salvador: This is the capital from which the country gets its name. Subject, like Guatemala City, to earthquakes, the city was destroyed in 1854. There are thus no colonial buildings, and the modern ones have been built bearing the probability of earthquakes in mind. San Salvador is situated in a basin surrounded by mountains, at an altitude of over 2000 ft. The population is 350,000, a tenth of the country's total.

The heart of the city is Plaza Barrios. Near here are the majority of the more important buildings, the National Palace (seat of government), the new cathedral, National Theatre, the Archbishop's Palace and a rebuilt church, La Merced, of historical note. The area is also liberally sprinkled with parks. There are many cheap hotels near the TICA Bus Terminal.

Of the other towns of interest, Panchimalco is very close to the capital, 15 kilometres (9 miles) away. The Pancho Indians, pure descendants of the Pipil, live around here. Among the dwellings set amongst huge boulders is a fine Baroque church. 15 kilometres east of San Salvador lies Lake Llopango. In pre-Columbian times this was used for sacrificial purposes.

Currency: The national unit of currency is the colon, which is divided into 100 centavos. Prices in El Salvador are often quoted in US dollars, so always be sure which currency is being used to avoid being caught out.

Customs and Immigration: Citizens of the United Kingdom, USA, West Germany and Australia do not normally require either a visa or tourist card if staying for less than 90 days. Recently however some travellers have been asked to purchase tourist cards, so check on this. If you do obtain a tourist card prior to entering the country, these are usually issued free. There is an exit tax of one colon. Normal amounts of tobacco and alcoholic beverages are allowed in. The address of the Immigration Bureau is 25a Avenida Norte 11 – 15, and the National Tourist Board is situated at Calle Ruben Dario 519, San Salvador.

Language: Spanish again, but English is widely understood.

Climate: As in other mountainous countries, this depends on where you are. In the uplands temperatures are usually in the 70s°F (21–26°C) and not very variable. The rainy season is May to September. November through January is the best time to travel. The coast and other lowland areas experience a tropical climate, hot and humid, although malaria has now been largely controlled.

Health: Visitors can become ill from the food and drink, and there is still some malarial risk on the coast. You should therefore be careful what you eat, drink only 'Agua Cristal' bottled water, and continue taking your malaria pills.

San Salvador
Arterial Roads and Landmarks

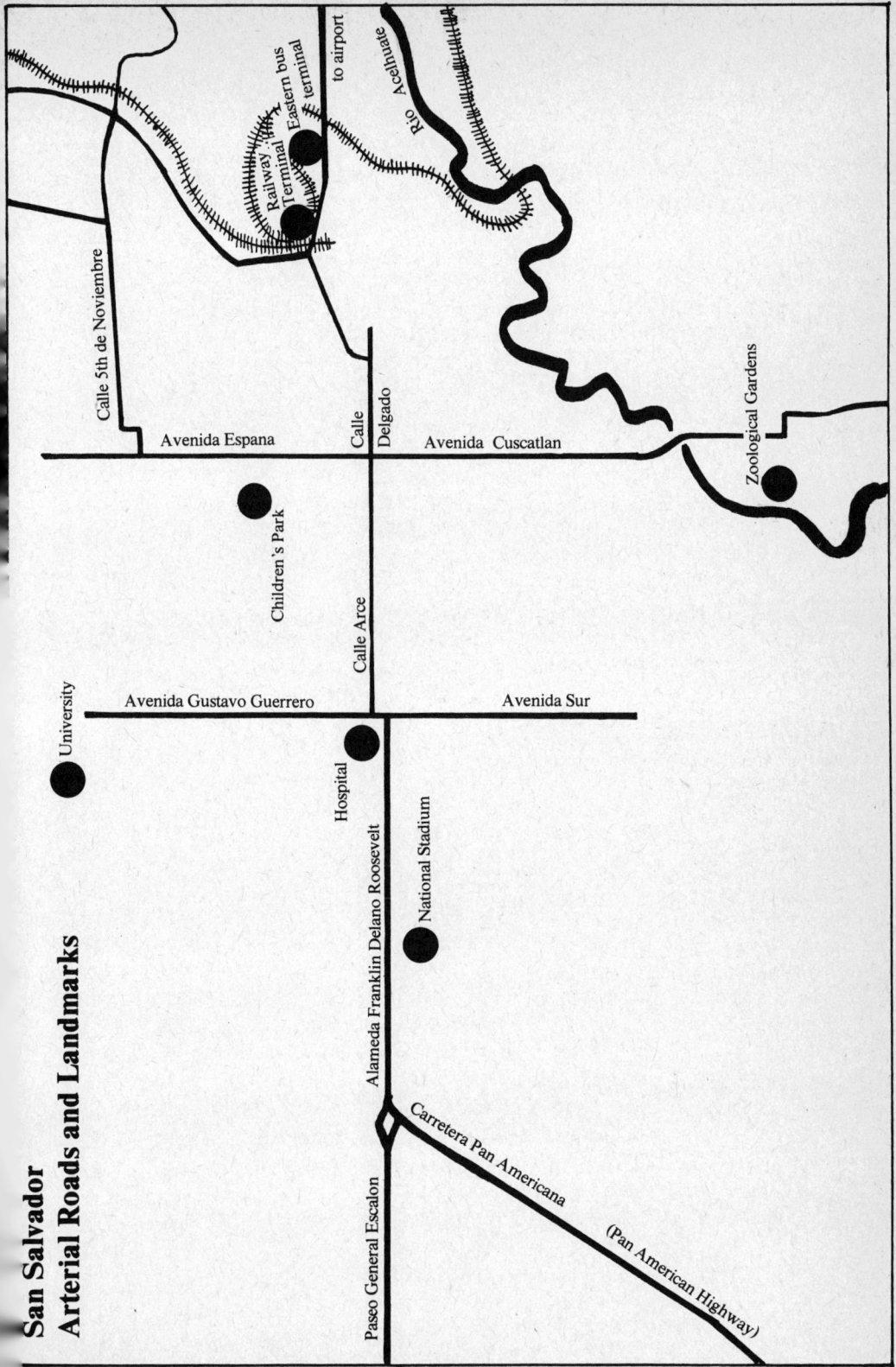

Calle 5th de Noviembre

Railway Terminal

Eastern bus terminal

to airport

Río Acelhuate

Zoological Gardens

Avenida Espana

Calle Delgado

Avenida Cuscatlan

Children's Park

Calle Arce

University

Avenida Gustavo Guerrero

Avenida Sur

Hospital

Alameda Franklin Delano Roosevelt

National Stadium

Paseo General Escalon

Carretera Pan Americana

(Pan American Highway)

Guatemala City to San Salvador

'This is a relatively short bus journey. We left Guatemala City at 13.00, arriving at 18.30. For accommodation in San Salvador try the St. Bruno annex, 6 colon. This hotel is next to the bus station and has plainly furnished rooms situated round an open courtyard where the washing facilities are available. After one night I changed to the San Carlos Hotel, C2, with bathroom, which was very good value; the proprietors were very helpful. This place however is next to the TICA Bus Co. parking lot and certain bedrooms can be noisy.

'Food in San Salvador is no problem, especially if you like chicken, which is served up in great quantities and cooked in a savoury manner. In a good class restaurant chicken, chips, roll and mineral will cost about C3.

'In the city are wide modern roads with busy traffic; the points of interest are easily accessible by the local bus service.

'From San Salvador a number 102 bus will take you to La Libertad for C1, a ride which takes about an hour. This large fishing port is certainly worth a visit, especially if you like surfing. The huge waves come pounding in all along the beaches near here to provide some of the most exhilarating surf rides obtainable anywhere; in other parts of El Salvador I was told of fabulous beaches with huge Pacific 'tube' rollers thundering down upon the shores, and they may well outdo the La Libertad variety. However, along the sands adjacent to this port the high curving, creaming waves will test the abilities of any surfer to the limit.

'The beaches seem to extend endlessly in both directions. The black volcanic sand, left glistening wet by the receding waves, produces a bright radiance along the shore as the water converts it into a huge mirror. The glassy surface reflects the sky, trees and birds, not to mention the distant views which shimmer like mirages. Local fishermen, unable to launch their sixteen-foot boats through the maelstrom of surging water, are assisted by a jib crane standing at the end of the pier. I walked the 100 yards or so along the open wooden decking of the pier. It extends beyond the breaking surf to the clear turquoise water, which rose and fell many feet as the incoming waves built up for their final onslaught on the shore.

'Quite a number of Libertadians were on the pier as this was the time for landing catches. The jib of the crane swung out over the sea and dropped its hook to the boat waiting forty feet below on the swelling waters. Suspended from ropes attached to the gunwales, the boat complete with its crew of three was quickly hoisted up and over on to the pier deck where the locals swarming round the craft quickly emptied it of its catch.

A member of the crew signalled to the crane operator and in no time at all the jib had delivered the boat and fishermen back to the briny to pursue more of the large, strange-looking fish they had just landed.

'Fish dishes are naturally a speciality in this town and can be obtained in two restaurants 400 yards from the pier, where prices are somewhat high. Around the market are several stalls selling slices of red watermelon which I thought acted as the greatest thirst quenchers of all time; the flesh was cold, crisp and oversaturated with delicately-flavoured liquid. They were cheap and in that tropical heat I enjoyed my lunchtime sitting by the stall, keeping the boy busy cutting slices for me from a melon which measured two feet in diameter. Not much in the way of protein or calories, but in that climate very, very satisfying.

'Accommodation is available in this small town where I met several people from the USA making long sojourns. Rooms can be rented in a house on the beach and complete bungalows cost about US$100 per month. Bigger residences, small ranches, are popular with retirees such as the night club owner from New Orleans I encountered in this out of the way place.

'The countryside of El Salvador is undulating, with rivers flowing between fields of cotton bushes white with blossom, or past tall green sugarcane ready for cutting. Always, not so far off, are the mountains, some with the ominous symmetrical shape of a volcano which reminds one of the country's unstable terrain. Back in the capital, San Salvador, I visited the tourist office where I was shaken by the hand and given a most cordial welcome and all the information I desired.

'It appears that TICA Bus, who operate a service through Central America, are permitted one bus per day across the El Salvador/Honduras border. This results in passengers being delayed several days unless they hold a through booking between Guatemala and Panama; in these cases stopovers are limited to certain countries. It was suggested that instead of waiting three days for a seat on TICA Bus, I used local transport and made the journey in several stages. This I decided to do.'

HONDURAS: background information

Honduras is the archetypal 'banana state'. Not only do bananas comprise half the exports, but Honduras displays those national facets often portrayed in western literature and film as peculiar to Central America: an economy based on tropical agricultural produce, politics of a volatile nature with the army playing a large part, countryside covered with jungle, the odd mountain range rising above, bad communications and general underdevelopment.

The Spaniards at first found few Indians here and little reason to stay themselves. Those that did come intermarried freely so that now 90 per cent of the population is Ladino. Of the remainder the majority is black, mainly living along the Caribbean coast, whilst only 1 per cent is pure Indian, and another 1 per cent is of pure Spanish ancestry. This underpopulation persists. There are $2^1/_2$ million inhabitants, 1 million less than El Salvador which, in area, is one-fifth of the size. 45 per cent of the country is jungle, most of the people living in the western part of the country; this is reflected in the communications. Some 150 kilometres (90 miles) of the Pan American Highway pass through Honduras, across the narrowest part of the country, along the Pacific coast, some 120 kilometres (75 miles) from the capital, Tegucigalpa. There is a major artery running from the Pan American Highway through Tegucigalpa to the northern, banana-growing, area. The only other paved roads are in these northern and western areas, along the coast and to the Guatemalan and El Salvadorean borders. Of the very limited railway system, which is entirely in the north and does not even serve the capital, only 95 kilometres (60 miles) serve passenger traffic. The railway's main function and 'raison d'être' is to carry bananas.

The people are very poor, two-thirds being peasants or agricultural labourers, living on the bread- (tortilla-?) line. The middle class is miniscule. Primary education is compulsory by law and the current constitution, but cannot be enforced as there are insufficient schools, especially in rural areas. Illiteracy is at least 55 per cent.

The constitution of 1957 is a liberal one. It gives universal suffrage over 18, some rights to workers, allows civil marriage and divorce, and recognises the right of Habeas Corpus. Government has not been smooth however. The Liberal government elected in 1957 was deposed by the army in 1963; from 1965 to 1971 General Osvaldo Lopez Arellano governed as President, making way for a civilian coalition government under Ramon Ernesto Cruz. At the end of 1972 General Lopez Arellano decided it was time for him to take a hand again, which he did until another military junta ousted him in 1975.

Along with the bananas, coffee is the main export crop. Maize, beans, rice, sugar and tobacco are grown mainly for domestic consumption. Three-quarters of the population live off the land. The economy is the poorest in Central America and was not helped by the destruction caused by Hurricane Fifi and the subsequent floods in 1974. There is very little industrialization.

Tegucigalpa: The city is built in a basin, its two parts separated by the Choluteca River. Tegucigalpa itself is built at the foot of, and up the sides of, Mount El Picacho, one of the steep mountains overshadowing three sides of the town. Tegucigalpa's twin city, Comayaguela, on the other side of the river, is built on flat ground in the basin. Tegucigalpa can be very picturesque, as it is mainly comprised of low, colonial period dwellings, often close together and sometimes attractively painted, winding up the hillsides. There are a few taller modern buildings. For the curious and perceptive traveller Tegucigalpa can be a very interesting and exciting city. Comayaguela market, with the nearby display of native handicrafts is an arresting spectacle; the eighteenth-century cathedral features many art treasures, including a fine silver altar. Then there is the seedy, dangerous and exciting nightlife of Belen; and, of course, the splendid towering mountains.

North of Tegucigalpa: To the north, northeast and northwest of the capital lie areas of interest. The Caribbean coast, to the north and northeast, is a rapidly developing area, as it is here that production, particularly in regard to exports, is centred. In the Caribbean itself the Bay Islands offer a contrast and history. And more ancient history, for those who can never tire of Mayan remains (they do exist!) lies at Copan in the west, northwest of the capital.

The most important towns in the north are Puerto Cortes, Honduras' main port, San Pedro Sula, second only to the capital in terms of population, and La Ceiba. Puerto Cortes and San Pedro Sula can be reached by bus from Tegucigalpa. Delta Line and San Cristobal both operate regular coach services, and there are minibuses from the market area. Both these towns are progressive by Honduran standards, the centres of what industrialization there is, and holding the keys to distribution and exports. La Ceiba is specifically a banana port, with nearby the colonial village of Jutiapa and good beaches. It is also a good point from which to take an excursion to the Bay Islands, an archipelago with a history and present differing from that of the rest of the country. Utila, Roatan and Guanaja are the three largest islands. Approximately half the population are blacks, whilst the other half are of British descent, and still speak English. The islands were bases for pirates in the eighteenth century; Port Royal, on Roatan, the largest of the islands, was perhaps the most famous of the buccaneers' bases. It is now of no importance.

Only the most enthusiastic of fanatics will want to see more Mayan ruins, but if you are among this number you will find them in Copan, in the extreme west of Honduras, on the Guatemalan border. They can be reached, but with some difficulty, from Guatemala City. The easiest way to reach them from inside Honduras (not including plane, which is expensive) is to take a bus from San Pedro Sula. It can also be done from Tegucigalpa using local buses via Siguatepeque, Gracias and Florida. There are other ruins, not yet fully excavated, between Florida and Copan.

Currency: The lempira (the name of a famous Indian chief), also known as the peso. It is divided into 100 centavos.

Language: Mainly Spanish, but English is spoken in the Bay Islands, in the north and by West Indian settlers on the Caribbean coast.

Customs and Immigration: With the exceptions of visitors from the USA, United Kingdom or West Germany, a visa is required, as is an exit permit. The usual amount of tobacco and alcohol is allowed in, and there is no duty on personal property.

Climate: As is usual in Central America, the climate is dependent on altitude. Whilst the capital and other high areas enjoy a reasonable climate, the coastal areas are always hot and humid; avoid the north in December and January.

Health: As you would expect, intestinal parasites proliferate and dysentery is common, especially among unwary travellers. Try to obtain a mosquito net if travelling to the northern coast. Make sure you have been innoculated against typhoid and tetanus if you stay more than a day or two (a good idea anyway for Central and South America). Do not drink the water; avoid fresh fruit and vegetables unless in a very good restaurant.

San Salvador to Tegucigalpa

TICA Bus run a through service from San Salvador to Tegucigalpa, which takes about 9 hours. Alternatively, you can travel in short stages, as described below.

San Salvador to San Miguel: 'Take no.29 bus to Bus Terminal Oriente, then no.113 to Cojutepeque. Fare C$^1/_2$. Depart 10.30, arrive 11.30. From here walk 300 yards through the town and pick up the next bus to San Miguel – bus no.301, fare C3.50, time two hours. As San Miguel appeared an interesting place, I stayed overnight at Hotel Hispano Americana – C10 with bath, in a new (unfinished) block. San Miguel is a busy small town with plenty of food and drink stalls (most welcome as the temperature was in the upper 90s°F/37°C). Restaurants near the park and by the bus station are cheap and generous. None of the many banks in town would change a US$10 note into ones. The surrounding countryside is very scenic and mountainous.'

San Miguel to Amitillo (frontier): 'Depart 10.00, arrive noon. Fare C2 (change buses at San Rosa). The frontier lies amidst beautiful scenery with a river that invites one to linger by its wooded banks – but it is prudent to attend to frontier crossing formalities on arrival. Retain the stamped clearance paper for presentation to the guard on the El Salvador side, then walk across the bridge and show the same paper to the guard on the Honduras side. After customs clearance look out for a minibus going to the capital. When I arrived there were very few vehicles about.'

Amitillo to Tegucigalpa: 'This takes 3 hours, passing on the way the junction road for Costa Rica (this is where the bus leaves the Pan American Highway). The bus stops here by a café near which is a tree with large apes clambering about its branches. The road entering Honduras goes through an area covered with the yellow blossom of mimosa trees, whilst here and there strange pointed hillocks rise above the carpet of flowers. Solid wooden-wheeled painted bullock carts complete the rural scene. Climbing up from the junction road to the capital we could see heavy dark clouds obliterating most of El Picacho mountain. Rain came later, alternating with drizzle which occured on several days whilst I was in Honduras (in January). The minibus stops near the second-class bus terminus and a hundred yards downhill from here accommodation can be found at the large hotel for 4.50 lempira. In the centre of the city the Hotel Marichal offers single rooms with bathroom and hot water for L9.

'Food is obtainable in a restaurant a few yards from the hotel, but, in common with other eating places, was expensive by Central American standards. I found a Chinese restaurant which was the cheapest; steak, chips, and vegetables cost L2.50. On the other hand, a breakfast of cornflakes, ham, egg, coffee and bread at the hotel cost L3.50.

'The market is worth a visit; there are varied handicrafts on sale as well as fruit and vegetables by the pavements. Inside the covered area venders of meat and fish occupy small booths whose walls are made from mosquito-proof wire mesh netting, giving them the appearance of cages. Many of the buildings are modern and this, with the light-skinned people thronging the streets, gives the city a European appearance. I wandered into the public library and saw a dozen American magazines on the rack; the librarian explained that there was a largish American community in the vicinity. They had selected this country for their retirement.'

NICARAGUA: background information

Like Honduras, Nicaragua has a population of $2^1/_2$ million, of whom 90 per cent are crowded into one part of the country, if 'crowded' is a word that can be used regarding this underpopulated country. Like its northern neighbour, Nicaragua has large potential resources, partly in available agricultural land, partly in minerals, partly in other potential industries, which have yet to be developed. Although still an agriculture-based economy, 42 per cent of the population live in towns, these being almost entirely in that belt of the country running southeast along the west of the country. Along one side is the Pacific Ocean; the other natural boundary is made up of a chain of volcanoes, Lake Managua and Lake Nicaragua. Not including the two lakes, the majority of the rest of the country comprises a large, central mountain land, sparsely inhabited. Its eastern slopes are covered in deciduous trees. These mountains descend into a wide eastern coastal plain, inhabited mainly by blacks of West Indian extraction, racial mixtures of Indians and blacks, and some Indians. These lowlands were largely neglected by the Spanish because of the unhealthy climate in which heavy rainfall predominates. This is known as the Misquito Coast. The first attempts at development here were British-inspired; Jamaicans were introduced to Bluefields and Greytown (San Juan del Norte). There are still many English-speaking communities on this coast.

The northwest part of the country includes part of that same chain of volcanoes that are an inherent part of Guatemala, San Salvador and Honduras. There are three volcanoes in Lake Nicaragua and one overlooking Lake Managua. But volcanoes have their uses; their ash provides good agricultural land, and so Nicaragua's population can live in just this quarter of the country and find adequate land for everyone.

Communications are somewhat better here than in Honduras, at least in the inhabited areas. The railway is only 350 kilometres (220 miles) long, but at least it serves the most densely populated areas and the capital. Half the 2,000-odd kilometres (1,250 miles) of road is paved, which includes the Pan American Highway. Good roads join all the major towns, and many of the rivers in the eastern plain are navigable. The possibility of building a canal across Nicaragua, utilizing the lakes, was explored before Panama was chosen as the site.

Something over three-quarters of the people are Ladino, whilst almost one-tenth are black, 5 per cent Indian and a very small proportion of European ancestry. In this, as in many other characteristics, Nicaragua is very similar to Honduras.

But Nicaragua is not a banana state. Many of the usual pre-requisites for banana production are here: a black population of West Indian ancestry, tropical climate, port facilities to export them. About 70 years ago the United Fruit Company tried to develop this industry here, but it languished when the crops were attacked by Panama disease. Bananas then became an insignificant part of Nicaragua's exports, but are now a developing industry. Main exports are cotton, sugar, coffee and meat, with tobacco and rice becoming important.

Managua: With the advent of the Spanish, the two towns which they founded and which became most important were Leon and Granada. Granada was the richer of the two, and conservative, whilst the poorer Leon was liberal. Because of its proximity to the Pacific Leon was chosen as the administrative capital. During the stormy history of the first days of independence, conflict between these two towns was rife. Managua was chosen as the new capital in 1858, and is normally regarded as the commercial centre.

I say normally. In 1931 Managua was destroyed by earthquake, and fire finished the job five years later. It was rebuilt in modern style then again flattened by earthquake in 1972. The city is now being rebuilt, again with modern buildings (many of which neglect the probability of future earthquakes in their design). Overlooking Lake Managua is Mt Momotombo, the still active volcano, at the foot of which lay the original town of Leon, Leon Viejo. This was destroyed by earthquake in 1609 and the town moved to its present site, 32 kilometres (20 miles) away.

Leon: Leon is still the intellectual centre and retains its liberal traditions. There is a university, the largest cathedral in Central America, many colonial churches and religious colleges. This city has been untouched by earthquake and so still retains the colonial-style buildings it had when it was the capital.

Granada: Granada is the third city of Nicaragua, situated at the foot of Mombacho volcano on the edge of Lake Nicaragua. Preserved from natural disaster, this town has seen violence at the hands of Leon liberals, British and French pirates and the American expedition of William Walker in 1856. There is much to be seen here from the colonial days, and the old traditions are preserved.

Lake Nicaragua: This lake, 150 kms (93 miles) long and 55 kms (34 miles) at its widest point, is peppered with small and not-so-small islands, mostly inhabited. Although a freshwater lake, the fish are of the saltwater varieties, adapted to this environment, which suggests that this was once part of the sea, formed into this lake by earthquake, volcanic activity, or both. Or maybe some other catastrophe such as The Flood. This whole area is one of outstanding scenic beauty and well worth a visit if you have the time.

Bluefields and the Misquito Coast: The weather here is very inclement, hot, humid and very wet. It is potentially a development area as it is underpopulated yet the centre for the banana trade, cocoa, mahogany, other wood, and gold mines in the interior. The ports are little used for imports (which come into the Pacific gateways) but handle the region's exports.

Although the name 'Bluefields' comes from the Dutch pirate Bleuwveldt, there is a British influence, if only in the language, West Indian English. The residents are largely of black Caribbean ancestry, originally brought over as slaves and labourers. The religion here is Protestant Christian, dominated by the missions. There is a good road from Managua to Rama, and you can take a bus for US$4 approximately. From Rama there is a daily boat service taking about 8 hours. It leaves at 13.00. If stopping over in Rama try the Hotel Lee. Try the Hueto, Hollywood or Dario in Bluefields. Besides the exports above mentioned, Bluefields supplies the USA with frozen fish, shrimps and lobsters.

Off the coast are two small islands, Islas Maiz (Corn Islands) which embody most of what is desired in a Caribbean island. But beware; they are becoming popular with tourists (mainly localized).

Currency: The cordoba is the unit of currency, often referred to as a peso. It is divided into 100 centavos. Currency restrictions are stringent and there is a black market.

Customs and Immigration: British passport holders can stay in Nicaragua for up to three months without a visa or tourist card, but this is always worth checking. Most other nationalities, including US travellers, require a visa or tourist card, available from Nicaraguan consulates. Often a ticket out of Nicaragua is required before entry is allowed, but if you are long-haired-and-beard-less, clean and tidy and are carrying sufficient funds you should have no trouble. If you are forced to buy an airline ticket at some stage, get it direct from the airline if possible, for it will then be easier to arrange a refund in most cases. There is an 'Earthquake Tax' of US$1.50

on entering, which is put towards the reconstruction of Managua, and another C$6 is charged for crossing on a Sunday. Avoid any attire or baggage with military overtones.

Language: Officially and mainly Spanish, but as noted before Caribbean dialects of English are spoken on the eastern coastal land. Some Indian dialects.

Climate: All down to altitude again. The differences here are that firstly Managua is at a lower altitude than most of the other capitals (55 metres), and therefore on average hotter (average daily temperatures range between 80–90°F (27–32°C), with high humidity), and the tropical Caribbean coastline is wetter than normal.

Health: The above means that you should exercise caution in what you eat and drink. Drinking water is often safe, but not always, and you should avoid fresh vegetables and fruit unless in a very good restaurant. Meningitis is endemic.

Tegucigalpa to San Jose

Tegucigalpa to Managua: 'The bus left Tegucigalpa at 09.00, arriving in San Jose at 18.00. The fare, including the next stage to San Jose (Costa Rica), is 35 lempira.

'Managua has very few buildings left standing after the 1972 earthquake; garden gates are frequently the only indication of where a house once stood and large open spaces form the larger part of the city. An Englishman I met on the bus had settled in Honduras and thought it would be a good idea to stay in an earthquake-proof hotel. With so much evidence of havoc, this seemed a sensible suggestion. Accommodation in a single storey hotel cost C$18. The few restaurants were a long way apart; barbecued chicken and rice cost C$8.'

Managua to San Jose: 'Depart 08.00; arrive 17.00. The road passes through fairly flat country devoted to growing corn, sugar and cotton. Accommodation in San Jose near TICA Bus station, in the Pension Salamanca, cost C23 (see map, page 133). The rooms are small cubicles, with communal washing facilities, but clean.'

Nicaragua and Costa Rica

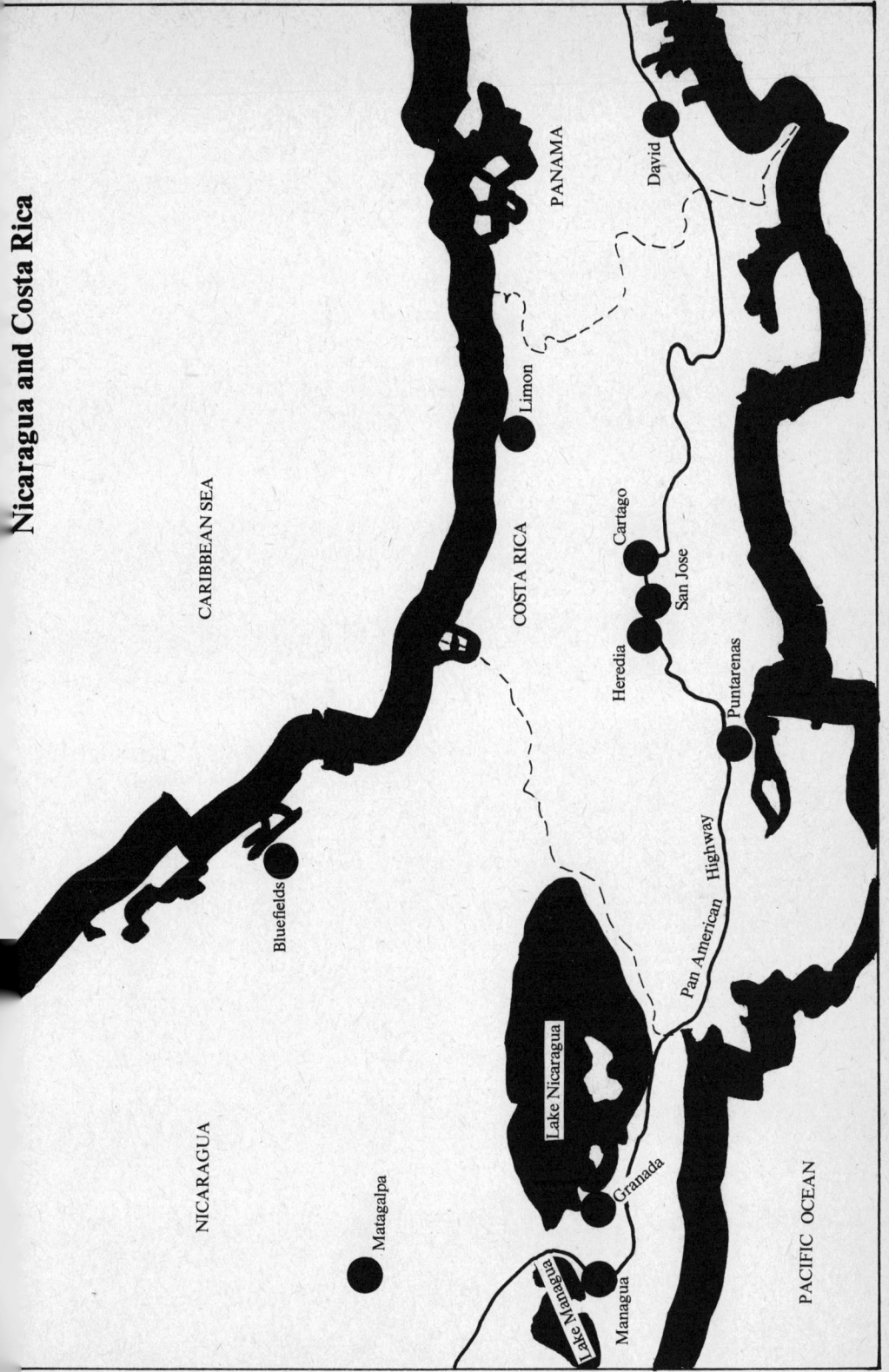

CARIBBEAN SEA

NICARAGUA

PANAMA

David

Limon

COSTA RICA

Cartago

San Jose

Heredia

Puntarenas

Bluefields

Pan American Highway

Lake Nicaragua

Granada

Matagalpa

Lake Managua

Managua

PACIFIC OCEAN

COSTA RICA: background information

You will find Costa Rica something of a constrast to the other Central American republics. In area only El Salvador is smaller, and in population terms Panama is the only republic with less inhabitants. Unlike elsewhere in Central America the majority of the racial mix is of European ancestry, though racial distribution is uneven. The Indians of Costa Rica were drastically reduced by disease so that until relatively recently the country was underpopulated. The settlers concentrated in what is now the most densely populated and most important area, the Meseta Central, Central Basin. Two-thirds of the population live here.

Overlooked by volcanoes, some of which are still active, this central basin is covered in rich volcanic ash. Part of Costa Rica's present-day prosperity must be traced back to the fact that this was the first country to realize the value of this soil for the cultivation of coffee. In 1751 the total population of this central basin was only a little less than $2^1/_2$ thousand. Today it has expanded to some $1^1/_4$ million. With the rise in numbers the area in agricultural use in this basin has also expanded. The population of the area has however remained fairly homogenous. Though here mainly of European ancestry, clusters of Indians, Ladinos and blacks live in the country: on the Pacific coast Ladinos comprise half the citizenry, in Limon (on the Caribbean) one-third are blacks of West Indian descent, whilst there are only 5,000 pure Indians surviving in the country.

Costa Rica is a genuine democracy, if such a political state can be said to exist. A President, elected for a four-year term (all over 20 have the vote, which is free and secret), has executive powers, whilst the Legislative Assembly is also elected every four years. In 1948 the army was abolished on the ground that a peaceful nation doesn't need one. There is a national guard however. The country has the highest standard of living in Central America, the highest literacy rate, the greatest degree of economic and social progress. Many large areas of the country have yet to be developed, there are many resources to be exploited and industrialization has only just begun; which is as well, because Costa Rica also has the fastest population growth. Main exports are coffee, bananas, meat, sugar and cocoa. Beans, maize, potatoes and sugar are grown for domestic consumption. Farming methods are more efficient here than elsewhere in Central America, one of the main reasons for Costa Rica's relative wealth.

Very broadly speaking, there are two mountain ranges, a main one running right through the country from the northwest to the southeast, the Cordilleras Guanacaste, Central and Talamanca; and a smaller one on the Nicoya Peninsula. There are lowlands along both the Caribbean and Pacific coasts, and a large bay, the Golfo de Nicoya. The Caribbean coast is in parts swampy, and it is on Costa Rica's Caribbean coast that Central America's first banana plantations sprung up. These went into decline when hit by Panama Disease, but are again becoming an important export industry.

Cartago was the Spanish administrative centre and the capital on independence in 1821. It was not long however before San Jose, more important commercially and more powerful, became the capital. The seeds of Costa Rica's economic success were sown before independence. Coffee was introduced from Cuba in 1808 and its development encouraged by the government's free land grants beginning in the 1820s. Railways were built to transport it to the Caribbean port of Limon.

The population density of the Caribbean coastland is still low, because the ever-increasing numbers in the central basin have tended to remain in that area, slowly expanding outward; there have been very few who have travelled to the undeveloped areas in the manner of the pioneers of the Old West. This largely accounts for the very different racial make-up of both the coastal areas.

Communications are fairly good. The number of paved roads is increasing, with special emphasis naturally on the more populated regions, particularly in the Central Basin. The Pan American Highway runs for 680 kms (420 miles) from Nicaragua in the north to Panama in the south, passing through San Jose which is in the approximate centre. This is entirely paved. Railways link Limon with the Central Basin; the railway was largely established for the banana industry.

San Jose: Architecturally San Jose is what you would expect from the capital of a country like this, progressive but proud of its heritage; a mixture of colonial with modern architecture, with increasing emphasis on the latter. The climate is agreeable, though evenings can be chilly.

San Jose is not the most exciting town for the traveller, but it is a good centre for excursions into the surrounding countryside. The central basin with its volcanoes and coffee plantations can be easily visited on the good roads; Puntarenas is linked to the capital by rail; and the towns of Cartago can be visited en route to Limon.

Accommodation and Restaurants in San Jose: For accommodation try the following:

131

Downtown San Jose: Key

1	LACSA	5	Costa Rica Railway Station
2	COPA		
3	Braniff	6	Pacifico Railway Station
4	TICA Bus		

Hotel Astoria, Avenida 5, Calle 5 no. 7; near Plaza Morazan. US$2/US$2.50 per person.

Pension Internacional, Avenida 5, Calle 1–3. US$3 with breakfast.

Pension Salamanca, Calle 9–11, Avenida 2. US$2.50.

Restaurants worth trying:

Café Mallorquina, Calle 9, reputedly good and cheap.

Kuang Chaou, Calle 11, Avenida Central -2. Chinese.

Morazan, near Morazan Park.

Puerto Limon: This is the centre of the Caribbean banana-exporting industry (bananas are also grown on the Pacific coast). Columbus landed here on his last voyage. It is now a well laid-out town with a promenade, parks and cultivated tropical vegetation. Most of the 36,000 inhabitants are black, of West Indian descent. English is spoken along this coast, which is largely undeveloped and empty. To attract tourists the government has declared it a national park. Many parts of this coast have excellent beaches bordered by jungle which can be explored along the rivers by small boats. Probably worth a visit if you are not pushed for time.

Accommodation in and around Puerto Limon: Here are some suggestions for the area; there are not yet any flashy, expensive hotels.

Puerto Limon: Hotel Miami, US$5 including bathroom and breakfast.

Hotel Palace, US$2.50 per person.

Hotels Elegante, Limon, Venus, US$2.00.

Cahuita: Hotel Lamm, US$2.50.

Siquirres: Hospedaje Wilson, Oriental, Nena; all US$2.50 approximately.

Puntarenas and the Islands: This town is built on a small peninsula in the Gulf of Nicoya, on the Pacific side of the country. It is a centre for local tourism and deep-sea fishing. The islands in the Gulf can easily be visited

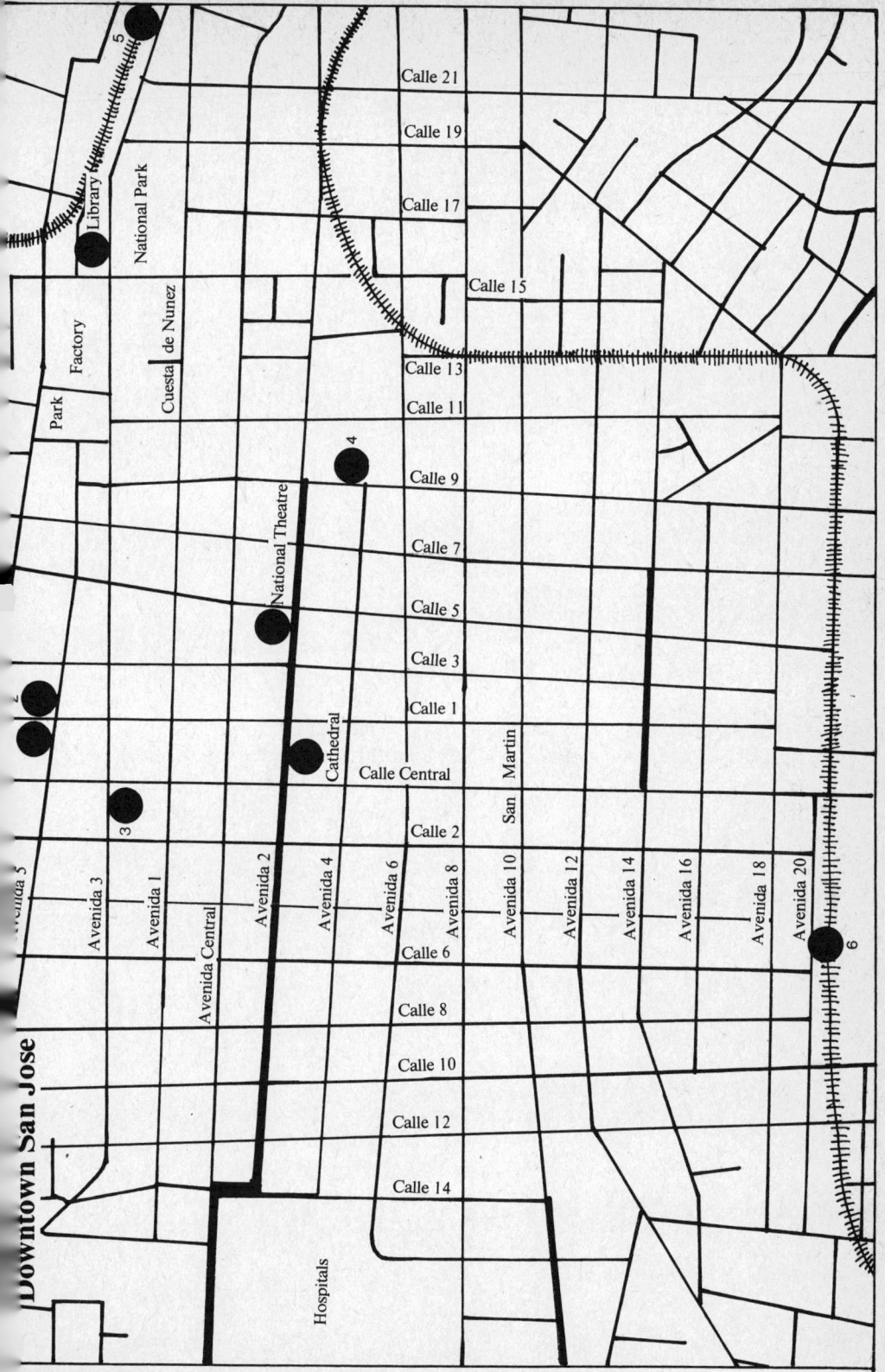

Downtown San Jose

Calle 21
Calle 19
Calle 17
Calle 15
Calle 13
Calle 11
Calle 9
Calle 7
Calle 5
Calle 3
Calle 1
Calle Central
Calle 2
Calle 6
Calle 8
Calle 10
Calle 12
Calle 14

Library
National Park
Cuesta de Nunez
Factory
Park
National Theatre
Cathedral
San Martin
Hospitals

Avenida 5
Avenida 3
Avenida 1
Avenida Central
Avenida 2
Avenida 4
Avenida 6
Avenida 8
Avenida 10
Avenida 12
Avenida 14
Avenida 16
Avenida 18
Avenida 20

5
4
2
3
6

by fishing boat. Local industries are bananas, rice, cattle and coconuts. Accommodation here is more of a tourist nature, and prices are seasonal, but you could try:

Hotel de Verano, US$2; Hotel La Riviero US$2.50.

Cabinas Centrals and Hotel El Prado, about US$2.

Hotel Los Banos, US$2 to US$2.50.

All the prices are those for low season; prices will be higher (sometimes double) in the summer season, January to March.

If you travel to Puntarenas visit San Lucas island. In addition to having a superb beach and fine scenery, it is the site of an experimentally-liberal penal colony whose administration would cause retired British Brigadier-Generals apoplexy. You are not likely to visit Cocoa Island (Isla del Coco) as it is 400 km (240 miles) off the coast. It is uninhabited, but is reputed to be the place where Henry Morgan and/or other pirates buried their loot.

Currency: Back to the colon again, divided into 100 centimos. Although Cost Rica has the highest standard of living in Central America, by no means does it have the highest cost of living.

Customs and Immigration: A tourist card or tourist visa is normally necessary and gives up to 30 days in the country, extendable for six months. Any tourist staying less than 90 days does not need an exit visa. British, United States, Canadian, West German and Swiss citizens do not require tourist cards or visas normally, but this should always be checked. An ongoing or return ticket is reputedly required before entry is allowed; the authorities may consider that a TICA Bus ticket to Panama City or a trans-Atlantic return air ticket serves this purpose. Customs allowances are as elsewhere, and there are no currency restrictions. Hitch-hikers are frowned upon at border posts.

Language: Spanish of course, with a little Caribbean English around Limon.

Climate: Tropical in the lowlands, with the Caribbean coast wetter than the Pacific. The rainy season is June to November. San Jose has a very agreeable climate, usually 60–82°F (16–28°C) during the day, but chilly at night. In the higher mountains it can be quite cold with frosts.

Health: Although Costa Rica is noticeably more developed than the other republics, don't get carried away. Water is probably safe in San Jose, but not elsewhere, so you should still avoid fresh fruit and vegetables. And beware of malaria, particularly on the Caribbean coast.

San Jose to Puerto Limon

'The railway station was closed because of flooding and landslides so I took a bus to Turrialba. I left at 08.00 and arrived at 10.00. Fare 5 colones. I took the train from Turrialba. This leaves at 11.00 and arrives in Limon at 15.30 (there are two a day in each direction). Fare C14.

'The railway follows the river past picturesque waterfalls, through deep cuttings and by small hamlets; through coconut forests, banana plantations, fields of tapioca and luxuriant foliage where the huts on stilts are enveloped by tropical growth. The train climbs through this splendid scenery then drops down to sea level where it continues its progress a short distance from the beautiful beach. All the scenery I saw in Costa Rica was colourful and it was the flowers which lent so much dazzle to the scene; indeed whatever else had prompted this country's name, the richness of the abundant blooms may well have contributed to the thought. Or should they have named it Costa Flora? The train has frequent stops when youngsters board with refreshments. Halts are also made to pick up produce and milk from the farm hands who come down the track on horseback, looking very rural.

'In Limon accommodation can be had for C35 with bathroom; and a main meal costs 12 to 17 colones. This is a small town where it is necessary to walk two miles before a suitable spot can be found for swimming. Although isolated, some very good beaches can be found about twenty miles along the coast. The weather here was very hot.

'The bus back to San Jose departs at 14.00; change at Siquirres. The fare is C18. The roads are mostly unpaved, particularly between Puerto Limon and Siquirres, and therefore a bit bumpy. The scenery is not as good as by rail.'

San Jose to Panama City

'I was informed previously by TICA Bus that there were no vacant seats on the coach to Panama and a delay of four days was anticipated. On my return to San Jose I enquired about the position and was told an extra bus was leaving in fifteen minutes with one vacant seat. I collected my gear and without even time for a coffee was on my way that same evening. San Jose attracts a lot of visitors but, apart from the museum, I did not discover a great deal to interest the sightseers, who appeared to be using it as a centre for excursions to the surrounding countryside.

'Departed San Jose at 20.00 and arrived in Panama City the following day at 16.15. There were two 20-minute stops during the 16-hour journey.'

PANAMA: background information

Panama is a bigger country than you may think, although most of the action is centred around the canal. The building of this canal was the ultimate proof of Panama's position as the 'Crossroads of the World', as it has been described. From this strategic position Panama has always gained its importance, even before the canal was built.

It was the Spanish colonizers who first realized Panama's value in the field of communications. Most of the gold they found, both in the form of natural deposits and fashioned ornaments, was in South America, in what is now Colombia and Peru. Transporting this to Colombia's Caribbean coast for shipment to Europe would have been a time-consuming, hazardous and costly undertaking, so it was simply shipped from the Pacific ports to Panama (Balboa) and taken by mule across a natural declivity in the isthmus to Colon. The Chagres River, which is navigable down to the Caribbean, was also used. There were two reasons for loading the ships up river: the climate is more amenable there, and there was a greater degree of protection from the pirates with which the Caribbean was rife.

This did not deter the pirates, however, many of whom were British. The knowledge that so much wealth was going to the undeserving Spanish prompted some of the more colourful figures of naval history to collect their share. In 1573 Sir Francis Drake ventured as far as Cruces, looted the town and stole the gold. In 1599 he had another go. But the most famous attack is that of Henry Morgan in 1671. The Spanish had built forts to protect this vital link, the most famous being that at San Lorenzo. Undaunted, Morgan captured San Lorenzo and sent an expeditionary force inland which attacked, looted and burnt the town of Panama Viejo (Old Panama) on the Pacific. His returning troops needed nearly 200 mules to carry their ill-gotten gains. But the most important attacks were those of Admiral Vernon in 1739–40, when he captured Portobelo and San Lorenzo. This ultimately forced the Spaniards to ship their treasure round Cape Horn; a glance at any world map, and a rudimentary knowledge of the primitive sailing ships of the time, will show that this alternative route was costly in time, manpower and ships.

The word 'Panama' means 'abundance of fish'. So guess what you'll find plenty of on the menu. It was in Panama that Columbus made his only landing on the mainland of the Americas in 1502, founding Portobelo. In 1513 Balboa hiked across the isthmus and discovered the Pacific.

137

The people are the most cosmopolitan in Central America. About 75 per cent are Ladino, and there two groups of blacks: Spanish-speaking descendants of slaves brought from Africa, and English-speaking of West Indian ancestry. There are still communities of Indians, rural-based, largely in the least accessible places including the Darien Gap and on many of the islands. In addition there are numbers of Chinese and East Indians. There are about 45,000 civilian and military personnel in the Canal Zone.

48 per cent of the population is urban, a fact which is in itself unusual in Central America. Literacy is 75 per cent, with the majority of the illiterate in rural areas. 25 per cent of the annual budget is invested in education, whilst another quarter supports health, social security and public works.

Receipts from the use of the Canal go to the United States, but despite this the Canal has still been traditionally the main source of income for Panama. This has been in the form of services provided for the US military and employees. With Panama's other, natural, resources, this makes the country ideal for American tourists. This could only be adversely effected by a worsening political relationship between the two countries.

Almost 40 per cent of the population work in agriculture, but this is mainly for domestic consumption, and a lot of it is at subsistence level in isolated rural communities. Agrarian reform is on the way, and the next few years will see both the agricultural and the manufacturing industries increase in importance. There are also minable natural resources. Banking is one of the fastest-growing sectors of the economy; there are many offshore banks, and one can have an anonymous numbered bank account, as in Switzerland.

Panama has more than 800 islands scattered in the Pacific and the Caribbean. In the Bay of Panama, an hour from the city by ferry, is Taboga, 'the Capri of the Pacific'. Pizarro built his ships for the conquest of Peru here. Also in the Bay of Panama are Las Perlas (the Pearl Islands), about 100 in number, 20 minutes' flight from Panama City. Most are uninhabited, but the principal ones are being developed for the international jetsetter. Off the other coast are the San Blas islands, home of the Cuna Indians, a 200-mile archipelago of about 385 islands, some of which are minute. None are of any size.

Currency: The Panamanian unit of currency is the balboa, shown as B/. As it is on a par with the US dollar, and US currency notes and coins are used alongside the balboa, we show all prices in this section in US$; in fact there are no Panamanian banknotes – US dollars are used exclusively. Coins are in the same denomination, of the same material, and are the same size as US coins. No problem. There are no currency restrictions, and you will find it easy to use your credit card here. If you have run out of money by this stage you can take your credit card to a bank and draw cash in American dollars. The minimum withdrawal allowed is US$100.

Customs and Immigration: Most nationalities, including citizens of the United States, need a visa or tourist card. These are valid for 30 days. The tourist card is renewable, costs US$2, and can be bought from an airline if flying in, or otherwise from a Panamanian Consulate. Neither British or West German citizens need a tourist card or visa; they can stay for up to 30 days.

Any personal possessions you are likely to have with you, and 500 cigarettes can be brought into the country. Drugs without a doctor's prescription will be confiscated, as will subversive literature.

If you have not got an onward or return air or ship ticket, and/or less than US$150, you may not be allowed in. And get a haircut.

Language: Spanish is the official language, although English is the second language, compulsory in schools. Half of the Caribbean state of Bocas del Toro is English-speaking. There are two English-language daily papers. American is spoken in the Canal Zone.

Food: You will find food throughout Central America largely the same as in Mexico. Whether the accent is on the basics, such as tortillas, enchiladas and fresh fruit, or on the more sophisticated meals depends partly on the country and largely on where you are eating and the type of restaurant. But food in Panama is worth a specific mention because there is more variety, particularly in the capital.

Since the population of Panama is international, so is the food. Chinese, Italian, French, Argentine, Spanish, Japanese, Mexican and Panamanian. And because Panama is located between two oceans, the food of the sea – particularly lobster, shrimp, corvina and red snapper – is prominent. Sancocho is a filling soup, carimanola a yucca filled with chopped meat, patacones are fried plantains; besides of course empanadas, tortillas and tamales. And besides the 'ethnic' restaurants there are those which specialize in seafood. And as the tourist literature charmingly puts it: 'If you want Colonel Sanders Kentucky Fried or Krispy Chicken, ice cream from Dairy Queen, or a MacDonald's hamburger, in Panama you can have this too.'

Mexico and Central America

Information: For information on Panama, once you have arrived in the country, try the Information Office, El Panama Hotel Grounds (Via Espana), Panama City, Panama. Postal address: P.O. Box 4421, Panama 5. Telephone 64–5316.

For advance information and tourist card (if you need it) try the Panama Tourist Bureau, McAllister Hotel Arcade, 10 Biscayne Boulevard, Miami, Florida 33132, USA. Telephone 358 9330.

Climate: Can be wet. May to December is the wet season, particularly along the Caribbean coast, which has twice the annual rainfall of the Pacific coast. You will encounter less rain December through April. The sun shines every day, although sometimes clouds get in the way. Temperatures are normally 73–81°F (23–27°C) on the Pacific side, and 73–84°F (23–29°C) on the Caribbean side. It is cooler at night and in the mountains.

Health: Thanks to the Canal builders, most of the worst tropical diseases which were endemic in this area have been eliminated. The water in Panama City and Colon is safe to drink (Panama claims to have the best water in the world and also applies strict standards of hygiene to food preparation).

Fiestas: Panama is proud of its many festivals. The typical dances are El Tamborito and La Cumbia. The brightly coloured, white lace-trimmed national dress is the pollera; the women also wear hair ornaments called tembleques. The men wear distinctive national dress at the festivals.

Holy week festivities are at their best in the interior, although the carnival in Panama City, held on the four days before Ash Wednesday, is perhaps the most spectacular.

Balboa: About 40 per cent of Panama's total population, approximately 85 per cent of its urban population, lives in the four towns at the two ends of the Canal; Panama City and its twin, Balboa, on the Pacific, and Colon with its twin, Cristobal, on the Caribbean.

Balboa is situated between Panama City and the Canal, on the Canal. It is in the Canal Zone, and thus somewhat lacking in typical Latin atmosphere. Taboga Island can be visited from Balboa; boats leave twice daily from pier 18, take about an hour and cost US$2 return. Accommodation can be found on the island at the Hotel Chu. The cost is US$7 a day, and meals are reputed to be good. 'There is no traffic on this small island, which seemed to me to be a good place to relax for a few days, although things were a bit expensive compared to the mainland. I returned the same evening taking in the sights as we chugged across the edge of the Pacific and under the high bridge which spans two continents and then into the canal which joins two oceans.'

Cristobal: This town was founded as the port of entry for suppliers during the building of the Canal, and is in the Canal Zone. There is potential danger both here and in Colon of being attacked and robbed. The main importance of this town is its situation at the entry to the Canal.

Colon: This town, which runs into Cristobal, is actually an enclave in the Canal Zone. Its population is almost 70,000 and it is the second largest town in Panama. Portobelo is 50 kilometres (31 miles) along the coast from here and may be worth a visit.

The Panama Canal: A world map is really necessary to appreciate the value of Panama and its canal. In 1849, when thousands of Americans from the east coast scampered off to California for the gold rush, they found that the quickest way was to take a boat down to Panama, cross the isthmus, then take another boat up to California. The trans-continental railways were not yet built in the USA, and it was a long way by horse or wagon train. But that world map shows why the canal had to be built; not only is the journey around Cape Horn far longer, but until recently it was dangerous, especially in winter.

King Charles V of Spain was the first to be interested in the idea. He had a canal route survey done in 1524. But it wasn't until 1880 that the Frenchman Ferdinand de Lesseps, the director of the Suez Canal project, started work in Panama. As mentioned earlier in this book, Nicaragua was also considered as a possible site for a canal, utilizing the lakes. But Panama had three advantages: the length of canal required would be shorter, a natural declivity existed in the topography, and, most important, there would be far less risk of earthquake damage. De Lesseps was defeated by financial problems and tropical diseases in the 1890s.

At the time Panama was part of Colombia, who authorized the French company to sell its rights and properties to the USA. The Colombian Senate then reneged on the treaty, and the USA encouraged Panama to secede, which they did in 1903. The new republic then signed a new treaty with the USA which granted sovereignty of the Canal Zone (which extends 8 kilometres along both sides of the canal) to the United States for ever. The current Panamanian government does not accept the treaty; both Panamanian and US flags now fly in the Canal Zone, and the

American government make an annual payment of almost US$2 million.

Tropical disease was first eliminated by William Crawford Gorgas before construction began in 1904; Colonel George Washington Goethals was in charge. The first ship passed through in August 1914. The total cost was US$387 million; the canal is 50 miles long and ships take 8 hours to pass through. The average cost for a ship to go though is US$9,000, but then it costs US$60,000 to go round the Horn.

'An excursion to the Canal, to see how it operates, is very worthwhile. From the bus terminal a fifteen-minute ride will take you to the entrance to Miraflores locks, which are at the Pacific end of the Panama Canal. A walk of about a mile brings you to the canals and the viewing area. Opposite the Control Room is an observation area where visitors may sit and watch the operations. I had an invitation to join a party who were first taken to a small cinema where a film showed how the locks and canal were constructed. Then we were given a ten-minute ride through the Canal by means of a speeded-up film. We walked across the gates of one canal (there is one for up and another for down shipping) and entered the Control Room in which the engineers controlled the operation of the locks. One man gave instructions to the team who responded by regulating valves and equipment which controlled the level of water, or relayed back to him a reading from one of the recording instruments. A continuous watch was maintained through the enclosing windows of all movements below.

'The ingenious design of the canal can be appreciated at close quarters when one sees leviathan ships being raised and lowered by operating a lever which can be turned by the fingers; no pumps are used to transfer water from one lock to the other – gravity alone is used as a motive force. A man-made lake judiciously sited provides an inexhaustible supply of water to fill the locks as required to raise the ship; to lower the ship, water is emptied into the sea. By this process the largest vessel can proceed along the fifty miles of waterway, being raised or lowered some eighty feet en route.

'We went on to the gantry outside the Operations Unit and watched a 40,000-ton cargo ship moving slowly through the Miraflores Locks. The pilot, standing on a temporary platform erected on the deck, gave instructions by radio as the ship – with only inches to spare – was hauled along by "mules", motorized land tugs running on switchback rails.

'Beyond the precincts of the locks, the jungle is visible. Here primitive conditions exist in tremendous contrast to this man-made area, where vast natural forces are controlled in such a seemingly easy manner. The administration offices of the Canal are on Balboa Heights, which you will pass on the bus. The building stands on top of a mound with flags flying and an impressive stairway leading to the entrance. Nearby are the residences of the Canal Zone workers and also a post office selling the special stamps of the Zone; and to remind us that we are in Panama there are a few Indian women nearby with gold rings in their noses, selling handicrafts.'

Panama City: The capital city has a population figure of something less than half a million. It was founded after Henry Morgan had looted and burnt Panama Viejo (Old Panama), six kilometres (four miles) away and easily visited. The new town was strongly fortified and thus uninviting to the pirates who attacked elsewhere. Much of this remains, although most of Panama City is modern.

It has a very cosmopolitan flavour, and is full of contrast. Besides the colonial reminders, one sees the obvious signs of American influence and the bazaar atmosphere of Hongkong-type shopping facilities attracted by low import duties and American money.

Minibuses, 'chivas', ply the streets of Panama City. Fares are from 5 cents to 25 cents. There are two kinds of taxis: 'chicos', small ones, and 'grandes', larger ones. Chicos are cheaper. There are no metres and fares are charged on the zone system.

If this is the end of the road for you, this is the place to buy anything you may want. Local handicrafts are very good, items such as cameras are subject to low import taxes and can even be bought duty-free if you are flying out. It is also reputedly possible to use the American PX stores in the Canal Zone; you are not supposed to, but if you play your cards right ... If you have no money left, remember that it is easy to use you credit card here.

'The Hotel Ideal (annex) next to the TICA Bus depot costs US$8 with bathroom, and is comfortable. Restaurants and cafés abound in this busy city and meals to suit all pockets are available. Opposite the hotel you will find quick service counter cafés very reasonable and ideal for breakfast.

'Avenida Central separates two very different areas in Panama City. On one side lie the modern buildings and shops of Panama City and on the other side is the colourful old district called Caledonia.

'I made my way through the Caledonia District late one afternoon, passing by the wooden houses standing cheek by jowl to each other, all with large overhanging balconies and lines of brightly coloured washing fluttering like bunting all around. Wherever a clear space occurred it was occupied by scores of children running and shouting, so adding movement and sound to the theatrical setting. There are great opportunities here for cameras to capture scenes which possibly have not changed for over a century.

'On the waterfront which borders the district I came upon the fruit and vegetable market. It seemed that the traders, having sold as much as they could for that day, were busy eating up the residue. People sat on the kerb or leaned against the sea wall, devouring watermelon, pineapple, oranges and other fruit in vast quantities. No-one took anything away in a bag; it was eaten there and then. I thought I would join these Panamanian fruit-eaters and asked for a slice of melon. The vender shook his head, and cutting a huge melon in four, handed me a quarter, weighing at least three pounds. Nothing less than this was worth selling or worth interrupting his own massive eating marathon.

'I returned to the shopping area of Panama City which is as modern as in any western city, as exotic as any eastern bazaar, and with variety enough to satisfy the most avid souvenir and bargain hunter.

'The next day I joined the crowds on the pavements – not in search of goods, but in an endeavour to find the best way to continue my journey from Panama to Colombia. I had spent four weeks travelling from Chetumal in Mexico to Panama and had covered 1700 miles. They were miles during which I was always in contact with the people and the way of life of the countries I passed through. Travelling by local bus had provided me with an opportunity to see, and to be part of the native scene, an experience which is often denied to travellers using other modes of transport. But now I had arrived at a point where the road ended; no ordinary vehicle could traverse the wild area between Panama and Colombia known as the Darien Gap.

'Admittedly a British Army expedition had once forced a way through, and it was also possible to go with the aid of Indian guides through the jungle to a point in Colombia where the road began again and connected with the Pan American Highway; but that takes seven days, is costly and difficult. I therefore enquired for more conventional methods of reaching Barranquilla in Colombia.

'A shipping agent suggested I might make the one-day journey by passenger boat at a cost of US$135, but I settled for the COPA Airlines flight which took one hour and cost US$50. So on a Sunday afternoon I took the local bus to the airport and flew away from Panama City across the Caribbean Sea to Barranquilla.'

Note: Information on flights from Panama City to Miami and other major cities in the USA is provided in Appendix 1: Homeward Bound, page 161–2).

Part 5
A Taste of South America

145

Before that dreaded return to the grey skies of home, you may wish to sample a titbit of that third America – the undiscovered continent, and one of the pearls of the Caribbean. All that can be found in South America is encapsulated in Colombia. The beaches of Cartagena and Barranquilla, the Amazon jungle retreat of Leticia, the splendour of the Andes, the colonial heritage and big city bustle of Bogota. And Barbados, the most easterly of the Caribbean islands, is usually described as a paradise by those to go there.

In this chapter we give some brief background details on Colombia, Venezuela (Caracas) and Barbados. These are only meant to be sufficient for those using this as an interesting route home. This book does not claim to give full details of travel in South America and the Caribbean. If you will be travelling extensively in South America you can do no better than to buy *South American Survival* by Maurice Taylor; if you wish to visit many of the Caribbean islands, another work entitled *Caribbean Island Hopping* is available by this author, Frank Bellamy. Both are published by Wilton House Gentry (London).

Information on return flights from Colombia (Barranquilla and San Andres) and Barbados is provided in Appendix 1; Homeward Bound, page 161.

Panama to Barranquilla (Colombia)

To reach South American from Panama, you have to fly or go by boat. As the shipping companies are reputed to increase their fares half-way across, you may as well fly. Two airlines ply the route – Lacsa, charging US$56, and Copa, charging US$48. Copa runs three flights a week – on Wednesdays, Fridays and Sundays.

Colombia

Documents: No visa is necessary for US, British or most European passport holders. Officially an onward ticket is required before entry can be allowed, but you may find that an air ticket from Barbados is accepted for this purpose.

Climate: Very much dependent on altitude. As the Equator passes through Colombia, there is no way to define the seasons except in terms of rainfall, which varies from place to place. Bogota can be cold and wet whilst the coastal areas are hot and humid. Therefore, if you are travelling extensively in Colombia you will encounter almost every type of climate.

Currency: The peso, divided into 100 centavos.

Food and drink: Colombian food is very varied indeed, blending dishes from all over Latin America with traditional Indian dishes. Of the many chicken meals, pollo en salsa de Mostaza is a favourite, but also try ajiaco de pollo. Other dishes to look for åre locro de choclos and bandeja antioquena. The local speciality is canastas de coco. Aguardiente is the popular rum-type drink. Beer is good.

Accommodation: Colombia is one of the cheaper countries in South America. Some recommended and inexpensive hotels are:
Barranquilla: Colon or California
Cartagena: Bellavista or Roma
Medellin: Neuvo or San Francisco
Bogota: Aragon or Halia
Leticia: Residencia Pullman

Travel: Colombia has more airlines than any other Latin American country, a situation resulting from the difficulties imposed on surface transportation by mountainous terrain and thick jungle. Air fares are not standardized. Avianca operate a scheme valid for 30 days of travel, but with certain restrictions:
10 stopovers including Leticia and San Andres: US$200
10 stopovers including Leticia but not San Andres: US$175
10 stopovers including San Andres but not Leticia: US$135
10 stopovers not including San Andres or Leticia: US$110
The ticket must be issued outside Colombia. US, French and Spanish residents can obtain information from any Avianca office; UK citizens should contact Pan American in London, or glean information in Miami.

For single journeys, SAM are usually cheaper than Avianca. Some sample fares from Bogota are:
Barranquilla: US$24
Cali: US$16
Cartagena: US$23
Leticia: US$51
Medellin: US$14
San Andres: US$43
Trains are the cheapest way to travel, but the railway system is very

limited. Some sample train fares from Bogota are:
    Neuva: US$1.25 (10 hours)
    Puerto Salgar/Santa Marta: US$12 (24 hours)
  Bus services are poor, with crowded vehicles and bad roads. Some sample fares from Bogota are:
    Cali: US$5 (1st class, 10 hours)
        US$4 (2nd class, 12 hours)
    Medellin: US$4/US$5 (16 hours)

San Andres: This Caribbean island is part of Colombia, yet situated off the coast of Central America. Besides being worth a visit in its own right, it is conveniently situated to provide savings on return air fares (see Appendix 1: Homeward Bound, page 162).

Colombia to Caracas and Barbados

For entry into Venezuela all nationalities need a visa or tourist card. This document will not be granted unless and until you can show the authorities an onward air ticket, one specifically out of Venezuela. This is most easily done by purchasing a through air ticket, Barranquilla/Caracas/Barbados: you may even be able to get your tourist card issued by the airline when you buy your ticket. The fare is approximately US$160. There is no cheap air fare available, except the small reduction a through fare offers over two separate tickets.

  It is possible to travel by bus from Colombia to Caracas. But the journey is long, arduous, and − allowing for meals and accommodation − probably more expensive than a flight. Allow at least a week for the trip. If you do decide to travel overland, you should buy a Caracas/Barbados ticket in Colombia. Viasa (the Venezuelan national carrier) flies the route and should be able to issue you with a tourist card. The fare is US$94 (the plane flies through Trinidad, where you can stop over at no extra cost, provided you have a ticket issued on this basis).

Caracas (Venezuela)

Climate: Tropical with little seasonal variation. The dry season in Caracas is December through April, when the nights can be cool.

Currency: The bolivar, divided into 100 centimos. Venezuela is both the richest and the most expensive South American country, with its revenues largely based on its oil deposits and processing. The currency is more likely to be revalued than devalued. Inflation is minimal.

Food and drink: You'll find much international food in Caracas – not the bland airline type, but among the best of European, Latin American and Oriental cuisine offered by specialist restaurants. Native food includes sancocho – the stew or soup also found in Panama, arepas – a hard maize bread, pabellon and empanadas. Local beer and rum are good, though there are no local wines. The coffee is excellent.

Travel: a 17-day excursion air ticket, valid for unlimited mileage on all AVENSA flights within Venezuela, can be purchased for US$120 outside Venezuela. Sample one-way fares from Caracas are:

Canaima: US$45
Cuidad Bolivar: US$35
Maracaibo: US$30
Merida: US$29

There are no rail services to speak of. Venezuela has the best road network in South America, jungle and Andes permitting, and the buses are generally of good standard. Some sample fares from Caracas are:

Maracaibo, San Cristobal, Merida – all US$8.

Barbados

This most easterly of the Caribbean islands is known as 'Paradise Island' to its visitors and 'Little England' to its neighbours. 21 miles long by 14 miles wide (at its widest), Barbados' reputation and importance are far greater than this small size would suggest.

Barbados is known throughout the world, though particularly in the USA, Canada and Britain, as the Caribbean's leading tourist island, a reputation enhanced by a perfect climate and some of the friendliest people you could wish to meet. Over the last few years Barbados' tourist figures have been artificially boosted by an increasing volume of stopover traffic – travellers bound for South America who have discovered that they can save money by making their journey via the Caribbean.

Climate: Perfect all year. Usually in the 80s°F (27–31°C), though often in the 90s°F (32–37°C). Cool breezes from the Atlantic.

A Taste of South America

Customs and Immigration: Most nationalities do not require a visa. But you will not be allowed into the country unless you possess an air ticket out of Barbados. Customs allowances are normal with strict quarantine regulations and a ban on meat imports.

Currency: The Barbados dollar. Prices are quoted in either Barbados or US dollars, so check. You will find Barbados the most expensive place so far. Remember that December through April is the high season here, when the cost of accommodation is doubled and other prices are also affected.

Accommodation: Most accommodation is expensive. The cheapest places to stay are generally situated fairly close to the airport, between it and Bridgetown. Here are some suggestions.

Margate Gardens, Hastings. From US$5.50 per person per night. An apartment hotel, self-catering, near the beach, with swimming pool, etc. Recommended by those who have stayed there and one of the cheapest apartments available.

Roman's Apartments, Enterprise Road, Christchurch. Very close to the airport, this place specializes in short-stay traffic – travellers going on to South America or Venezuelans going home through Barbados. Most of its clientele therefore stay one or two nights only. This is probably the cheapest accommodation available, if only because it does not deal with tourists as such.

YMCA, Bridgetown. Phone first from the airport, to check if space is available.

Appendix 1
Getting There and Back

North American Connections

Following the route of this book, US and Canadian travellers will cross the US/Mexican border at El Paso, or fly direct to Mexico City, thus missing out the north Mexican itinerary. (The latter is recommended if you are on a fairly tight schedule and want to spend some time in Central America). Alternatively, some travellers from the northern US or Canada may wish to start their trip in Miami, travelling down through the Southern USA (details of this journey are given in Appendix 2, pages 163–97).

We give below details of the types of incentive air fares available to North American travellers, and examples of some regular and excursion fares to Miami, El Paso and Mexico City (correct at the time of writing). For further information, you should consult your travel agent.

Group Fares: Certain airlines offer cheaper fares for groups of four or more travelling together on both outward and return flights. These fares are usually available on foreign airlines and are valid on international flights.

'No Frills' Fares: Many US airlines, including National, are now offering very cheap fares on regular domestic services. It is thus possible to fly from many US cities – New York is just one example – to Miami for a cost roughly equivalent to the bus fare. The conditions are generally as follows: although on a regular flight, you pay for the seat only, and receive no catering service; you need to book your flights at least seven days before departure, and there are only a certain number of seats allocated for this purpose.

Excursion Fares and Night Fares: Excursion fares are available on many international flights and domestic services within the USA. Conditions and validity vary, so check with your travel agent. Night fares are available on many US domestic services.

Student flights: If you are a student it is always worth checking with your local student union body or travel organization on the availability of cheap flights to your required destination.

SOME FARES TO MIAMI

From	One Way	Return	Excursion
New York (night)	$76	$152	
Los Angeles (night)	$139	$278	$219
San Francisco	$189	$378	$238
Atlanta (night)	$51	$102	$90
Boston (night)	$84	$168	
Chicago (night)	$82	$163	$143
Detroit (night)	$78	$159	
Montreal	$125	$250	
Seattle	$200	$400	$280
Toronto	$118	$236	
Washington DC	$85	$170	

SOME FARES TO EL PASO

From	One Way	Return	Excursion
New York	$150	$300	$240
Los Angeles (night)	$57	$114	$104
Boston (night)	$128	$256	$256
Chicago (night)	$86	$176	$155
Toronto	$147	$294	
Washington DC	$138	$276	$220

SOME FARES TO MEXICO CITY

From	One Way	Return	Excursion
New York	$176	$352	$330
Los Angeles	$116	$232	$189
San Francisco	$134	$268	$224
Atlanta	$126	$252	$213
Boston	$187	$374	

SOME FARES TO MEXICO CITY

From	One Way	Return	Excursion
Chicago	$145	$290	$225
Detroit	$156	$312	$268
Montreal	$194	$388	$305
Seattle	$191	$382	
Toronto	$176	$352	$270
Washington DC	$162	$324	$279

Trans-Atlantic Flights for non-US Travellers

Using Miami as a gateway to the Americas, trans-Atlantic flights can cost as little as £161 up to a maximum of £274, depending on season and date of booking. Some of the suggested flights and fares are listed at the end of this appendix. Details of the journey from Miami through the Southern USA and down to the Mexican border are given in Appendix 2: Southern USA, pages 163–97.

First of all, here is a short explanation of the different types of discount fares available to European travellers.

Advance Booking Charter (ABC): A concept introduced by the British government in 1973 to stamp out illegal ticket discounting, ABCs have become an increasingly popular means of visiting the Americas, and are generally the cheapest way. There are a few basic rules to which you must adhere:

Your ticket must be booked and paid for at least two months before departure. In practice, you should book before this to be sure of getting a seat.

Cancellation within the two-month period means loss of the full cost. Neither outward nor return date can normally be altered after booking.

If you miss the plane, you've had it.

The two biggest ABC operators are Laker and Jetsave, although at the time of writing Laker have no programme to Miami and Jetsave's programme is limited to three-week round trips. A third company, growing quickly and with a good reputation for efficiency and service, is Airplan. They have a Miami programme which allows for three- or six-

157

week round trips. All ABC companies charge the lowest ABC fares allowed by law. Your travel agent will be pleased to give you further details.

22/45 Day Excursion Fare: Excursion fares giving a minimum 22 days and a maximum 45 days in the Americas are available on all scheduled flights to Miami. Both British Airways and National Airlines operate daily services using wide-body aircraft (747 Jumbo Jets and DC10s). These fares show big savings on normal return fares.

APEX Fares: Advance Passenger Excursion Fares were introduced by the scheduled airlines as a counterblast to ABCs. Valid 22/45 days, they are obtainable on all scheduled flights to Miami, although you should note that only a limited number of seats are allocated for this purpose. They must be booked and paid for two months in advance and carry cancellation penalties. As the cost saving is small over normal excursion fares, this makes them a dubious buy in our opinion.

International Air Bahamas: IAB operate regular scheduled flights between Luxembourg and Nassau. As you have to get to Luxembourg however (flight cost from London £38.50 each way) and then from Nassau to Miami (about £15 each way) this method is only attractive to British residents who are looking for a one-way fare or a stopover in Nassau. These fares are very competitive with other fares available from continental Europe however, where air fares are generally higher than those in the UK because of the international currency situation.

International Caribbean Airways: Barbados to Luxembourg. International Caribbean Airways, the national airline of Barbados, operate scheduled services between Barbados and Luxembourg/London. There is no advantage in flying direct to London with this company, as they are forced to charge the same high fares as everyone else. But they do offer cheap fares into Luxembourg. From Luxembourg to Barbados the one-way cost is £98 Low Season (November 1 to March 31 approx) and £117.50 Normal Season (April through October). That was the good news. Now the bad news: due to the vagaries of international air fares it will cost you more to fly back as return fares are in Barbados dollars, which means that as the pound sinks lower the fares go up. Approximate fares are given in the table below.

Youth Fare: If you intend to stay more than six weeks and are under 23 on the date of travel, and intend to return from Miami, a Youth Fare may be best for you. This can only be booked within five days of travel and your return ticket will be open and valid for up to a year. If this is of interest you can get full details from your travel agent or British Airways (telephone number (01) 828 9711).

Aerovias Quisqueyana: This airline is based in Santo Domingo (Dominican Republic) and flies once a week Rome/Madrid/Santo Domingo/Miami. They are able to provide connections with other airlines and offer cheap fares to many destinations. The fares quoted overleaf include a connection from London.

Travel agents: It is always better to consult a good travel agent rather than an airline direct, as the agent is in a better position to give you unbiased information and will be able to advise you of any bargains introduced subsequent to the publication of this work. The following agents are particularly experienced in this type of travel. They will be able to advise you on your trip and to save you money.

Trail Finders Ltd., 46/8 Earls Court Road, London W8 6EJ. Tel: (01) 937 9631. This is the Overland Information Centre where trained travel consultants, all with intercontinental overland experience, specialize in selling overland tours and advising independent travellers. Any flight arrangements you require can be bought here, in addition to many bus and train tickets (Continental Trailways, Amtrak and Tica Bus). Tell them what you want to do and they will advise you on the best way to do it. They also sell maps, guides, books such as this one, travel insurance and have a visa service.

International Flight Services, 1 Kensington Mall, London W8. Tel: (01) 229 4302. This company specializes in cheap flights to the Americas with no other services except insurance. Advance Booking Charters with Laker, Airplan or Jetsave can be bought here, and they are also agents for International Caribbean Airways and many South American carriers. IFS usually have exclusive low fares to many points in the Americas, so although they cannot help with overland travel information, it is worth giving them a call if your travel plans are firm.

LONDON/MIAMI/LONDON

	Low Season 1/11 to 31/3	Shoulder Season Apr/May/Jun/Oct*	High Season 1/7 to 30/9*
ABC	£161	£170/£182	£182/£218
22/45 Excursion	£198	£225	£274
APEX	£173	£197	£244
One way direct	£167	£176	£210
Youth Fare direct	£245	£268	£295

* The seasons given above are for westbound traffic. When travelling eastbound, June is High Season and September Low Season.

LUXEMBOURG/NASSAU/LUXEMBOURG
International Air Bahamas

	Low Season		Shoulder Season		High Season	
	£	LF*	£	LF*	£	LF*
22/45 Excursion	£131	12460	£144	13750	£188	18410
LUX/NAS one way	£110	11040	£116	11040	£136	12920

* LF = Luxembourg francs

LUXEMBOURG/BARBADOS/LUXEMBOURG
International Caribbean Airways

	Low Season*	Normal Season*
LUX/BARBADOS one way	£99	£118
BARBADOS/LUX one way	£112 approx	£135 approx
LUX/BARBADOS/LUX	£197	£235

* Seasons are as follows: Low Season October, November and 25 December to 14 April; Normal Season 15 April to 30 September and 1 to 24 December.

AEROVIAS QUISQUEYANA Low Season Fares

LONDON/MADRID/MIAMI one way	£135
LONDON/MADRID/MIAMI return	£265

Homeward Bound

From Merida: If you are taking the Mexican itinerary only, and not continuing into Central America, a flight from Merida to Miami, and then on to your final destination, is probably the best method. Pan American runs four flights weekly (on Mondays, Thursdays, Fridays and Saturdays); single fare: US$77. Alternatively, North American travellers might prefer to fly from Merida to Mexico City. This is a daily service. Single fare: US$63. Air fares between Mexico City and North American cities are given on page 156. There are few other international flights from Merida.

From Panama: Again, the best method is probably to fly from Panama to Miami and then on to your final destination. There are three different economy fares available on this route, depending on which airline you use. Braniff, Pan American, Lan-Chile and Ecuatoriana charge US$155; Air Panama US$152; and Lloyd Aero Boliviano US$143. LAB run three flights a week, in the very early morning (approx. 02.00) of Tuesdays, Thursdays and Saturdays.

If you definitely intend to return this way, you may find it advantageous to purchase your ticket beforehand from the very helpful Miami office of LAB. Having this ticket in your possession can be an advantage when passing through immigration procedures on your way through Central America, as it is proof that you intend to leave the isthmus. Although this means you will have to pay the US Transportation Tax of 8 per cent, you will find that there is a 5 per cent sales tax on tickets bought in Panama anyway. (There is also a US$4.50 airport tax.)

We list below details of other fares from Panama.

Mexico and Central America

PANAMA TO

New York	$245
Los Angeles	$319
San Francisco	$334
Miami	$143 (LAB)
Chicago	$251
Detroit	$249
Washington DC	$245

From Barranquilla: The Colombian airline, AeroCondor, operates regular scheduled services between Barranquilla and Miami, using Boeing jets. AeroCondor charges US$120 as opposed to a regular fare of US$155 (their first-class fare is only US$143). They run a daily service, leaving in the afternoon. This ticket can be bought in Colombia, Miami or Europe (though not at the time of writing in the UK, unless combined with a trans-Atlantic fare, for example Nassau/Luxembourg). At a slightly higher cost, you are allowed a stopover in the Caribbean island of San Andres. If preferred, you can fly from Cartagena to Miami with the same airline at the same cost.

From San Andres: AeroCondor has two flights a week, on Thursdays and Sundays, from San Andres to Miami. Single fare: US$90. This would be an interesting (and economical) way of returning home. You can fly to San Andres from the Colombian mainland (see page 148).

From Barbados: There is at present no financial advantage in US or Canadian citizens returning via Barbados, although services to North American cities are regular. International Caribbean Airways hopes to begin operating regular scheduled services to North America in 1977.

Europeans can benefit from the cheap trans-Atlantic flights offered by International Caribbean Airways, the national airline of Barbados. Forced to change the same extortionate Barbados/London fare as everyone else (over £250 even in the low season), ICA also flies to Luxembourg, a route on which they are allowed to charge much lower fares. Details of these fares are given on page 160.

If you decide to return to Europe through Barbados, it is advised that you buy your air ticket before departure. Besides being essential to allow you entry into Barbados, it can often be used at other immigration points as proof that you intend to return to Europe.

Appendix 2
The Southern USA

The southern USA: background information

This appendix is designed primarily for European travellers taking advantage of the cheap trans-Atlantic flights to Miami, and thus approaching Mexico through the southern USA. I hope it may also be of interest to North Americans who are not familiar with this part of the country.

I took this route myself and found that, far from being just a means to an end, it considerably enhanced the whole trip. There is so much in the south. From Miami Beach's sophistication to the primeval Everglade swamps, a few miles away. Most of America's distinctive music styles were generated here: blues from Memphis, the rock 'n roll of Elvis Presley and Chuck Berry, Bluegrass hillbilly music, country and western from Nashville Tennessee, and of course New Orleans jazz.

Traditionally the south has been regarded as the most backward part of the country. Loved for its colourful character, splendid antebellum houses, magnificent Florida coastline, yet the springboard for man's excursions into space. But also the land of racial intolerance, rednecks and the crazy hillbillies. Now this is changing. In many instances the south is setting an example to the north, in new social attitudes and exciting business opportunities. And 1976 saw ex-Georgia Governor Jimmy Carter's spectacular presidential candidature and election.

A brief history: Although independence celebrations were centred on the north-east, the first European settlement in the New World was actually in South Florida. Juan Ponce de Leon, a lieutenant of Christopher Columbus, came ashore in 1513 searching for the Fountain of Youth. He was followed fifty years later by a band of Conquistadores who settled in what is now St. Augustine. In 1803 the United States bought the territory of Louisiana from France for $12 million.

With the flourishing wealth of the great cotton plantations, slavery became one of the major issues which led to the Civil War. Not the only issue. The south was prosperous and resented taxation and control from a distant government. The Confederacy consisted of South Carolina, Mississippi, Florida, Alabama, Georgia, Louisiana and Texas. After four bloody years the south was in ruins and is only now recovering. The heroism of the Confederate troops is still a source of pride in the south, as evidenced by monuments to President Davis, General Robert E. Lee and General 'Stonewall' Jackson.

The war was such a shattering experience that locally history is divided into two periods, antebellum — prewar, and after the war. The whole lifestyle changed. Previously the powerful plantation owners had ruled like barons with great estates. They cultivated a gracious and civilized way of life which still lingers on. But it has taken a hundred years for a new south to emerge from the ashes and begin to impress itself on the nation.

Florida: Over the last hundred years the American Dream has come true in Florida. It is undoubtedly superficial and materialistic, a trend encouraged by the large numbers of retired people who move south to enjoy the fruits of their lives' labour. But everything is clean, the climate is perfect and corruption seems minimal. Life is unhurried, even in a big city like Miami, and it is very difficult to feel despondent. Even if down and out in Miami one can at least lie on the beaches.

Towards the end of the last century Florida was developed by the great American pioneering spirit. First Henry Morrison Flagler, then Julia Tuttle moved down, built hotels, a railroad and a town — Miami. And once Miami/Miami Beach had become the world's foremost holiday playground, and begun to decline, new areas were developed. Spacecity at Cape Canaveral, Mickey Mouse Land at Orlando.

Although the little hick town of Tallahassee in the northwest is Florida State's capital, Miami/Miami Beach is the hub of the state. Known as the Gateway to the Americas, Miami's busy international airport links Florida with Europe, Mexico, the Caribbean and Central and South America. Inevitably this gives Miami a very cosmopolitan aspect. In addition to the Americans who have drifted south to The Beach — many of whom were immigrants anyway, with a strong Jewish element — Spanish-speakers from Central America, Colombia and Venezuela proliferate. And of course the strong and increasingly important contingent of Cuban emigrés. Miami has lost its exclusivity as the fashionable place to live as the rich find new havens. Palm Beach, Naples and the Florida Keys are examples. In addition to residents, some industry is moving out of Miami, notably to Fort Lauderdale up the road.

Louisiana: The contrast to South Florida's Spanish-American flavour is the French legacy of Louisiana. Between the Mississippi delta and the Texas border is Acadiana, bayou country with fishing villages and smallholdings set amongst the swamps. This area is French-speaking.

Towards the end of the sixteenth century the French colonists arrived, but for a hundred years found times hard. The French solution was to export large numbers of the weaker sex from France to ginger up the menfolk. New Orleans is a city founded on this philosophy. The French colonizers were joined by Germans, Canary Islanders, American refugees from the Revolution, black slaves. Mix them up, add salt and stir and you have the Creoles. Although the Creoles are today less obvious as such, there still remains one distinctive local breed, the Cajun. Now a hardy, poorly educated, land-based and traditional folk, they were the result of France's decline in the Americas. When in 1713 Acadia (now Nova Scotia) fell to the British, those residents who were unwilling to take a new oath of allegiance were tipped out. Many came down to the deep south.

Although Baton Rouge is the state capital, New Orleans is the outstanding city. Vieux Carré, the French Quarter, is unique. Whilst downtown New Orleans is climbing heavenwards with new constructions of concrete and glass, Vieux Carré has been designated a national monument. Its narrow streets with pastel-painted houses adorned with filigreed wrought-iron balconies make it a photographer's paradise. The atmosphere is uninhibited. Grossly over-commercialized, it must be one of the few places in the world which the tourist is too overawed to ruin. Maybe its joie de vivre makes it a natural for exploitation – because the locals are not self-conscious about its stripclubs, porno shops and prostitution they do not obtrude. And the food of course. Not really French but Creole.

With drinking laws amongst the most liberal in the USA and the best place to stay recommended in this book (see page 188), you'll have a ball.

Texas: The history of Texas is hard-fought and progressive. Colonized by the Spanish along with Mexico, Texas became independent with Mexico in 1821. The English-speaking settlers in Texas were as little impressed with rule from Mexico City as they were with Madrid, so making Texas an independent republic in 1836. Up until 1845 when she became the 28th state, Texas was The Lone Star Republic.

This century had barely started before oil was discovered in Texas. This was the first step towards turning a predominantly agricultural economy into an industrial one. Now Texas boasts huge skyscrapers in its major towns, Houston, Dallas, Austin. A good reason for avoiding them.

Following this book your only experience of Texas will be San Antonio and El Paso. Perhaps appropriately, as the Battle of the Alamo was one of those defeats that ultimately led to victory. But more than that, San Antonio is a very pleasant, smallish town. By using the Paseo del Rio (Riverwalk) you can amble throughout the centre of the town without being bothered by city bustle. And its strong Mexican flavour sharpens the taste buds for that country to the south.

The southern USA: travel information

Visas and customs: Non-US citizens should get their United States visas at the earliest opportunity. Normally Britons should have no trouble, but Australians and New Zealanders resident in the United Kingdom may experience difficulties. A visa for the USA is usually multi-entry, valid for the life of your passport. So you should apply just as soon as possible. Remember that if you are refused a visa, this is not accepted by insurance companies as a valid reason for their accepting your liabilities in respect of cancellation penalties.

US customs' regulations are quite liberal. One quart of alcohol, and 300 cigarettes may be taken in, as may $100-worth of gifts. Your reasonable private effects are also duty-free.

Currency: The dollar ($), divided into 100 cents. All US notes are the same colour and size, green on one side, grey the other, so be careful. It may help to keep your billfold in sequence. Notes come in $1, $2, $5, $10, $20 and some larger denominations. Coins are one cent (penny), five cents (nickel), ten cents (dime), 25 cents (quarter), and 50 cents (half dollar).

Banking hours are usually 9am to 2pm/3pm, although it should not be necessary to visit a bank in the States as most hotels, restaurants and large stores will take traveller's cheques, giving change in cash. It doesn't take long to start thinking in dollars.

Language: This should cause no problems as most Americans speak a language very similar to English; indeed parts of the American vocabulary are now being incorporated into vernacular English. The only other language you can expect to encounter readily is Spanish, in Miami, Texas and Mexico.

Food: Cheap American food is generally better than its English equivalent, less greasy and more spicy. You will probably find yourself eating often in cafeterias although you would never do so at home. Don't forget to allow for the sales tax and, when eating in restaurants, tip. In New Orleans you will be able to eat good food at reasonable prices – $3 to $5 for a meal. Cheap meals generally will cost maybe $1 to $1.50 for breakfast, $1.50 to $2.50 for lunch and $2 to $4 for dinner. Please remember that it is unfair to judge a country's food by its cheap eating places; if you only eat at such places, do not base your opinions of American food on them. The occasional good meal will increase your

168

enjoyment of the trip and give you a fairer indication.

Accommodation: We want to keep you off Skid Row. Generally therefore we have not chosen the very cheapest possible accommodation except in rare instances. If this trip is going to cost you anything between $500 and $1000 (excluding long distance connections) it is ridiculous to try to save $30/$50 by eating and sleeping on Skid Row, where the health and theft risks are higher and enjoyment of the trip lower.

The suggested accommodation is commensurate with the lowest practical price for cleanliness and security. Where possible the hotels are close to bus and/or railroad terminals, on the basis that it is better to walk without your luggage than with it. By coincidence this is generally where the cheaper hotels are found.

Climate: Autumn, winter and spring are the best times to travel. Although in some areas, such as South Florida, winter is the high season, the price difference on the overall cost is insignificant. Additionally European travellers should note that trans-Atlantic fares are at their highest in the summer (see Appendix 1: Trans-Atlantic Flights, page 157), so that the overall cheapest time to travel is winter. South Florida enjoys a tropical climate, which is what made Miami Beach one of the world's foremost holiday playgrounds. Nowhere should the weather be cold, but in the summer it can be really hot. Winter evenings can be cold in some places.

DAYTIME AVERAGE TEMPERATURES

City	Minimum		Maximum		Average	
	°F	°C	°F	°C	°F	°C
Miami/Miami Beach	60	16	100	38	80	27
New Orleans	56	13	83	28	70	21
San Antonio	55	13	89	32	75	24

Time Zones: There are four time zones in the USA, three of which you pass through. Miami is in the Eastern time zone, five hours behind GMT. West of Tallahassee you move into Central Time, whilst El Paso is another hour behind on Mountain Time.

Tipping: Taxi drivers and waiters expect 10/15 per cent tips and look askance at less than 50 cents. A tip is expected even if service is bad (which doesn't necessarily mean you give it).

Post Offices and Telephones: Post offices in the States work long hours, so when you find one it should be open. Officially main central post offices in major cities are open 24 hours a day, and others open between 8 am and 6 pm Monday to Friday and Saturday mornings. Generally they are marked on the town plans later in this book.

Stamps can also be bought from hotel clerks at a supplementary charge. In such cases you will also find a mail box handy.

Note that telegrams in the USA are sent by a commercial company (Western Union) and other commercial companies run the telephone system (mainly Bell). The telephones here are of a good standard; most local calls cost a dime (10 cents) from public booths and are free from private phones.

Forward mail: We do not recommend that you have mail forwarded to you, but if you must we suggest the following:

The YMCA, 40 NE 3rd Avenue, Miami, Florida (reliable if you convince them you are returning).

'L'Auberge', 717 Barracks Street, French Quarter, New Orleans, Louisiana (make sure it is marked 'To be Collected').

Post Restante is not a good idea. It is called 'General Delivery' in the USA. General Delivery mail must be collected in person and should be addressed as in the following example:

Your Name
C/O General Delivery
Main Post Office
San Antonio
Texas, USA.

Electricity: Usually 110/115 volts, 60 cycles AC.

Shopping and Cleaning: Shops tend to work long hours, the drugstores (many of which are quite large with a wide variety of products on sale) usually staying open until 9 pm, as well as being open on Sundays. Laundromats can be found in large towns. These usually cost 50 cents (two quarters) for the wash and 10 cents for the dryers. Washing powder can be expensive.

Drinks (alcoholic) and Cigarettes: Drink laws are humorous in their anachronisms and lack of uniformity unless you drink a lot, in which case they can be frustrating. New Orleans is very liberal as the indigenous population likes to have a good time. Drink with meals, when available, tends to be expensive.

The price of cigarettes does not vary according to brand. The standard price is 60/65 cents, but places can be found which sell them for 50 cents. No-smoking regulations proliferate in public places and on public transport. Watch for the signs.

Other Drugs: You may be offered marijuana on this trip. The use of this is more likely to get you imprisoned than deported as the drug has not yet been legalized and strong attempts are still being made to eradicate its use. Don't touch it.

USA Transport

Fare reductions for non-US citizens: All travel arrangements booked and paid for in the United States are subject to an 8 per cent transportation tax. Thus, European travellers who have made their plans in advance and purchase all possible travel tickets before departure can make considerable savings. In addition, there are certain discounts on US travel available to foreigners.

1: Amtrak train fare. If purchased by non-Americans outside the USA, the fare New Orleans/San Antonio/El Paso will cost $50 (standard fare: $65 plus tax). This discount is also available in the USA on production of your passport, provided the ticket is bought within 90 days of your arrival; with tax it will cost you $54.

2: If you intend to travel Miami/El Paso in a week or less (which is really moving), you could go all the way by bus, utilizing the Trailways one-week Eaglepass ticket, which costs $76 (available outside the USA only). Greyhound have a similar fare on their Ameripass scheme.

USA Coach Operators: There are two big national bus consortia, Greyhound and Trailways, operating between them some 8500 vehicles. Greyhound are better known outside the USA and are stronger in the north; they have a reputation for noisier and dirtier buses. Trailways' head office is in Dallas, Texas, and they are stronger in the south. On this route, their vehicles are operated by Tamiami Trailways, usually the new Silver Eagle buses with waterproof luggage storage, toilets, reclining seats, air-conditioning and tinted windows (essential in Florida).

Mexico and Central America

When I made this trip, I used Trailways. I found their buses clean and quiet, and was impressed by the cleanliness of the Trailways' terminals in all towns visited. In both New Orleans and El Paso, I found that although Greyhound had newer, bigger and grander terminals, they were dirty — particularly in El Paso, where the litter stood out in stark contrast to the splendour of the building. In Miami, Naples, Saint Petersburg and New Orleans — the points where you will be carrying baggage to or from a bus station — we found the Trailways' terminals conveniently located.

It is possible to go right through from Miami to El Paso by bus. The saving is small however, and the journey is far more interesting if you use the excellent Amtrak service from New Orleans to El Paso, as detailed in the text.

Amtrak: Due to what is generally regarded as mismanagement in the eyes of most Americans, the rail system — as far as passengers were concerned — was until very recently allowed to become run down. Most of the main inter-city routes have now been nationalized under the name Amtrak. The American taxpayer subsidizes this enterprise and will continue to do so in the forseeable future, whilst new rolling stock, locomotives and other facilities are introduced.

The benefits to you are immediately evident in New Orleans. In spite of the beaurocratic time-wasters in the ticket office (mentioned in detail below), your immediate impressions of the trains should be good. The coaches are double-decker, with baggage space, rest rooms and conductors' quarters downstairs (where you enter). Upstairs you will find the seats, all forward-facing. These are reclining — really reclining, they go right back, leg rests pull out and there is more legroom than in any other kind of transportation. Pillows are provided at night. The rest rooms are very good indeed: very clean, plenty of hot water, soap, towels, easy chairs, shaver sockets, etc. Each carriage has at least one conductor.

Apparently there is no smoking allowed, although there are no signs to this effect. Smoking is allowed in the buffet car, which is in practice used as a bar by those who like to while away the time drinking, playing cards, chatting, etc, and in the restaurant car. After New Orleans the food served on board will fail to excite your palate, but the prices are not unreasonable.

Amtrak Reservations: If you have already purchased your Amtrak ticket it is probably open, and you will need to make a reservation for the particular dates you want to travel. The long distance toll-free Amtrak New Orleans telephone number is 800–874–2800. You can thus make your reservation by telephone if you wish.

Should you not have bought your ticket in advance do it shortly after arrival in New Orleans. Reservations and ticket issue are the most obvious weak link in Amtrak. When there's three trains a week rather than three trains an hour, the systems become rather cumbersome. The ticket itself is rather like an airplane ticket with all the work that involves. Your booking is put on computer. The clerks are slow and unco-operative. Even then they managed to overbook the train on my trip! Be sure to take your passport and insist on your 25 per cent reduction if you are a foreign national.

City Buses: Most city buses work on a flat fare system (for example Miami is 30 cents). You have to pay the exact fare on entering the vehicle.

Taxis: American cabs may come as a pleasant surprise – you pay the fare on the meter (although they expect a tip)! Charges vary but you can expect 75 or 80 cents the first 1 mile and 20 cents thereafter.

Suggested Transport Schedules

Carrier	From	To	Departure Times	Arrival Times	Cost
Tamiami Trailways	Miami	Fort Lauderdale	9.00 am 12.00 pm 12.15 pm	10.00 am 1.00 pm 1.15 pm	$50.60
	Fort Lauderdale	Naples	4.15 pm	6.35 pm	
	Naples	Saint Petersburg	11.25 am 6.35 pm	4.20 pm 11.10 pm	
	St Petersburg	New Orleans	7.30 pm	02.05 pm (next day)	
Amtrak*	New Orleans	San Antonio	1.00 pm	2.25 am (next day)	$53
	San Antonio	El Paso	2.40 am	2.15 pm	

* Amtrak: three per week. Departs lunchtime Monday/Wednesday/Friday, arriving San Antonio in the very early hours of Tuesday/Thursday/Saturday. Departs San Antonio very early hours of Tuesday/Thursday/Saturday, arriving El Paso at lunchtime the same day.

Please note: The transport schedule above is a very rough guide. Full details are in the text.

The Americans do not use the 24-hour clock. To avoid causing confusion with the bus and train schedules you will pick up en route, herein we use 'am' and 'pm' with regard to travel times in the USA.

Miami

Arrival in Miami: Immigration officials will ask all non-US nationals how long they intend to stay in the USA. Tell them the approximate duration of your trip. They will generally give you a slightly longer period.

Your traveller's cheques will of course be in US dollars. If you need some dollar bills in change you can get these upstairs in the terminal building. If changing traveller's cheques for this purpose do not use the moneychanging window – they charge a commission. Instead walk down to the bank near the Eastern Airlines desk.

To get yourself downtown use the Redtop sedan service; just wait near the taxi rank until one comes along. Either ask to be taken to one of the hotels we suggest, or a well-known point such as the Columbus/ McAllister Hotels. The fare is $3. There are also Orange Streaker buses (make sure you take one downtown bound) but the Redtop is the best bet. The cheapest way of all is the number 20 bus. Make sure it is southbound, and get off at the corner of East Flagler Street and NE 1st Avenue. You will need to pay the exact fare of 30 cents on entering the bus; ask the driver to give you a yell when you reach Flagler (don't rely on it).

Although slightly cheaper hotels, or hotels of the same price, can be found in parts of Miami Beach and in the outskirts of Miami, downtown is the best area to stay. Here are the Trailways' terminal, Mexican Consulate, Pan American office, banks, etc.

Don't let anyone tell you Miami is expensive. It isn't. If you have too much money and would like to be relieved of some, then the people here will be only to glad to help. But the main tourists here are the consumer-conscious Americans, mainly lower income groups (the richer Americans go further afield – you will see many in Mexico), and the residents possibly earn less than the national average wage. Both factors tend to keep prices down. Cheap hotels and eating places can thus be found with a little shopping around, and this book gives you a head start.

Miami Beach is, if anything, cheaper. Its halcyon days are over. On a weekend when a big football game (the World Championship) attracted tens of thousands from out of town, Miami/Miami Beach still had accommodation at all prices. Miami Beach is probably more of a Brighton than a Saint Tropez. In fact for a cheap seaside place with beautiful uncrowded beaches it is ideal.

Street names in Miami run from the junction of Flagler Street and Miami Avenue (see map on page 177). Avenues run north/south and streets east/west. Always note the prefix to street/avenue names (NE/NW/SE and SW).

Where to Stay: Miami has hotels to suit all pockets. Please note that when refering to prices we give the high season rates. Summer prices will be lower and may be negotiable. We didn't check out the big, flashy, obviously expensive hotels such as the Columbus; hotels mentioned here range from medium-priced to cheap.

At the top end of our scale is the Ponce de Leon at $12 for a single and $16 for a double. Rooms are air-conditioned with bathrooms, television, etc, and the hotel is conveniently situated on Flagler Street, as downtown as you can get. Snapping at its heels pricewise is the Hotel Leamington at $11 for a single and $14 for a double. Bathrooms, air-conditioning, radio, etc.

The Hotel Colon on NE 2nd Avenue is the hotel most strongly recommended. There are no flashy extras here at all, and it looks forbidding from the outside, but $9 single or $10 double buys you adequate accommodation with bathroom. If you are looking for the cheapest accommodation commensurate with cleanliness and security and are willing to take a room without its own bath, then stay at the Bristol. At $5 for a single and $7 for a double it's not quite the cheapest in town, but it is better than a number of more expensive hotels (including the Bradford next door which should be avoided). Unprepossessing from the exterior, it is situated on NE 1st Street. The Colon and the Bristol are the recommended hotels in Miami.

Should the above hotels be full, other hotels you can try are the Park (243 NE 5th Street) at $8 single, $10 double; the Gibson, NE 2nd Avenue, similar prices, and the Ritz Hotel in Flagler Street. All are owned by the same company. The YMCA at 40 NE 3rd Avenue is a reliable address for mail forwarding if you are staying there. The YWCA is a modern building but a little out of the downtown area.

Where to Eat: Good cheap eating places can be found on or near the main streets in Miami and Miami Beach.

Downtown Miami: Key

1	YMCA	22	Pan American Airlines
2	YWCA	23	Mexicana Airlines
3	Hotel Senate	24	Loftleider/International
4	Hotel Avondale		Air Bahamas
5	Hotel Detroit	25	British Airways
6	Hotel Gibson	26	Eastern Airlines
7	Hotel Cortez	27	National Airlines
8	Hotel Columbus	28	VIASA
9	Hotel Colon	29	AeroMexico
10	Hotel Ponce de Leon	30	AeroCondor
11	Hotel Bristol	31	Trailways Terminal
12	Hotel Leamington	32	Post Office
13	Walgreens Drugstore/	33	Travelers Aid
	Cafeteria	34	Laundromat
14	America Cafeteria	35	Mexican Consul
15	McCrory		(Rivergate Plaza)
16	Bellamar Restaurant	36	Woolworths
17	Howard Johnson	37	Army and Navy Store
18	McDonalds	38	1st Federal Building
19	Honolulu Restaurant	39	Biscayne Tower
20	Pacifico Cuban Chinese	40	Dade County Courthouse
21	Burger King		

MIAMI: For cafeteria-style eating try Walgreens drugstore, upstairs, at the corner of Flagler and 2nd Avenue (SE). They have many specials and by taking advantage of these you can eat quite cheaply. Pancakes with syrup, butter and coffee breakfast cost about $1 (including tax). Lunch or dinner should cost you $2 to $3. The America Cafeteria is a small, Cuban-run eating place where you sit on a stool at the long counter. Food is good, prices reasonable, service varies from good to indifferent. A good breakfast here of orange juice, toast, jam and cofee costs 60/65 cents including tax. Don't have the pancakes here. They have a little shop out front which sells cigarettes at 50 cents (Europeans should note that when you buy cigarettes in the States you are normally given a book of matches as well).

MacDonalds are normally regarded as the cheapest eating places in the States, claiming to have served over 17 billion 'meals'. You are not likely to eat here twice. A better place for a quick, cheap snack, the same sort of

Downtown Miami

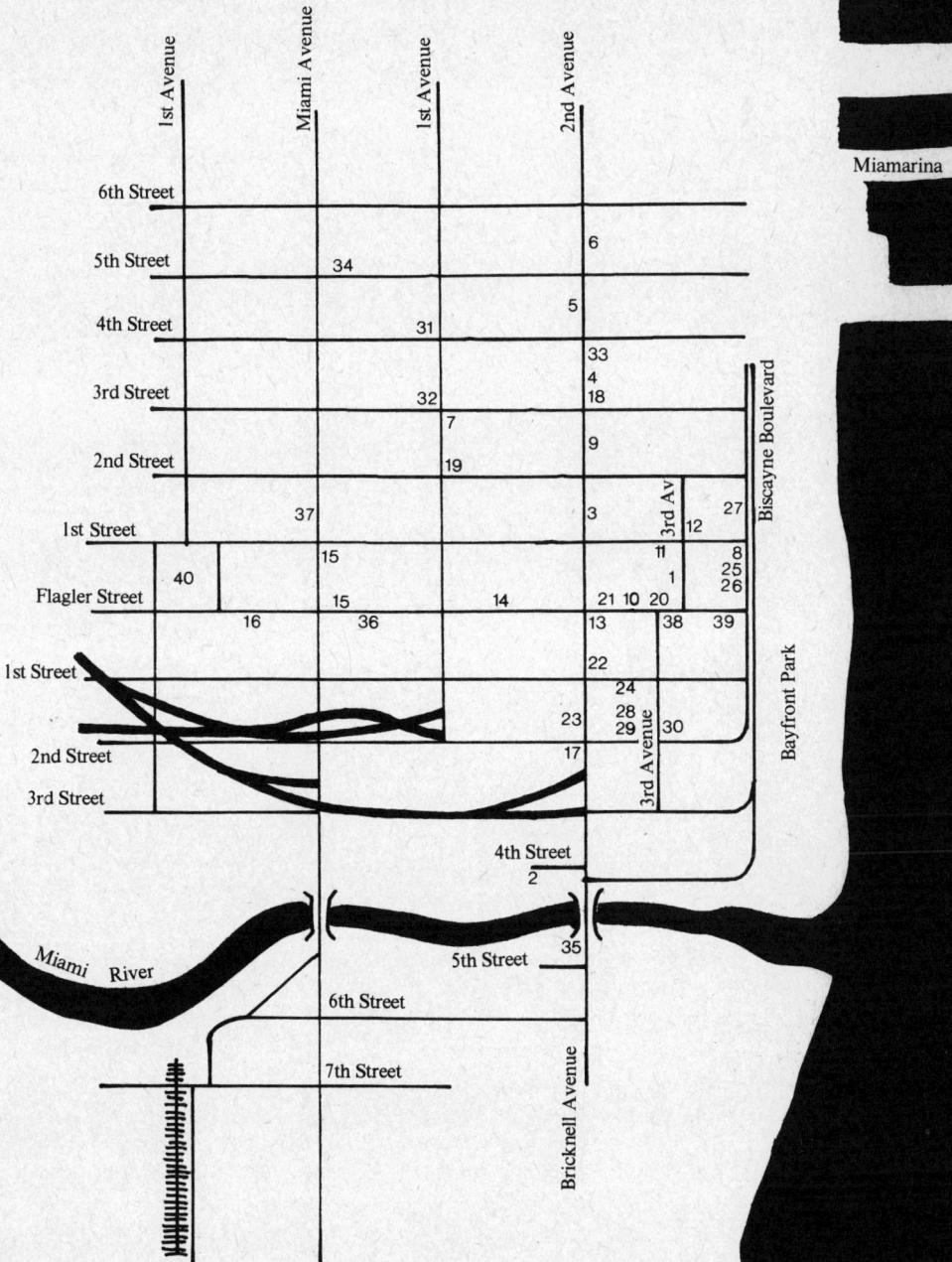

Miamarina

1st Avenue

Miami Avenue

1st Avenue

2nd Avenue

Biscayne Boulevard

6th Street

5th Street   34

4th Street   31   6

5

3rd Street   32

33
4
18

7

2nd Street   19

9

1st Street   37

3

3rd Av

27

12

15

11

8
25
26

40

1

Flagler Street   15   14   21 10 20

16   36

13   38   39

Bayfront Park

1st Street

22

24
28
29

3rd Avenue

23   30

2nd Street

17

3rd Street

4th Street

2

Miami   River

5th Street   35

6th Street

Bricknell Avenue

7th Street

Miami and Miami Beach: Key

1	Downtown area	10	Rickenbacker Causeway
2	Coral Gables	11	Venetian Way
3	Coconut Grove	12	Miami Seaquarium
4	North Miami	13	Miamarina
5	Normandy Isle	14	Parrot Jungle
6	Hialeah	15	Miami Jai-Alai
7	Miami Springs	16	South Miami Beach area
8	Julia Tuttle Causeway	17	Flame Steak
9	MacArthur Causeway		

---

food but better and, if anything, cheaper, is Burger King. Though the graphics and colours are similar to the British 'Wimpy Bars', and the clientele mainly the same sort of composition, there the similarity ends. This is 'The Home of The Whopper', which means the larger, American-sized hamburgers (the Wimpy-sized ones are also available at 35/40 cents a time). Besides your 1lb of beef you get tomato, lettuce, mayonnaise, etc. French fries (chips) are extra. The place is very clean, and counter service very, very quick, this speed generated by the use of production line techniques, sometimes causing confusion to the slow-witted customer. Try it when it's crowded, it's a riot. Staff are dressed in red and yellow uniforms and caps, looking like airline stewardesses from the sunshine state.

From time to time you will want a proper meal and there can be no better place than the Honolulu Restaurant. Although technically a Chinese restaurant, its popular menu is the international one, and it's good. Typical meal: fillet steak, mushroom sauce, sweet peppers, salad, vegetables, french fries, chinese crackers with butter, beer, dessert, coffee. Price $4.50 including tax but not tip. Verdict: delicious. Service is very good. The Bellamar, newly opened at the time of writing, is striving to reach the same league. Not yet as good in terms of value it may be worth a try. It serves Spanish-American food. The Pacifico is a Cuban-Chinese (?) restaurant worth trying. Avoid McCrorys.

MIAMI BEACH: A good place to get off the bus in Miami Beach is the junction of Collins Avenue and Lincoln Road. Walking southwards from here you find the unfashionable part of Miami Beach where the residents are mainly retired people. This means uncrowded beaches and lower prices. Near the intersection of Collins and Lincoln, on Lincoln, you will

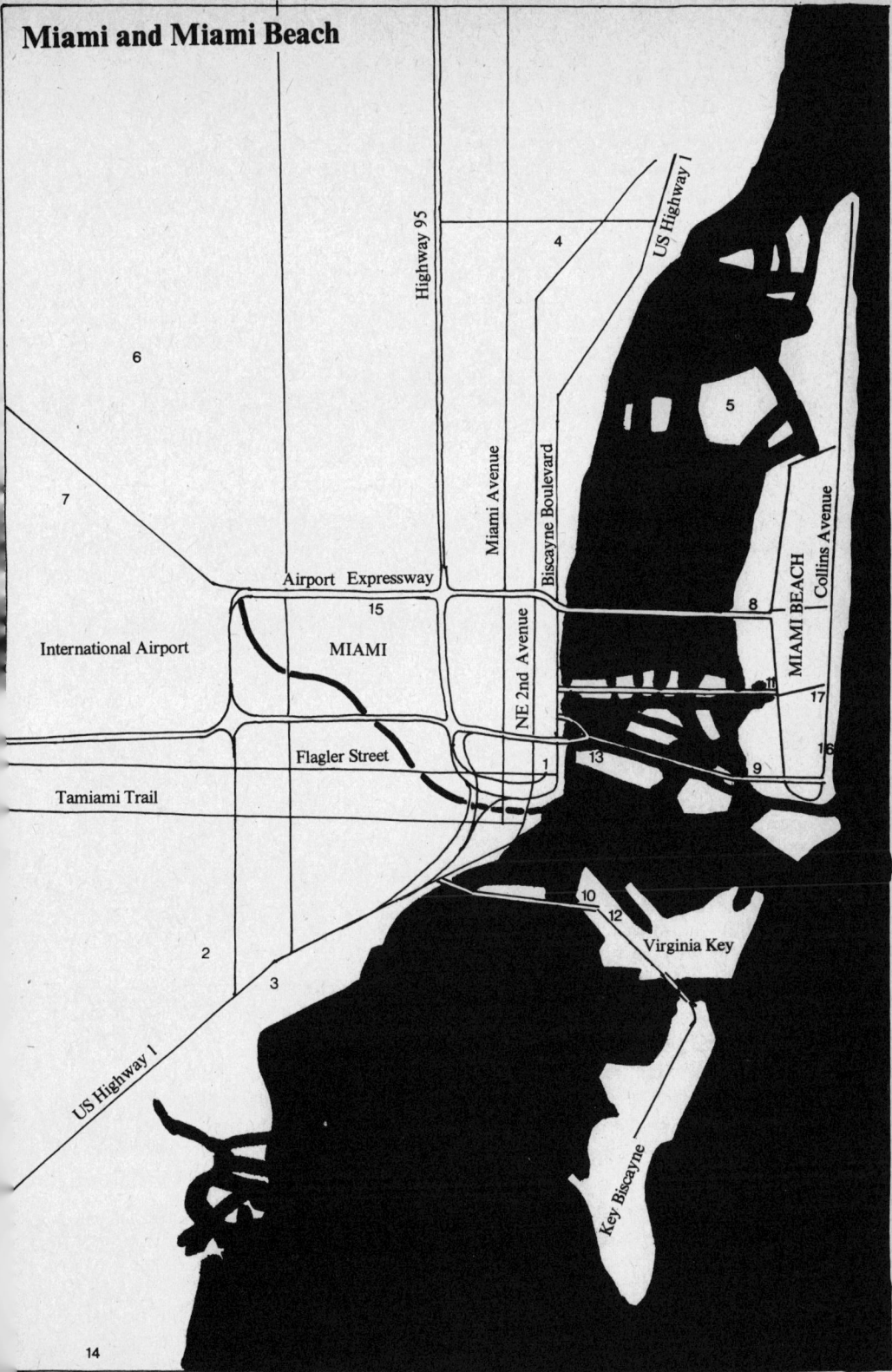

Miami and Miami Beach

International Airport

MIAMI

MIAMI BEACH

Virginia Key

Key Biscayne

Airport Expressway

Flagler Street

Tamiami Trail

Highway 95

Miami Avenue

Biscayne Boulevard

NE 2nd Avenue

Collins Avenue

US Highway 1

US Highway 1

1
2
3
4
5
6
7
8
9
10
11
12
13
14
15
16
17

find the Flame Steak. A 3lb sirloin or T-bone with baked potato, toasted garlic bread and dressed salad here will set you back $3, if ordered before 5 pm (50 cents more after 5 pm). If you cannot afford this, cheaper meals are available. Near the junction of Lincoln and Washington Avenue, on Washington, is a place (Big Daddy's) offering a 50 cent breakfast of orange juice, doughnut and coffee.

ELSEWHERE: If you have time to leave the downtown Miami and Miami Beach areas and see a Golden Nugget Pancake House at feeding time, try it. You'll wonder how they do it for the money (example: veal escalope, french fries, vegetable, warm roll and butter for $1.85).

Things to Do: First, work. If you haven't got them already, this is the place to get your return air ticket to Miami, and your Mexican tourist card. If you are undecided about your schedule, buy an open ticket and make your flight reservation later on. Details on flights and fares back to Miami from Mexico and Central America are given in Appendix 1: Homeward Bound, page 161.

The Mexican Consulate is at 444 Bricknell Avenue (continuation southwards of 2nd Avenue), the first building on the right past the bridge. Go in the morning. The Tourist Card is free, and they have brochures, some of which may be of interest.

You can get your Trailways ticket before you depart (if you haven't already bought it) or when you leave, if you arrive at the bus station 30 minutes before departure. The fare is $50.60, but you will be charged 8 per cent Transportation Tax. It will probably be issued Miami/Pensacola/New Orleans.

Now, pleasure. Call in at the Chamber of Commerce, 1200 Biscayne Boulevard. They have information and brochures on things to do. Or if you don't want to walk that far, go into any of the travel agencies and pick up the brochures which interest you.

The main attraction is Miami Beach. Take a number C, K, L or S bus from NE 1st Avenue at the corner of Flagler. Get off at Lincoln and walk down Ocean Drive, where you find the better and less crowded beaches. Then there is the Seaquarium on Rickenbacker Causeway (Virginia Key), near ex-President Richard Nixon's winter quarters. Take the B bus from SE 3rd Avenue, opposite the 1st Federal Building. Entrance is about $3, but you can easily spend a day there. Or you could take a blimp ride, 30 minutes for $5. The Goodyear Blimp is moored at the near end of MacArthur Causeway. You can take the beach bus or walk. You may need to book in advance.

One of Miami's best known attractions is its Monkey Jungle. This has now become territory to which the monkey has become indigenous, most of the present population having been born there. The climate is of course perfect for them. The humans are caged for their protection. The address is 14805 SW 216 Street. Expect to pay about $2 entrance. The Parrot Jungle at 11000 SW 57 Avenue (South Red Road) has macaws pulling off tricks they were never designed to do. Plus of course all the exotic birds you can imagine.

Also in Miami you have Jai Alai (pronounced 'HiLi'), 'a game that moves so fast it has the fans jumping out of their seats and the players literally climbing the walls'. This is the Basque game of Pelota (most of the players are Basques) but played indoors and featuring gambling – minimum bet $2. Address of Miami Jai Alai is NW 36th Street at 36th Avenue. Then there's the Planetarium, Everglades National Park, Little Havana, Coconut Grove (artists'/hippy quarter, quiet leafy roads), Miamarina with its dozen or so cruise liners, outdoor concerts in Bayfront Park, winter concerts of the most famous entertainers, etc, etc.

If you have, or make, friends in Miami get them to take you to the Everglades National Park. Otherwise there are bus tours to the area. These wild primeval swamps – 2188 square miles in area – are still the homeland of the alligator, sea cow and egret. Its Indian name is 'Pahayokee', grassy water. There are roads, tracks, trails and waterways for the tourist to wander. But the area is so vast that tourism, commercialism and development will take a long time to destroy it, if ever.

Miami to New Orleans

Leaving Miami: You can go direct to Saint Petersburg, or you can take in Fort Lauderdale and Naples on the way. Recommended schedules for each way follow.

If checking in your luggage with Trailways make sure you tell them where you are getting off. And tell the driver when boarding. Remember that your ticket will normally be issued Miami/Pensacola/New Orleans, and it is important that you do not allow the driver to tear off the coupon until you leave Saint Petersburg. Similarly make sure your checked baggage goes to the same place as you (mine was left on the bus at New Orleans and if not for my vociferous rescue would have gone on to Houston). You should note that you are only allowed to smoke (by law) in the rear 10 seats of the bus.

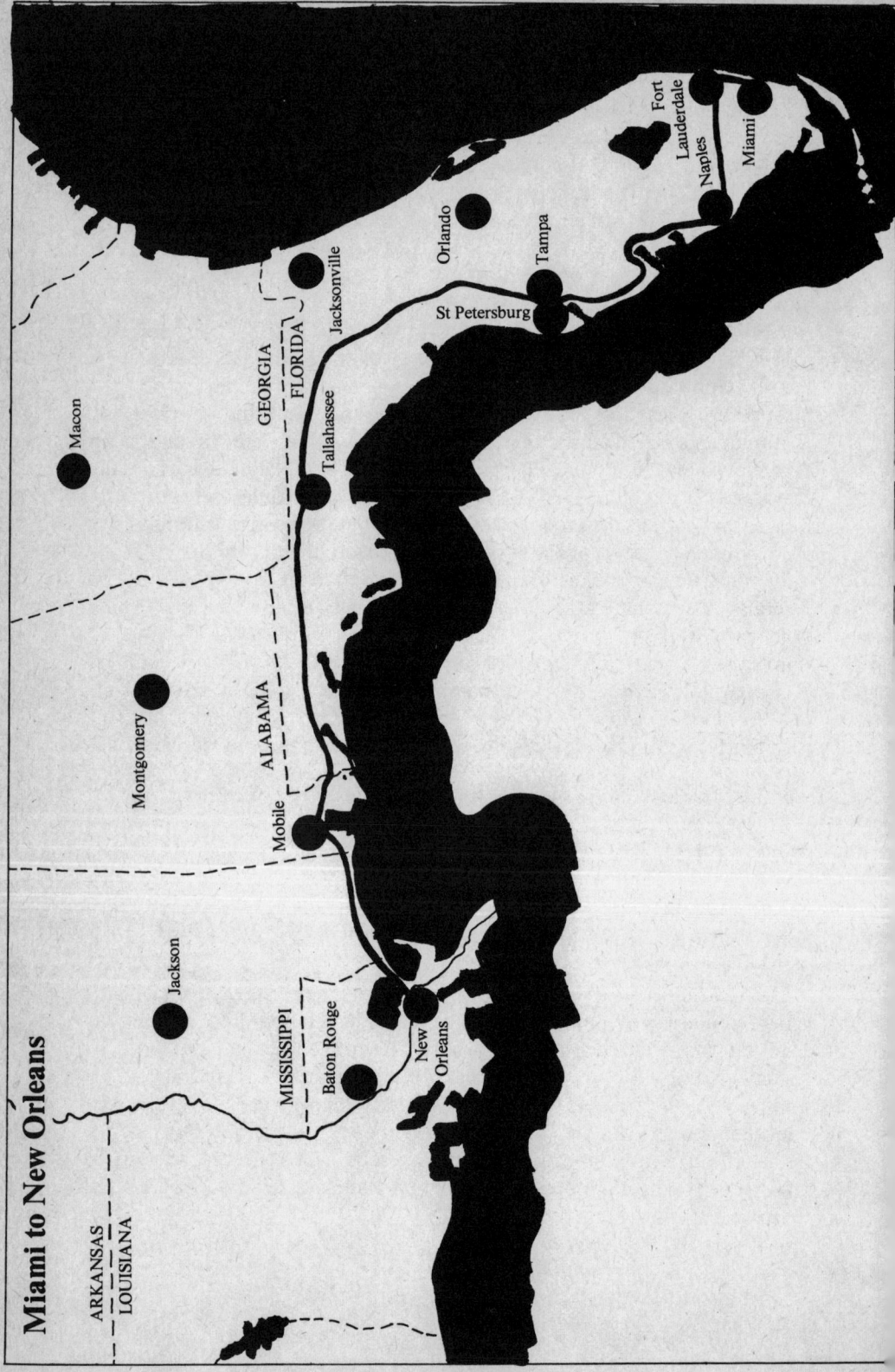

Miami to New Orleans

ARKANSAS
LOUISIANA

MISSISSIPPI

Jackson

Baton Rouge

New
Orleans

ALABAMA

Montgomery

Mobile

GEORGIA
FLORIDA

Macon

Tallahassee

Jacksonville

Orlando

Tampa

St Petersburg

Fort
Lauderdale

Naples

Miami

The Southern USA

---

1   Miami/Fort Lauderdale/Naples/Saint Petersburg

Depart Miami:	9.00 am	Arrive Fort Lauderdale:	10.00 am
	12.01 pm		1.00 pm
	12.15 pm		1.15 pm

| Depart Fort Lauderdale: | 4.15 pm | Arrive Naples: | 6.35 pm |

| Then next day: | | | |
| Depart Naples: | 6.35 pm | Arrive St Petersburg: | 11.10 pm |

| Or after two days: | | | |
| Depart Naples: | 11.25 am | Arrive St Petersburg: | 4.20 pm |

---

2   Miami/Saint Petersburg Direct

Depart Miami:	9.00 am	Arrive St Petersburg:	4.15 pm
	12.15 pm		7.25 pm
	3.15 pm		11.10 pm

Fort Lauderdale: Away from the main drag, Fort Lauderdale (known as the Venice of America) is quieter than Miami. Not necessarily deader, but it has the stillness and serenity you associate with waterways.

On your way in, moored by a bridge which the bus crosses, you will probably see a Mississippi-style riverboat, the *Southern Belle*. A walk along the canal on which it is moored, on the opposite side to the boat, and in a quarter of a mile you will notice the stillness.

The Spanish American/Cuban element is absent here, which makes the

183

town less colourful. The snack bar/restaurants within a few blocks of the Trailways terminal are more expensive, and the one I tried, Holly's Luncheonette, not as good as those in Miami. You can leave you luggage in a locker at the bus terminal for 25 cents.

From Fort Lauderdale the bus passes through the northern part of the Everglades National Park, down Alligator Alley. Not as exciting as it sounds, this is flat marshy scrubland, although wildlife, mainly of the winged variety, can be seen from the bus.

Naples: The population is almost entirely English-speaking Caucasian. There are reputed to be more millionaires in Naples than any other town in the USA. It certainly looks it. That tatty look with which you will be familiar after Miami is absent. Besides being a millionaire's paradise it is also a noted seaside resort. Because of its prosperity there is no cheap, basic-level accommodation here. Motels comprise most of the accommodation – their managers will express surprise when they see you are car-less. The town is rather spread out, although the population is small, and locals and visitors tend to use their cars for even short journeys. There is no public transport system. The beach here is superb and never crowded. Naples is not as yet commercially exploited. The town is built along the Tamiami Trail, which runs between Miami and Tampa.

For accommodation try the Sea Shells Motel, in the centre of town and near the Trailways terminal. Maximum price for one of the smaller rooms (plenty big enough) in December/January/February is $18 for two persons. Prices would of course be cheaper out of season. This is very good value for the money. The rooms are very clean and comfortable, with bathrooms, air-conditioning, colour television, telephone, etc. There is a swimming pool and gardens. There are also many little touches, such as a full ice bucket, book matches in each ashtray, not to mention the Gideon's Bible! Service is courteous and helpful. Recommended.

Over the road and towards the bus terminal are two good eating places, Howard Johnson and the Clock. Prices are slightly higher than Miami, but value is similar. All places here have the 'Bottomless Cup of Coffee' and excellent service. The best place to eat is the Plantation Pancake Inn, which the bus passes on the way in. A breakfast of five pancakes with whipped butter, maple syrup and coffee costs $1.20/1.50. They're so anxious to keep your coffee cup full they almost pour it down your throat. Prices are on a par with Miami's lowest and quality superb. Seems to close about 9/9.30 pm.

A little past the Plantation Pancake Inn, at the Days Inn (not recommended for accommodation, as its service and location are inferior

184

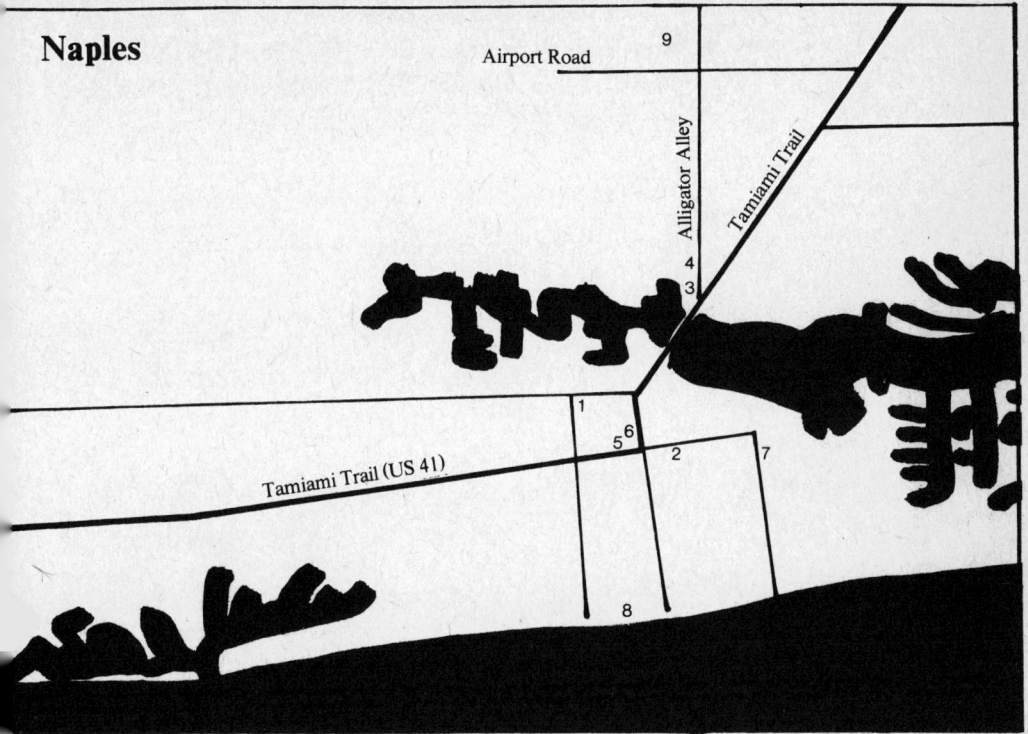

Naples

Naples: Key

1	Sea Shells Motel	6	The Clock
2	Trailways Terminal	7	Used Books Shop
3	Plantation Pancake Inn	8	Free Beach
4	Days Inn and Sambos	9	Buggy Racing
5	Howard Johnson		

to the Sea Shells Motel and its prices are higher – you are paying for international advertising) are two more restaurants, Sambos and a Chinese one. Sambos is in the same vein as the other places mentioned – the same sort of prices, but smaller portions and coffee on the watery side, food tending towards the anaemic. The Chinese was untried by us, but seemed to feature a set lunchtime menu.

Occasionally there is Swamp Buggy Racing in Naples. Programmes giving dates and details can be picked up in Miami.

Saint Petersburg: Whichever bus you take to Saint Pete you may as well check in straightaway at the Hotel Detroit. This hotel looks more expensive than it is; a single without bath costs $6.60, doubles with bath $10. This is an old-style hotel, a relief from the plastichemical overtones of Florida. It is situated on Central Avenue at 4th St. The clientele is predominantly aged and the service courteous and helpful. Amenities are good.

Attached to the hotel is a restaurant which appears to have personnel problems. It features 'Home Cooking'.

In the unlikely event that the Detroit is full, there are other cheap hotels in the same area of Central Avenue. Prices are likely to be the same throughout the year. In this same area there are eating places of the drugstore type, Walgreens, etc, and of course the Trailways terminal which has a very good breakfast menu, five set meals with variations on each, plus the usual hamburgers. There is no extra charge for your second cup of coffee, but you have to ask for it.

Although you wouldn't know it from the downtown area in which you arrive, Saint Petersburg is a beautiful city. If on a one-day stopover you can leave your luggage on checking out at the desk in the Detroit, or in the terminal left luggage (the latter costs 25 cents). Thus unencumbered you are free to enjoy your day in Saint Pete.

Wander down Central Avenue to the Marina area, then turn left and pretty soon you will see the tall masts of the *Bounty*. This is not Captain Bligh's vessel, which no doubt became firewood a long time ago, but one of the movie versions, from 'Mutiny on the....'. Interesting nonetheless. Moored alongside is an old riverboat, the *Tom Sawyer*. This does four cruises daily at $2.50 a time, at 11.30, 1.30, 3.30, and an evening 'Dinner Cruise' (more expensive).

Continue along the bayfront following the signs for The Sunken Gardens. It is a long walk, but a very interesting one, as it takes you through one of the residential areas of Saint Pete. The mainly wooden, one or two storey buildings are set amongst avenues of tropical vegetation. When you reach the main road, still following the signs, you turn right and continue along until you reach the gardens. The whole is cunningly designed so that you walk through 'The World's Largest Gift Store' before reaching the gardens proper. Admission is $3, and it is possible to spend hours there. The main attraction is the large variety of exotic coloured birds, although there are some animals (mainly of the monkey family) and thick, close tropical vegetation. It is a paradise for

St Petersburg

Bounty   *Tom Sawyer*

Central   Avenue

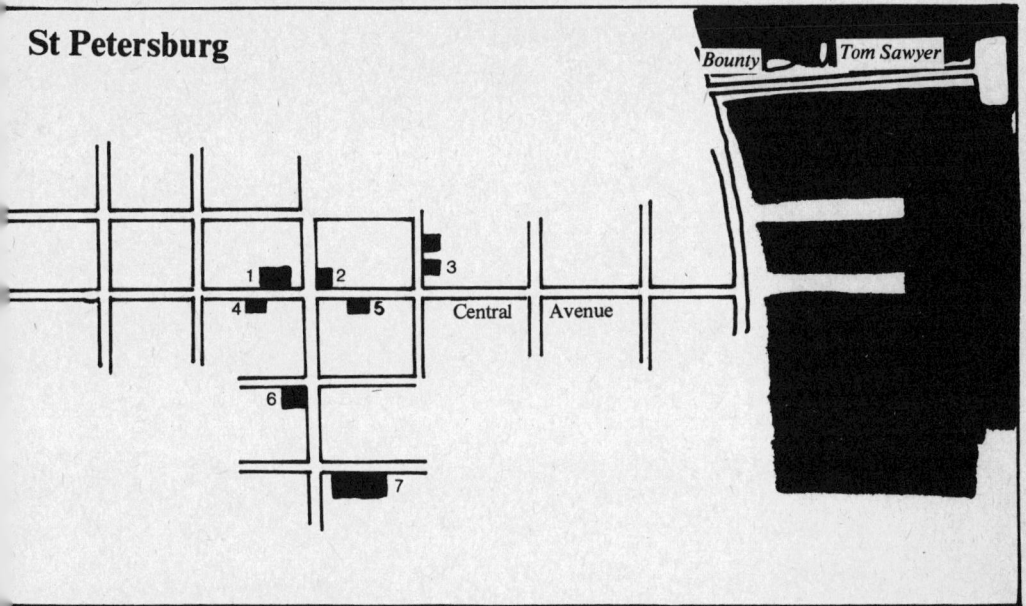

St Petersburg: Key

1 Hotel Detroit
2 Henri's Hotel
3 Restaurant
4 Taft Hotel

5 Bar
6 Trailways Terminal
7 Hilton Hotel

---

photographers. The birds are tame enough to allow close-ups to be taken.

If you are still not satisfied after this then there is an aquarium and zoological gardens on St Pete beach, with dolphin and sea lion shows, and a reef aquarium with big cats. About $3 for entry, and a bus ride is necessary to get there and back (it's out on the Gulf of Mexico).

If you are staying here for two days, Busch Gardens, Tampa, is possible on an excursion (allow a day) from St Pete. Old-style steam train, monorail, African animals, and a flume ride are amongst the attractions. And Saint Petersburg is the nearest stopover point on this trip to Orlando and Walt Disney World.

Saint Petersburg to New Orleans: Leave Saint Petersburg on the 7.30 pm

(Houston-bound) bus. It is your first overnight journey so you may have trouble sleeping. One tip is to take out of your baggage a soft article of clothing such as a sweater for use as a pillow. You arrive in New Orleans at about 2.00 pm the next day. During the journey you pass into the Central Time Zone, after Tallahassee, so put your watch back one hour.

Taking this bus you pass out of Florida at night, and can see Alabama and Mississippi from the bus the next morning. The change from Florida's wealth and sophistication to the comparative poverty of the deep south is noticeable. When taking advantage of the rest stops (for example Mobile, Alabama) you will see this reflected in the bus terminals. Though still clean they are old and shabby. Much of the route is along the coast, where you will see miles of flat, sandy, empty beaches. Then you arrive in New Orleans, the first big bustling city of the trip.

It's much like any big city – crowded, hustling streets with hurrying people. People seem less helpful than in Florida. This, the downtown area, is not a place in which one would want to remain long. But once you make the left turn off Canal Street into the French Quarter, you are in a different world.

New Orleans

Collect your baggage as soon as you leave the bus to be sure it doesn't end up in Houston. Then you have a long walk to your accommodation for the next few days. 'L'Auberge' is the place to stay. To avoid a possibly fruitless walk, telephone Nancy at (504) 523 1130 or 522 3807 to make a reservation. Then find your way to Canal Street and walk down until you reach Royal on your left. Walk along here until you reach the Tourist

---

New Orleans: Key

1	Trailways Terminal	10	Café Creole Vaucresson
2	Amtrak/Greyhound Terminal	11	Maxcy's Coffee Pot
3	'L'Auberge'	12	Chinatown Café
4	Tourist Office	13	Café du Monde
5	Post Office	14	Mena's Palace
6	French Market	15	Preservation Hall
7	YMCA	16	1st Saint Louis Cemetery
8	Hotel La Salle	17	Confederate Museum
9	Bonanza Sirloin Pit	18	International Trade Mart

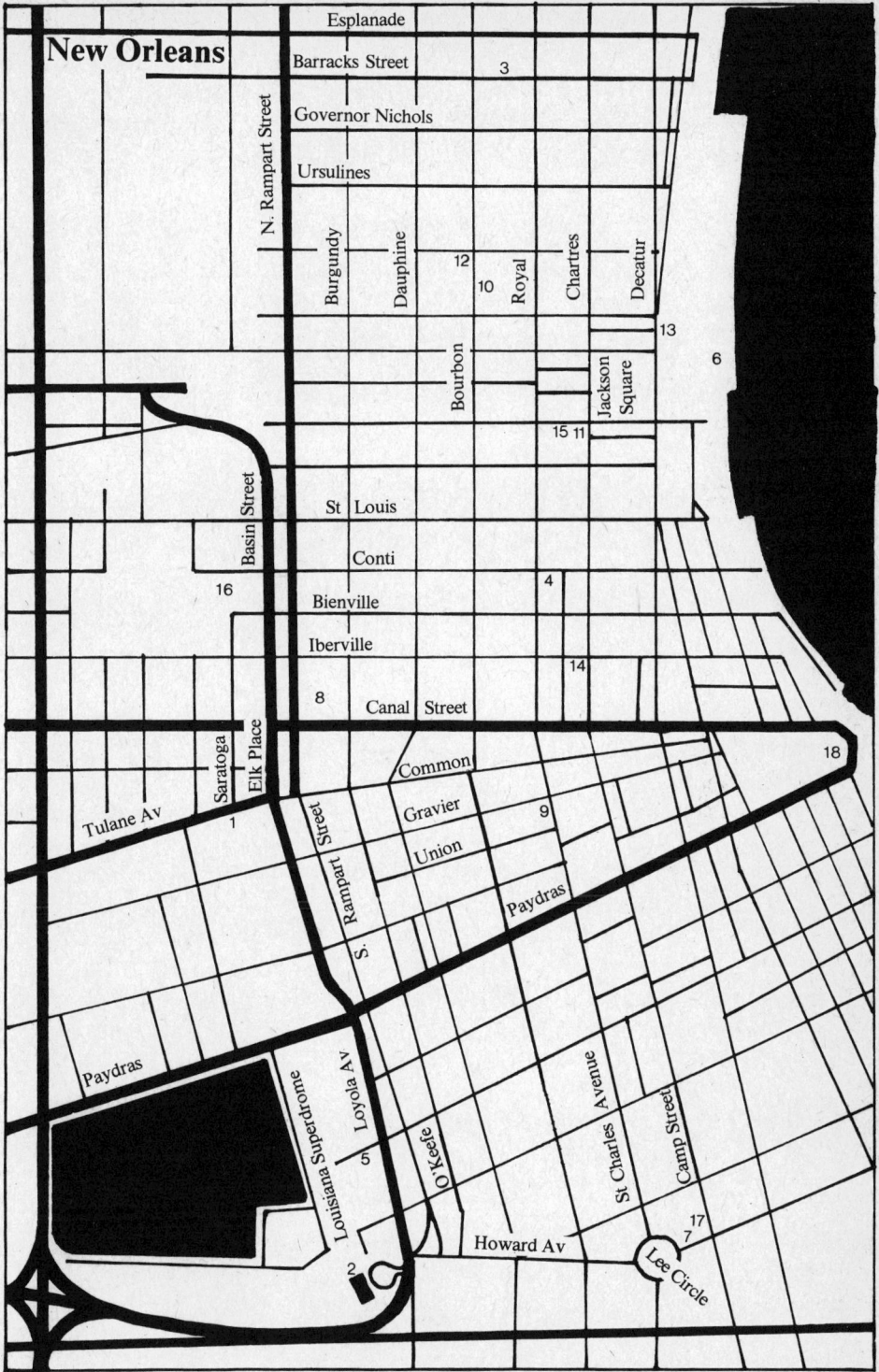

New Orleans

Esplanade

Barracks Street   3

Governor Nichols

Ursulines

N. Rampart Street

Burgundy

Dauphine   12

10

Royal

Chartres

Decatur

13

Bourbon

Jackson Square

6

15 11

Basin Street

St Louis

Conti

16

4

Bienville

Iberville

14

8

Canal Street

Saratoga

Elk Place

Common

Tulane Av

1

Gravier

9

S. Rampart Street

Union

Paydras

18

Paydras

Louisiana Superdrome

Loyola Av

O'Keefe

St Charles Avenue

Camp Street

5

2

Howard Av

17

7

Lee Circle

Office on the right. Enter, take what literature you require, and relax with your free cup of coffee. Then continue to 'L'Auberge' at 717 Barracks Street.

For people under 30 visiting New Orleans, 'L'Auberge' is perfect. At $8 a night it is the cheapest place in the French Quarter, but remember the address because there is no sign. If there is no answer to your knock, go round the back. The maximum number of guests is 8, but Nancy prefers just 5 or 6. There are kitchen facilities available here at no extra charge. Nancy's greatest pleasures are having a good time and housework, so the atmosphere is happy and lively and 'L'Auberge' is always meticulously spick and span.

Perhaps mention should be made of the other accommodation in New Orleans in case 'L'Auberge' is full.

Unfortunately French Quarter prices tend to be high, so you may find yourself outside this prime spot. The Hotel La Salle, 1113 Canal Street, charges $15 for a single. Cheap accommodation is available at a number of places on St. Charles' Avenue or Camp Street, but this is New Orleans' Skid Row. It cannot be recommended. If 'L'Auberge' is full the best bet may be the YMCA near Lee Circle; prices are $5, $7 or $9. It is about the same distance from the Trailways terminal (in the opposite direction) and nearer to the Amtrak terminal.

Most of your stay in New Orleans will be spent in the French Quarter, because this is what New Orleans is all about. The nightlife and most of the best restaurants are here or near here. Beware of all tourist guides, including those published by the Tourist Office. Many very good restaurants are not listed, whilst many listed restaurants are overpriced and/or bad. Nancy has a copy of the *Underground Gourmet* guide to eating in New Orleans, a publication which is even superior to this work on the subject of New Orleans food.

Bourbon Street is commercialized, crowded with tourists, usually (though not always) expensive, despoiled by strip clubs and porno. But it's still great. It's a fun place to be, and on a sunny day character oozes out of

---

The French Quarter: Key

1	'L'Auberge'	6	Café du Monde
2	Tourist Office	7	Mena's Palace
3	Café Creole Vaucresson	8	Preservation Hall
4	Maxcy's Coffee Pot	9	New Orleans Cathedral
5	Chinatown Café	10	Jackson Square

New Orleans: the French Quarter

Esplanade

1

Barracks

Governor   Nichols

Ursulines

St Philip

5

3   Dumaine

St Ann   6

Antoine Alley
Orleans   9
Pirates Alley   Jackson Square
St Peter   10

8   4

Toulouse

Burgundy   Dauphine   Bourbon   Royal   Chartres   Decatur   French Market

North Rampart Street

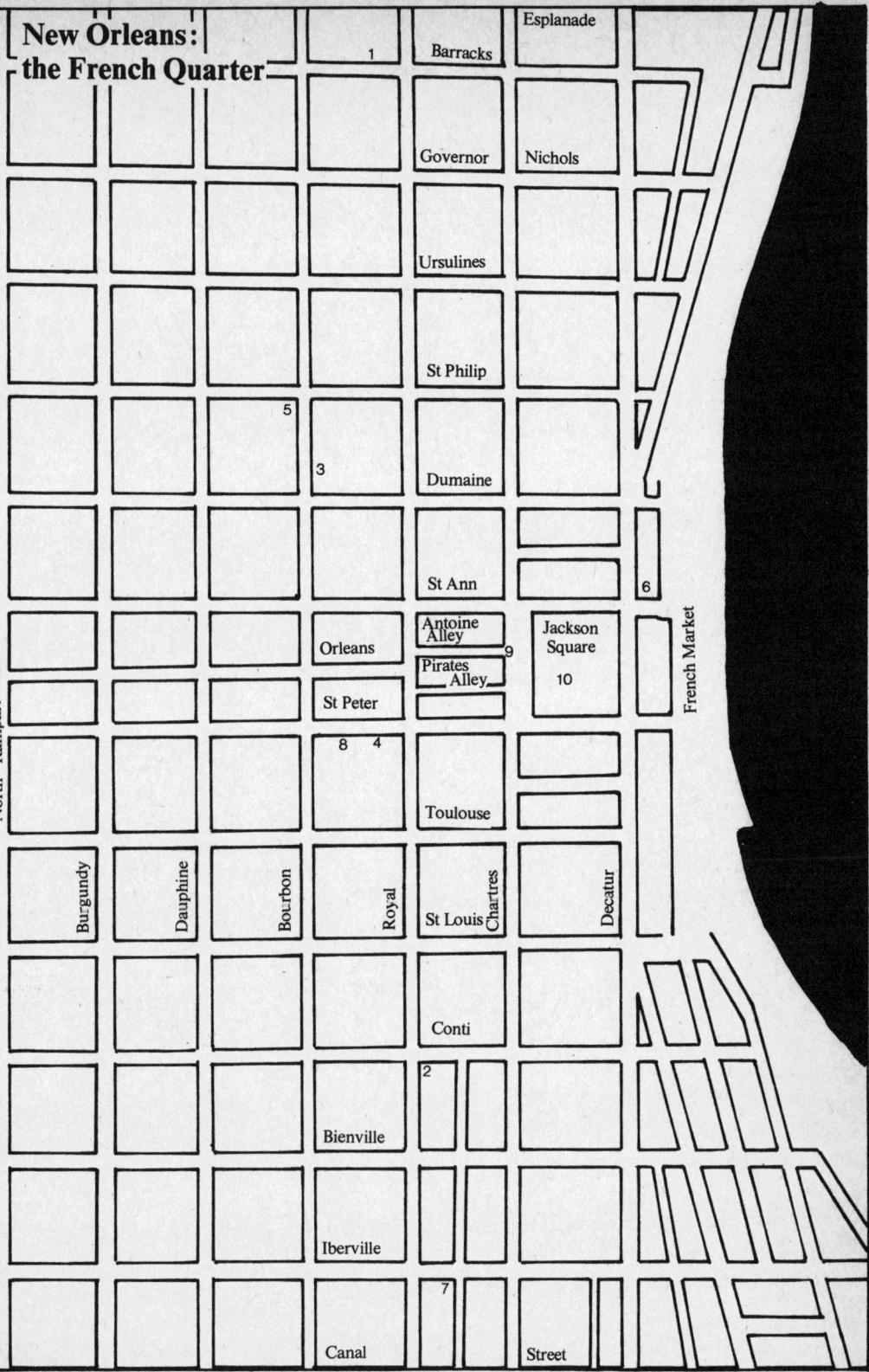

St Louis

Conti

2

Bienville

Iberville

7

Canal   Street

every pore. The same can be said of all the French Quarter, with its narrow streets, some of which are closed to traffic, pastel painted buildings, wrought iron balconies, and pseudo artists. It is choked with history. Prostitutes and drunks wander the streets at night, but it is not a dangerous place to be after dark.

If you insist on spending some money in Bourbon Street, you can do no better than the Café Creole Vaucresson at number 624. The Creole food is good here, and you can get away with change from $5 after a full and very good meal. It is not featured in the official tourist guide yet it is crowded; you draw your own conclusions. Maxcy's Coffee Pot at 714 Saint Peter Street can be unequivocably recommended. In the heart of the commercialized area, it is not dirt cheap, but it is cheap, the food is good, and it represents good value. Try anything here. The locals know about it however, so again it is packed out and service can be slow. The Chinatown Café doesn't serve the best Chinese food in town, and is not cheap, but the food is good and you get plenty. Service is first rate and it is conveniently situated at 627 Bourbon Street.

Another recommended restaurant (just outside the French Quarter) is the Bonanza Sirloin Pit on Saint Charles Avenue, near Canal Street. A sirloin steak, baked potato, toast, dressed salad and coffee (refillable) will set you back about $2.50 including tax. For those who like a late breakfast the Café du Monde, in the French Market, is unbeatable. A breakfast of coffee and hot, French-style doughnuts will cost 60/70 cents including tax. One place untried by us but recommended on good authority is Mena's Palace on Ibreville Street near Royal (it was closed when we tried). It doesn't look anything like a palace but the food is reputably good and cheap. Note that Pancho's Mexican Bar has moved from Gravier Street out of town.

There are of course so-so places and musts to avoid. Felix's Restaurant at 739 Ibreville Street must be in the former category. Perhaps because it is 'nationally famous' prices do not represent good value for the food offered. If you want to visit Felix's try eating oysters at the bar, near the door. You'll see why. Avoid the Desire Restaurant like the plague. It is typical of the majority of restaurants on or near Bourbon Street, providing for the needs of tourists with too much money and too little critical sense.

New Orleans of course is even more famous for its jazz than for its food. The most common music now in New Orleans is provided by the throbbing juke box. Over the last few decades a small dedicated group has tried to keep some authentic jazz in New Orleans, at the internationally famous Preservation Hall, at 726 St Peter St (between Bourbon and Royal). A smallish room, about 30 ft by 40 ft, it is open between 8.30 pm and midnight and features the original Algiers Stompers with Kit Thomas. It is usually crowded and dark and you may be unable to see anything (the band sit and the audience stand). Don't expect too much. The band are in their 70s and 80s and age takes its toll of all of us. Have a few drinks before you go along and get there early.

Sights of interest outside Vieux Carré include the 1st Saint Louis Cemetery at Basin Street (of 'Easy Rider' fame) where you can see old, opened and renovated tombs, the Confederate Museum on Camp Street near Lee Circle; on Camp Street, walking back into town, you will also see the down-and-outs, seedy cheap hotels, shops where you can buy 'New and Used Clothing'. Then proceed to the International Trade Mart, 2 Canal Street. At the top is the revolving cocktail lounge, or you can go up in an external elevator to the observation deck for $1.

On your walk you will have noticed the new New Orleans. Outside the French Quarter, which is being preserved, there is proof that creative architecture can utilize glass, steel and concrete.

Cruises along the Mississippi in the paddle steam ships *Natchez* and *President* can be taken from the end of Canal Street.

New Orleans to El Paso

This stage is travelled entirely by Amtrak, with a stopover in San Antonio (which can be omitted if your trip is less than four weeks' duration). Note that trains run only three times a week.

You should have made your reservation shortly after arrival in New Orleans (see page 172). Below we reproduce the current timetable.

Depart New Orleans	(Mon/Wed/Fri)	1.00 pm
Arrive San Antonio	(Tues/Thurs/Sat)	2.25 am
Depart San Antonio	(Tues/Thurs/Sat)	2.40 am
Arrive El Paso	(Tues/Thurs/Sat)	2.15 pm

Arrival in San Antonio: The train arrives in San Antonio at the ridiculous time of 2.25 am, which can have its advantages for the budget-conscious traveller. If you sleep on the station benches for a few hours, and dispense with your last night's accommodation, you save two nights' hotel bills, about $12. The itinerary on a two-day stopover would be as follows:

193

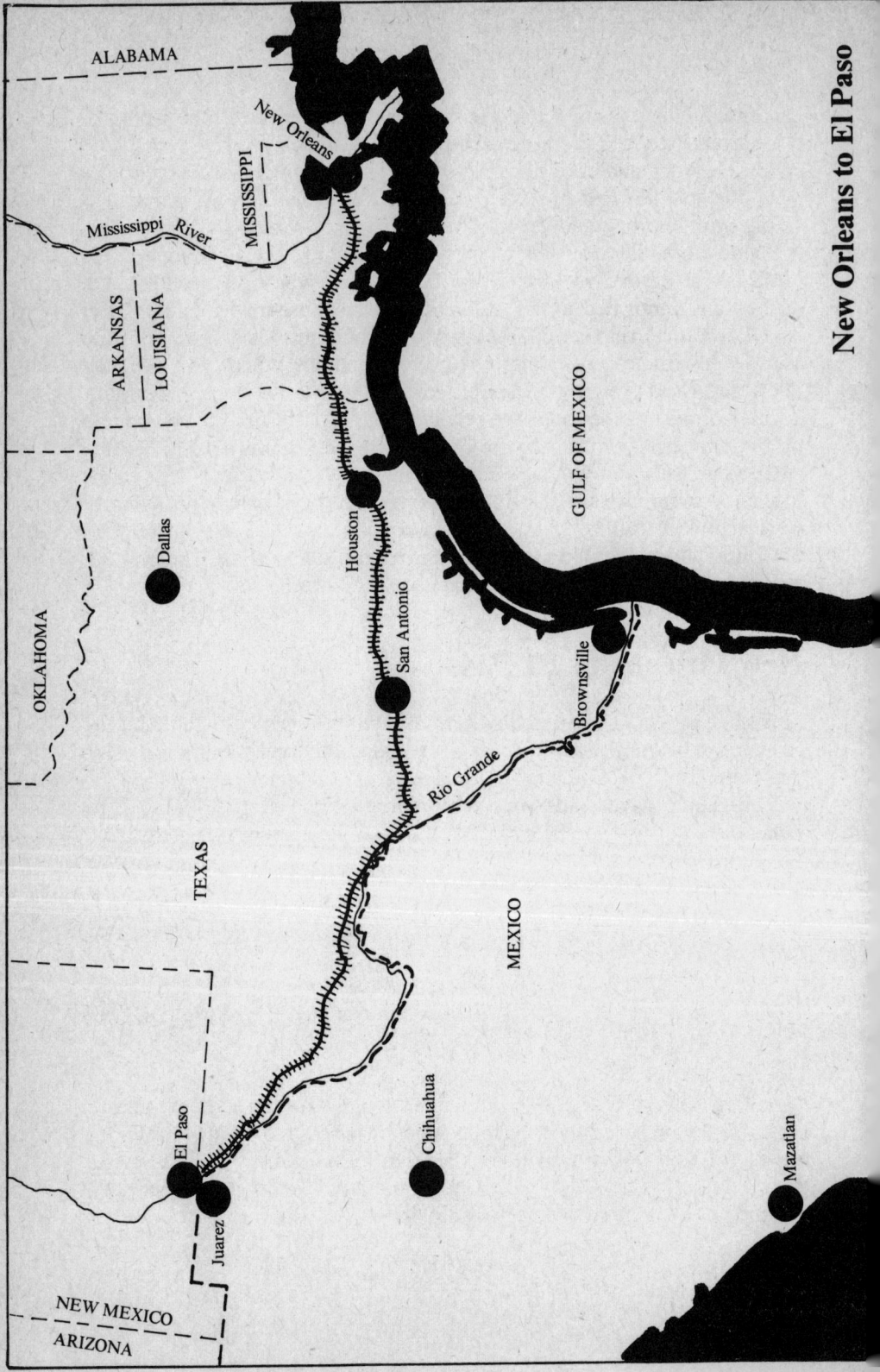

New Orleans to El Paso

The Southern USA

1st Day: Arrive 2.30 am, stay at station until about 8 am. Find hotel.
2nd Day: Check out of hotel, leave baggage at station (50 cents).
Return to station for 2.30 am that night (third morning).

The Hotel Navarro on Navarro Street is about the cheapest hotel in town. It is a shabby, seedy, rundown place though generally quite full. All rooms have a bathroom, hot water, and clean sheets (much repaired). As it is clean, however, it is a good bet. The prices stated inside the rooms are $4.50 for a single and $7 for a double. I was charged $6 however and doubles are now $9. The management claims those listed prices are very much out of date. As they are not so much yellowed, more browned with age, this could be true.

The best value hotel in town, the Riverside in College Street, had closed one week prior to my arrival. It may be worth checking whether it has re-opened.

The Travelers Hotel charges $7 single and $10 double, both without bath. This is a better hotel than the Navarro, but full on our visit. It is situated at 220 Broadway – do not confuse with South Broadway. Other budget hotels you could try are the Alpha Hotel, 315 N. Main Avenue, and the Robert E. Lee, W. Travis Street.

Watch the street names here; they all seem to be divided into North, South, East or West.

Arriving very early in the morning from the Amtrak station, you may find most breakfast places closed. You could try the Golden Egg on Commerce Street which has 24-hour service out of necessity; the food is bland, not cheap, and service atrocious (at least you will not have to leave a tip).

San Antonio is a very pleasant town, this being shown to best effect on the Riverwalk. Even the scores of tourists fail to destroy the pleasure of walking along the river on a sunny day. If you have the money and the inclination you can hire a pedalo. The Alamo is appropriately set in Alamo Plaza, in the centre of the town. As it is a low building it cannot be seen from a distance; if you have difficulty finding it make for the Crockett Hotel. The Alamo has been restored and lovingly commercialized, and is set in gardens interesting to the horticulturalist. Outside in the Plaza is a monument dedicated to the Alamo heroes (some of whom were British). The Alamo is open every day and entrance is free.

For lunch you must try Casa Rio on Commerce Street, by the Riverwalk. This Mexican restaurant is always full with a waiting area for customers, and no wonder! A very filling meal with two beers and coffee cost me less than $3. They serve a fair range of set meals, which are not cooked to order.

195

M Plaza

W. Commerce

M Plaza

W. Travis

M Plaza

W. Soledad

8

N. St Marys

N. St Marys

W. Houston

Travis

S. St Marys

Navarro

1

Market

S. Presa

N. Presa

6

Jefferson

College

Broadway

9

E. Neuva

Villita

10

7

4

S. Broadway

5

Alamo Plaza

Crockett

2

E. Commerce

Bonham

11

E. Commerce

Bowie

Elm

La Quinta

Gonzales

Sycamore

Hoelgen

Helman

3

E. Commerce

San Antonio

San Antonio: Key

1	Hotel Navarro	7	Hotel Travelers
2	The Alamo	8	GW Jrs
3	Amtrak	9	Plastic Breakfast
4	Casa Rio	10	Riverside Hotel
5	Hilton	11	Hotel Crockett
6	Walgreens		

The Walgreens here is of a reasonable standard with many cheap filling meals. Besides the normal Walgreens menu there is a selection of Mexican dishes available. GW Jrs is a cheap cheap hamburger place (there is a chicken restaurant next door) where you serve yourself with coffee – as much as you want. The food's not too good, but worth the money, and service very friendly. There are many cheap Mexican restaurants in San Antonio, but you may prefer to use them sparingly as you will soon be in Mexico.

The post office is situated on Alamo Plaza.

Leaving San Antonio: The ticket office is open at the Amtrak station between midnight and 5.30 pm. This means that if you get there before midnight you may find the doors locked. If this is the case go round the right-hand side and use the employees' entrance. You will not be prevented from entering or staying.

You should be able to get a good night's sleep on the train through to about 9.00 am. The spacious and uncrowded rest rooms provide adequate opportunity to attend to one's morning ablutions. Breakfasting is a more popular activity, and you may find yourself forced to wait awhile in the lounge. Although it is possible to take lunch on the train you may prefer to wait until you disembark at El Paso (one hour behind timewise).

Appendix 3
Travel Tips and Useful Addresses

What to Take

I believe that travel is the best education. But one needs to be educated in travel in itself in order to get the most out of it. Many readers will have travelled sufficiently not to need, and perhaps to resent, any hints from me: that is why this section as at the back. If you are an experienced traveller, read no further. But if your travel has been limited up to now, you may find that this section can enhance your enjoyment of the trip, and also save you money.

All essential information on what to take with you is given in Part 1: Preparing for the Trip. Yet after 14 years of travelling, I find that I still take the odd thing I could have done without and omit something useful. So here is a more detailed list of what I would advise you to take. Remember that it is essential to keep weight to the minimum.

Luggage: Rucksack or holdall? A rucksack will suit you best if you intend to walk a lot with your house on your back: that is what it is designed for. But if you are travelling long distances on public transport, confining your walks to excursions from an overnight base, you will find a strong holdall more convenient (and remember that Central American immigration officials are strongly prejudiced against rucksack carriers). Choose your holdall well: it should be strong, roomy, yet compact. If it is humble in appearance, it is less likely to be stolen. And a holdall leaves one shoulder free for cameras, lenses and a shoulder bag containing documents, film etc – the things you need to get at quickly.

Documents: Make sure your *passport* is valid for at least six months after the estimated end of your trip, and that it contains ample space for official stamps. Keep your *tourist cards* inside it. There is little point in having a *smallpox vaccination* if you leave your certificate behind. Immigration officials may require it, and will give you an injection on the spot (usually painful) or refuse you entry without it. Although *travel tickets* are often refundable, it is sensible to keep them with you at all times, ie not tucked away in your holdall. Keep a separate list of the numbers of your *Traveller's Cheques*: this will speed up any claim if they are lost or stolen. *Credit cards* are widely accepted in Mexico. I suggest Bank Americard (Barclay Card in Britain), American Express or Mastercharge. If you spend more than you expected to, a credit card can become the most important item you have with you. Remember that it can be used to obtain cash at a representative bank or American Express office. You never know whether you may use your *driving licence(s)* – so take it.

Business cards or cards with your home address are always useful. You will make friends, and this is the best way to keep them. Finally, remember *insurance certificates*.

Clothing: This is the most difficult subject to advise on, as it is largely a question of personal preference (I break most of the rules anyway). A parka is the most suitable coat as it provides warmth without weight. It is showerproof, thus doing away with the need for a raincoat, which would otherwise be necessary if you are travelling in summer, the rainy season. It also includes a hood which makes a hat less necessary, and ample pocket space.

How much clothing you take depends on how often you intend to wash it, and this depends on your speed of travel. I take enough clothes to last me about 14 days without laundry: a denim suit (suitable for immigration officials and semi-official wear yet strong and serviceable for hard travelling), two pairs of jeans, five shorts, four T-shirts, one sweater (for cool evenings), a necktie (just in case), swimming trunks and enough underwear, handerkerchiefs and socks for two weeks. Shoes are important. I take two pairs – a light pair (gym shoes, chukka boots, or nature shoes, etc.) and a pair of boots (fashion not ammunition). You could take two pairs of light shoes (I find them better than heavy boots for long walks) or light shoes and heavy boots, but avoid anything in between.

Toiletries: Take whatever you normally use, but remember that you may often have cold water only. Guys may find a battery operated electric shaver useful, though by no means essential. One towel per person is enough, as these are generally provided by hotels, etc.

Paper: Most of this is optional, as paper is heavy and will suffer during a long trip. But bear in mind the following: tourist office literature, general reading matter, airmail paper and envelopes (also useful for keeping a diary), address book, and of course this book.

Watch: Wearing a watch can save you time and prevent you missing buses. However, an expensive watch can mark you down as being wealthy and the possible subject of a robbery. Timex produce a waterproof plastic watch which reputedly keeps accurate enough time and costs only a few dollars. The thief is usually more interested in gilt than timekeeping – a plastic watch is useless to him and he may presume you have bought it because you cannot afford a glittering contraption with manifold knobs and dials. A Mickey Mouse watch may also do the trick.

Miscellaneous: The pills listed in Part 1 : Preparing for the Trip (page 23). Mosquito coils (though these can be bought locally). Sunglasses. Cigarette lighter. Polythene bags (useful for soiled laundry, leaky bottles, spare shoes and much else).

Photography

Cameras: For the purpose of snapshots – which is what most people want – there are no better cameras than the Instamatic or Polaroid. That's what they are designed for. If you have no interest in photography, but want a permanent record of the people you meet and the things you see, then you can do no better than to take the lightest and most compact Instamatic, plenty of film and some flashbulbs. A Polaroid is too expensive and possible too fragile. Forget the mystique, the full page advertisements in glossy magazines, and consider what you really need. It may well be an Instamatic.

If you want a permanent record of unusual photographs, and enjoy experimenting, spending time creatively building a picture, then you should be prepared to spend enough money for the right equipment. In short, this means a single lens reflex camera. In my opinion, nothing between an Instamatic and an SLR is worth buying.

The greatest advantage of a single lens reflex camera is that you look through the lens. You see what the camera sees, what the finished photograph will look like, subject of course to your exposures being correct and there being a film in the camera. This means that the composition of your picture can be perfect. The chances that you will cut off someone's head or plant a tree on his shoulders are quite negligible. Everything can be placed exactly where you want it within the rectangle which delineates the picture. This is especially useful when shooting into the sun: you can place the glowing orb exactly where you want it behind the silhouette.

Looking through the lens also gives you exact control over focusing. You don't have to guess how far away your subject is, or look through a separate rangefinder. Often, of course, you may want part of the photograph in focus and part out of focus (this gives depth to a photo): through the lens viewing gives you an accurate idea of what scope you have here, thus helping you to choose the correct aperture for your desired effect. Most modern SLR cameras are equipped with through-the-lens metering (TTL). In practice this means that a little needle, clearly visible when you look through the viewfinder, tells you what aperture setting and shutter speed you should use for a perfect exposure.

At present the Japanese are the undisputed leaders in the field of SLR cameras. Professional photographers, specialist magazines and enthusiastic amateurs all have their own prejudices, yet the Olympus OM1 and OM2 seem to stand a little above the crowd. One of the disadvantages of the SLR is that it is a relatively bulky and heavy camera. This is equally irksome to the professional, laden with second camera, lenses and accessories, as to the traveller, weighed down with luggage. Olympus designed the OM1 to be as small and light as possible, and its success has been proved by its huge worldwide sales. The OM2 is the automatic model. But this is not the end of the story. Other Japanese cameras of high reputation and good pedigree include Pentax, Nikkormat, Canon and many others. Like most British people, I could not afford a Japanese camera. To my compatriots I would recommend the Zenith and Practica ranges, manufactured in the Soviet Union and the German Democrat Republic respectively. These cameras are unavailable in the United States, but very popular in the United Kingdom, where they are freely available at discount prices.

When buying a camera you will need 'plenty money' and better advice than I can give, but here are some guidelines.
1. Read some specialist photographic magazines, which should give you an idea of reputation and price. They often include reviews of new and established models.
2. If buying second-hand, make sure the dealer is reputable and insist on a solid written guarantee (read the small print).
3. Many of the more popular cameras, such as the Olympus OM1 and the Pentax Spotmatic, can be bought new at a discount establishment, cheaper than older second-hand models available elsewhere. Again, the credentials of the dealer are important.
4. Try to use the camera before you make the trip, so that you can analyze the results beforehand.

Accessories: A camera case or bag is essential. I have a small camera bag which has a large zip-fastening compartment for the camera, and a small compartment which can be used for film, flash unit and documents, tickets etc. I find this ideal.

For a country such as Mexico, which experiences bright sunshine, your pictures need further protection. A lens hood will stop reflections spoiling your photographs when you shoot towards the sun. The cost is very small, and if you *want* reflections you simply remove the lens hood. I find the flexible black rubber type preferable to the stiff variety (usually plastic), because there is no need to unscrew it – you simply fold it back.

The most important accessory for this trip is a filter. During the day, particularly at mid-day, the sun is very bright. This intense light contains a high proportion of ultra-violet rays which give a blue cast to the finished photograph unless it is screened off. The most common mistake is the one I have made for years – namely, thinking it wouldn't matter if I gave just one stop less exposure. Don't follow my example. Buy an ultra-violet filter. Some people even use a yellow filter. I tried this on a recent trip to the Caribbean with some success, although it does tend to give a fairly strong yellow cast to the photograph. Companies such as Vivitar make a range of filters – in different colours, and also for special effects. It is worthwhile finding out more from a good dealer.

One major accessory I would strongly recommend is at least one additional lens. Most cameras are supplied with a lens of perhaps 55 to 48mm focal length. For the beginner and for most documentary photographs, this is quite acceptable, but as you become more ambitious, trying to make pictures rather than just recording what you see, you will require an alternative lens. Most photographers will purchase a telephoto first, possibly a 125mm or 210mm, or maybe one of the increasingly popular zoom lenses (eg a 75/210mm). The telephoto's effect is the same as that of the telescope: it brings distant objects near. Shipping, aeroplanes and sporting events are obvious uses. But a telephoto is also superb for photographing people. You can be so far away that your subject is unaware of you, thus enabling you to take natural rather than posed photographs. I use a 300mm Japanese telephoto – mainly because I once read an American photographer's advice to the effect that if one is taking bad photos, one should move closer to the subject! With a 300mm lens I let my camera do the walking. My lens is unbranded, cheap, fragile, yet it has produced some beautiful work.

A wide angle lens is quite the opposite to a telephoto. Professionals use them for interiors (that is why a hotel room looks much bigger in a holiday brochure than in real life). It is also useful for architectural shots when you are forced to get closer to your subject.

The spare lenses you will require will depend upon your style and needs. You may prefer to wait until you are used to your camera and its limitations. Remember that you do not need to buy lenses made by the manufacturer of your camera. Although there are different sizes of screw thread and various bayonet fittings, adapters are available to suit most popular makes of camera. Some independent companies specialize in making lenses which sell at lower prices than the major camera manufacturers, although the lenses may be of equal quality. Vivitar in particular enjoy a good reputation. Again, read the magazines and consult a reputable dealer.

Although you would expect to have little use for a flash on a journey such as this, modern systems are so light, compact and reliable that they are no encumbrance. I would suggest a small, electronic model (don't forget to buy the correct batteries) which will tuck into the corner of a small camera bag or fit easily into the pocket of a parka.

On a trip such as this, a tripod should be unneccesary. Theoretically, a tripod is essential with a 300mm telephoto, but the bright light in tropical countries is so abundant that you can shoot at high speed. I have never found camera shake to be a problem. Whenever I want to take a picture using time exposure, I have always found a handy wall and cable release adequate.

Finally, don't forget to take proper lens cleaning materials. There is little cost and no weight, but they can make a difference to your pictures.

Photo Technique: All rules can be broken, but only if you know why they exist and what will happen when you break them. These guidelines are thus intended to help and not to restrict you.

The best times for photography in tropical countries are late afternoon and early morning. Ultra-violet rays are at their strongest during the middle of the day and tend to bleach out colour. Although a filter may rectify much of this, your pictures will still tend to be bluer than you remembered. Whites and pale colours will be particularly disappointing. The human eye (or rather brain) can adjust where your machinery cannot. Sunrise and sunset have the opposite effect: although noticeably orange to the eye, the light is really stronger than it appears. This of course is usually beneficial in terms of photography, which is why people are rarely disappointed with shots taken at sunset. I prefer early morning and late afternoon because the shadows are longer and the colours stronger. It is possible to get interesting work by shooting into the sun, but remember that areas in shade will probably come out as silhouette. Taking photographs with the sun behind you (not necessarily directly behind you) should produce work richer in colour and interest.

The greatest problem faced by the novice is composition. Using a single lens reflex camera eases this problem considerably, but you still have to train yourself to look at what you can see through the lens very analytically. What you think you can see is often very different to what you – and the camera – are actually seeing. How many times have you taken a picture of a building and then seen that building leaning over backwards on the final print? You may assume it was the effect of the camera. Yet in fact that building appeared to be leaning over backwards when you looked through the viewfinder: your eye transmitted that information to your brain, but your brain was not to be deceived. It knew the building was standing upright and told you so. Next time, compare the verticals of the building with the verticals of your viewfinder.

You also need to train yourself to see everything within the frame of your viewfinder. Too many photographers look at their primary subject only, but it may be surrounded by a lot of rubbish – an uninteresting wall, part of a bus, the shoulder of a tourist ... If you are not looking out for this sort of thing, you will not see it until you get your pictures back from Kodak or the local drugstore. If you look at everything in the viewfinder, you will know when to move in closer, when to change the camera angle, and so on.

One last tip: you will never take unusual photographs doing the usual things. People have laughed at my antics when trying to get the effect I want, and of course I'm not always successful. But looking for the unusual is the only way you'll find it.

Film: The various merits of different sorts of film are outside the scope of this book.

The debate here is much more basic: whether you should use slides or prints (it goes without saying that for a trip to Mexico you should use colour). I always use slide film, Kodachrome 25 or Kodachrome 64, because – being an optimist – I hope to see my work reproduced in print, and nowadays conventional prints can easily be made from slides. But if you do not have projection equipment and/or facilities, you may prefer prints. These are easier to show to friends and neighbours as you recall anecdotes or recount indiscretions.

But whatever film you choose, buy plenty. And then buy plenty more. Remember that film is cheaper in North America and the United Kingdom than anywhere else.

American Express Offices

MEXICO
Viva Tours,
Olas Atlas Sur 21–A,
Mazatlan.
Tel: 64 10

Viva Tours,
Paseo Presidente Diaz,
Puerto Vallarta.
Tel: 2 00 03

Convisa SA,
Edf. Condominio B–1,
Guadalajara.
Tel: 4 44 14

American Express Co.,
Hamburgo 75,
Mexico City.
Tel: 533 0380

American Express Co.,
Costera Aleman 709A,
Acapulco.
Tel: 4 10 95.

Barbacjanos Travel Svc,
Loby Panamericana,
Merida.
Tel: 17640

GUATEMALA
Clark Tours,
Edf. El Triangulo,
Calle Mariscal Cruz & Av. 7,
Zona 4,
Guatemala City,
Tel: 60213/6

EL SALVADOR
El Salvador Travel Service,
Centro Comercial La Mascota,
Cerretera a Sta. Tecla,
San Salvador. Tel: 230177

HONDURAS
Mundirama Travel Service,
Edf. Fiallos,
Planta Baja 123,
Tegucigalpa.
Tel: 2 6979, 2 6111

NICARAGUA
Agencias Vassalli SA,
4a Calle NB No. 208,
Managua.
Tel: 2 6631

COSTA RICA
TAM Travel Agency,
Calle Central y la Av. Segunda,
San Jose.
Tel: 23 51 11

PANAMA
Boyd Brothers Inc.
(Panama Tours),
Calle 50,
Edf. San Miguel 58,
Panama City.
Tel: 64 7433

Tourist Offices

MEXICO
Avenida Juarez 92,
Mexico City

BELIZE
Belize Govt. Tourist Board,
Regent St.,
PO Box 325,
Belize City.
Tel: 3013

GUATEMALA
6a Av. 5–34,
Zona 1,
Guatemala City.
Tel: 24015, 24118

EL SALVADOR
Calle Ruben Dario 519,
San Salvador.
Tel: 21 7445, 21 4845

HONDURAS
Tourist Office,
Bank of London & Montreal Bldg.,
Cruce 6a Av y 3a Calle 209,
Tegucigalpa.

COSTA RICA
Calle Central,
Avs. 4 & 6,
San Jose.
Tel: 23 17 33

PANAMA
Instituto Panameno de Turismo,
El Panama Hotel Grounds,
Via Espana,
PO Box 4421,
Panama City.
Tel: 358 9330

Public Holidays

MEXICO

January 1	New Year
February 5	Constitution Day
March 1	Benito Juarez Day
	Easter (Friday through Monday)
May 1	Labour Day
September 16	Independence Day
October 12	Discovery Day
November 20	Revolution Day
December 25	Christmas

Mexico and Central America

BELIZE

January 1	New Year
March 9	Baron Bliss Day
	Easter (Friday through Monday)
April 21	Queen's Birthday
May 1	Labour Day
May 24	Commonwealth Day
September 10	National Day
November 14	Prince of Wales' Birthday
December 25–26	Christmas

GUATEMALA

January 1	New Year
	Easter (Friday through Monday)
May 1	Labour Day
June 30	Revolution Day
July 1	Bank Holiday
August 15	Assumption
September 15	Independence Day
October 12	Day of the Race
October 20	Revolution Anniversary
November 3	All Saints' Day
December 25–26	Christmas
December 31	Bank Holiday

HONDURAS

January 1	New Year
	Easter (Thursday and Friday)
May 1	Labour Day
September 15	Independence Day
October 3	Francisco Morazan's Birthday
October 12	Day of the Race
October 21	Armed Forces Day
December 25	Christmas

EL SALVADOR

January 1	New Year
	Easter (Tuesday through Sunday)
May 1	Labour Day
June 9	Corpus Christi
June 29–30	Public Holiday

August 3–6	August Holdays
September 15	Independence Day
October 12	Columbus Day
November 2	All Souls' Day
November 5	Anniversary of the First Cry of Independence
December 24–25	Christmas
December 30–31	Bank Holiday

NICARAGUA

January 1	New Year
	Easter (Thursday through Sunday)
May 1	Labour Day
May 27	Army Day
July 14	National Day
September 14	Battle of San Jacinto
September 15	Independence Day
October 12	Day of the Race
December 8	Immaculate Conception
December 24–25	Christmas

COSTA RICA

January 1	New Year
March 19	St Joseph's Day
	Easter (Thursday through Monday)
May 1	Labour Day
June 9	Corpus Christi
June 29	Sts. Peter and Paul Day
August 15	Assumption
September 15	Independence Day
October 12	Day of the Race
December 8	Immaculate Conception
December 25	Christmas
December 29–31	Civic Holiday

PANAMA

January 1	New Year
January 9	Day of National Mourning
	Easter (Friday through Monday)
May 1	Labour Day
August 15	Assumption (Panama City only)

October 11	National Guard Day
November 3	Independence Day
November 4	Flag Day
November 29	Independence Day
December 8	Mother's Day
December 25	Christmas

PANAMA CANAL ZONE

January 1	New Year
February 22	Washington's Birthday
	Easter (Friday)
May 30	Memorial Day
July 4	Independence Day
September 5	Labour Day
November 3	Independence Day
November 11	Veterans' Day
November 24	Thanksgiving Day
December 25	Christmas

US Representatives in Mexico and Central America

MEXICO
Embassy,
Cor Danubio y Paseo de la Reforma,
305 Colonia Cuauhtemos,
Mexico City.
Tel: 525 9100, 553 3333

Consulate,
6 de Septiembre 2286,
Ciudad Juarez,
Chihuahua.
Tel: 3 40 48

Consulate,
Centro Commercial Plaza,
Av del Mar s/n,
Mazatlan.
Tel: 2885, 2687

Consulate General,
Progreso 175,
Guadalajara.
Tel: 25 27 00, 25 29 98

Consulate,
Calle 56A No. 453,
Merida.
Tel: 60 30, 20 03

BELIZE
Consulate General,
Gabourel Lane & Hutson St.,
Belize City.
Tel: 3261

GUATEMALA
Embassy,
8a Av 11–65,
Guatemala City.
Tel: 23201/9

EL SALVADOR
Embassy,
No. 1230,
25 Av. Norte,
San Salvador.
Tel: 27 7100

HONDURAS
Embassy,
Av. La Paz,
Tegucigalpa.
Tel: 2 3121/4, 2 3127

NICARAGUA
Embassy,
Blvd. Somoza,
Managua.
Tel: 23881

COSTA RICA
Embassy,
Av 3 Calle 1,
San Jose.
Tel: 22 55 66

PANAMA
Embassy,
Av Balboa at 38th St.,
Panama City.
Tel: 25 3600

British Representatives in Mexico and Central America

MEXICO
Embassy,
Lerma 71,
Mexico City 5.
Tel: 114 880, 143 327

Consulate,
Lerdo de Tejada 2264,
Guadalajara.
Tel: 15 14 06

Consulate,
Hotel Las Brisas,
PO Box 281,
Acapulco.
Tel: 41650, 41580

Consulate,
Calle 58 No. 450,
PO Box 89,
Merida.
Tel: 16799

GUATEMALA
Consulate,
Edificio Maya,
Via 5, No. 4–50,
8 Piso, Zona 4,
Guatemala City.
Tel: 6132, 64375

EL SALVADOR
Embassy,
11a Avenida Norte Bis, No. 611,
Colonia Duenas,
Apartado 25–50,
San Salvador.
Tel: 21 9106, 22 3945

HONDURAS
c/o Embassy, Costa Rica

NICARAGUA
Embassy,
Av. Las Colinas,
(Lote 100),
Las Colinas (Apartado 13),
Managua.
Tel: 96256, 96207

COSTA RICA
Embassy,
3202 Paseo Colon,
Apartado 10056,
San Jose.
Tel: 21 56 88

PANAMA
Embassy,
Via Espana 120,
Apartado 889,
Panama City.
Tel: 23 0451/2/3

Canadian Representatives in Mexico and Central America

MEXICO
Embassy,
Melchor Ocampo 463–7,
Mexico City.
Tel: 533 06 10

BELIZE
c/o High Commission,
PO Box 1500,
Kingston 10,
Jamaica.

GUATEMALA
Embassy,
7a Av. 12–19, Zona 9,
Edificio Etisa 7th Floor,
PO Box 400,
Guatemala City,
Tel: 61560, 67227, 65393

EL SALVADOR
c/o Embassy, Costa Rica

HONDURAS
c/o Embassy Costa Rica

NICARAGUA
c/o Embassy, Costa Rica

COSTA RICA
Embassy,
6th Floor, Cronos Bldg.,
Calle 3 y Av. Central,
Apartado Postal 10303,
San Jose.
Tel: 23 05 88

PANAMA
c/o Embassy, Costa Rica

Index

* indicates hotels
** indicates restaurants

Acadiana, 166
Acaponeta, 17, 48, 53, **58**, 59, 62; town
   plan, 58
Acapulco, 20, 22, 39, 61, 63, 79, **80–2**
Acapulco*, 80
Acatlan, 82
ADO *see* Autobuses de Orient
AeroCondor, airline, 162
Aerovias Quisqueyana, airline, 159
Aha Una Ulu*, 109
Air Panama, airline, 161
Airplan, airline, 159
air travel: North American cities to El
   Paso, 156, Mexico City, 156–7, Miami,
   156, incentive fares, 155; Europe to
   Barbados, 160, Miami, 160, 161,
   Nassau, 160, incentive fares, 157–9;
   homeward from Barbados, 162,
   Colombia, 162, Merida, 161, Panama,
   161–2; Panama/Colombia, 144, 147; in
   Colombia, 148; in Venezuela, 150;
   Colombia/Barbados, 149; ticket
   reservations in Merida, 93, Mexico City,
   76, Miami, 180; tickets required for
   immigration, 24, 127, 134, 139, 147,
   149, 151, 162
Ajijic, 19, 20, **68–9**
Alabama, 165, 188
Alameda**, 89
Alamo, San Antonio, 195
Algiers Stompers, 193
Alpha*, 195
American*, 94
American Cafeteria**, 176
American Civil War, 165

American Community Centre, Chapala, 69
American Express: addresses, 208
Ameripass, Greyhound ticket, 171
Amitillo, 123
Amtrak, 171, **172–3**, 190, 193, 195, 197
Andes, Mts., 147
Antigua, 107
Arabs, 104
Aragon*, 148
Arellano, Gen. O.L., 120
Astoria*, 132
Atitlan, Lake, 112–13
Atlanta, 156
Atlantis, 31
Austin, 167
Autobuses de Orient, ADO, 49, 84, 87, 88,
   89
Autobus de Sur, 49, 90
Autobuses Gulfo Pacifico, 49, 88
Autobuses Teotihuacan, 00
Autobuses Turisticos, 86
Avensa, airline, 150
Avianca, airline, 148
Aztecs, Azteca, the Mexico, 30, 32, 36, 37,
   39

Bahamas, 31, 158, 159, 161
Bahia de Campeche, 90
Baja California, 40, 63, 64
Balboa, 100, 137, **140–1**
bananas, trade, 107, 120, 121, 126, 127,
   130–1, 134
banks: Belize, 105; Honduras, 123;
   Mexico, 41, 55, 58; Panama, 138, 139
Barbados, **150–1**; accommodation, 151;
   climate, 150; currency, 151; flights to
   and from, 158, 160, 162; visas, 24, 151
Baroque architecture, 79, 82, 116

216

Index

Index

218

Index

Index

Index

Index

Index

Area Code 403
Alberta Province
High River City